Advance …

"Johanna W. H. van Wijk-Bos's new commentary on 1–2 Samuel is elegantly written with the sensibility of a seasoned Old Testament scholar and the heart of a minister. She is sensitive to the theological and ethical issues regarding leadership raised by this sometimes difficult text, and she also reflects on the women's roles as few authors of commentaries have done before. This new volume in the Smyth & Helwys Reading the Old Testament series will be most helpful for preachers and teachers seeking a fresh word on familiar stories."

—*Alice Ogden Bellis*
Professor of Old Testament Language & Literature
Howard University Divinity School
Washington, DC

"At times biblical commentators tend either to paraphrase the biblical text more or less or almost to lose themselves in technical details. In her fine commentary on the two books of Samuel, Johanna van Wijk-Bos elegantly avoids both these pitfalls. In this meticulously researched book, she is constantly in dialogue with other scholars. She elegantly informs the readers of the significance of many of the Hebrew words for places and people, without losing herself in details. Arguably, one of the most important challenges for contemporary biblical commentaries is to what extent they take gender studies into account. Unsurprisingly, the two books of Samuel provide van Wijk-Bos with ample possibilities to discuss various aspects of gender issues, and she does it succinctly and with sophistication. This is a rich and thought-provoking commentary, allowing the narrative to speak for itself."

—*Jesper Svartvik*
Krister Stendahl Professor of Theology of Religions
Lund University, Lund, Sweden
and the Swedish Theological Institute in Jerusalem

"The stories in 1 and 2 Samuel may seem an easy read, some of the easiest in the Bible. Johanna van Wijk-Bos helps you read them slowly, notice the way the stories are told and notice the subtleties of their telling, and she thus helps you to get three times as much out of them than you might otherwise. She helps you understand the dynamics of the stories and think about the questions they open up. Like the books she is commenting on, her book invites and rewards careful, attentive reading."

—John Goldingay
Professor of Old Testament
Fuller Theological Seminary
Pasadena, California

READING SAMUEL

SMYTH&
HELWYS

Smyth & Helwys Publishing, Inc.
6316 Peake Road
Macon, Georgia 31210-3960
1-800-747-3016

Printed in the United States of America.

The paper used in this publication meets the minimum requirements of American National Standard for Information Sciences—Permanence of Paper for Printed Library Materials.
ANSI Z39.48–1984 (alk. paper)

Library of Congress Cataloging-in-Publication Data

Van Wijk-Bos, Johanna W. H., 1940-
Reading the Old Testament : Samuel / by Johanna W.H. van Wijk-Bos.
p. cm.
Includes bibliographical references.
ISBN 978-1-57312-607-6 (alk. paper)
1. Bible. O.T. Samuel—Commentaries. I. Title.
BS1325.53.V36 2011
222'.407—dc23

2011041556

Reading Samuel

A Literary and Theological Commentary

Johanna W. H. van Wijk-Bos

SMYTH & HELWYS
PUBLISHING, INCORPORATED MACON, GEORGIA

Also by Johanna W. H. van Wijk-Bos

Ruth, Esther, Jonah
(Knox Preaching Guides)

Reasoning with the Foxes:
Female Wit in a World of Male Power

Reformed and Feminist: A Challenge to the Church

Reimagining God: The Case for Scriptural Diversity

Called Out With: Stories of Solidarity in Support of Lesbian,
Gay, Bisexual, and Transgendered Persons

Ezra, Nehemiah, and Esther
(Westminster Bible Companion Series)

Ruth and Esther: Women in Alien Lands

Making Wise the Simple:
The Torah in Christian Faith and Practice

Acknowledgments

My thanks go to my academic institution, Louisville Presbyterian Theological Seminary, for its generous sabbatical policies that made it possible for me to write this commentary. I owe thanks to my colleague Amy Plantinga Pauw for her editorial comments on the introduction to the work. My editor, Mark Biddle, deserves profound gratitude for his patience, meticulous editing, and attention to detail. Throughout the process of writing, I benefited immensely from the work of J. B. Fokkelman and his extensive commentary on the books of Samuel.

Friends and family were of special importance during the last stages of completing the book, a period during which I suffered the unexpected death of my husband, David Bos. My thanks go to our son, Martin, his wife, Kim, and their daughter, Emma; to my sister, Hannah; and to my friends Aaron, Courtney, Kate, Chris, and Narges. All of them sustained me with their presence and healing laughter. During our time together, David was an unfailing support in my career and a conversation partner in my scholarly endeavors, offering encouragement and counsel also for my written work. He was my companion for almost forty-five years and shared with me all the values that we thought make a human life worth living. His departure from my side leaves a void for which I have no words. I count it a privilege to have been his marriage partner for such a long time.

I dedicate the book to his memory.

—*Johanna W. H. van Wijk-Bos*

IN MEMORIAM: A. DAVID BOS
February 15, 1935–February 12, 2011

"in gladness you will go out, and in peace be brought home."
Isaiah 55:12

Contents

Editor's Foreword

Reading the Old Testament shares many of the aims and objectives of its counterpart series, Reading the New Testament. Contributors to the current series, like those to its predecessor, write with the intention of presenting "cutting-edge research in [a form] accessible" to a wide audience ranging from specialists in the field to educated laypeople. The approach taken here, as there, focuses not on the minutiae of word-by-word, verse-by-verse exegesis, but on larger literary and thought units, especially as they function in the overall conception of the book under analysis. From the standpoint of method, volumes in this series will employ an eclectic variety of reading strategies and critical approaches as contributors deem appropriate for explicating the force of the text before them. Nonetheless, as in RNT, "the focus [will be] on a close reading of the final form of the text." The overarching goal is to provide readers of the commentary series with an aid to help them become more competent, more engaged, and more enthusiastic readers of the Bible as authoritative Scripture.

The title of the series prompts several comments. For the editor, at least, the term "Old Testament" is a convenient convention, since any alternative seems either awkward or provocative. The Hebrew Bible is the shared heritage of Judaism and Christianity, the body of believers whom Paul once described as branches from a wild olive tree who have been "grafted contrary to nature into a cultivated olive tree" (Rom 11:24). Since the beginnings of Christianity, questions concerning how and in what sense the Hebrew Bible/Old Testament functions as Christian Scripture have perpetually confronted the church. Nonetheless, throughout its history, in the spirit of Paul, the church has insisted that the God of Abraham, Isaac, and Jacob is the God of the New Testament. Rather than impose a detailed doctrine of the unity of the two Testaments or specify a particular hermeneutical approach, the editor and the publisher have chosen to invite contributions to the series from scholars selected because of their learning and insight, again in the spirit of Paul we hope, without regard to faith tradition or denominational identity.

The books of the Hebrew Bible were the fountainhead for the faith of both Paul and Aqiba. May it be that through the scholarship presented in the pages of this series, the books of the "Old Testament" water the faith of another generation.

—*Mark Biddle, General Editor*
Richmond, Virginia
November 2011

Introduction

Historical and Literary Context

The books of Samuel are a part of the great historical work in the Hebrew Bible that comprises Joshua, Judges, Samuel, and Kings. These books describe the span of history that covers roughly the period of the twelfth to the first part of the sixth century BCE. Not yet in the land at the opening of the long story, the people are no longer in the land at the end of it. The setting of Samuel is at the beginning of this history and the texts concern themselves with the origins and establishment of kingship, then with subsequent events under the first kings in ancient Israel at the end of the eleventh and into the tenth century BCE.

The book of Judges ends on the ominous note that in Israel there was no king and everyone did as was right in their own eyes (Judg 21:25), an ending that creates an appropriate beginning for the books of Samuel, since circumstances clearly cry out for more consistent leadership. Following directly on Judges in the order of books in the Hebrew Bible, 1 Samuel continues to speak of events in the last days of the Judges (Samuel), relates the early days of kingship (Saul), and eventually puts its focus on David as the chosen king, God's newly anointed. Second Samuel centers entirely on King David although it does not take the reader quite to the end of his reign, which is recounted in the first two chapters of 1 Kings. Anyone familiar with the material in these books is aware that kingship had a rough beginning in ancient Israel; the stories thus tell of obstacles that had to be overcome before David could take his seat on the throne to rule the loosely organized tribes as one people. David's rule is also far from trouble free; turmoil in his family and threats to his reign beset his later years, heralding the eventual break-up of the fragile union after the death of his heir Solomon. It is clear that neither in its beginning nor in its development did the course of kingship run smoothly in ancient Israel. This very fact made for fascinating narratives.

Although without external corroboration of the historical period involved we do not know exactly what occurred in the late eleventh and early tenth centuries in terms of political and military developments, it is safe to assume that there were numerous threats to the tribes that eventually became a centrally governed nation. The gravest military challenge at the turn of the first millennium came from the Philistines, part of the migrating groups that had moved into the Canaanite coastal plain around the middle of the twelfth century. They inhabited five major fortified urban centers, each with its own administrative leadership, called "overlords" or "petty kings" in the Bible. They had access to the recently developed iron technology and formed themselves into a confederacy that made them a serious enemy of the ancient Israelites. Neither side was inclined to settle disputes about the precious real estate they occupied in Canaan by peaceful negotiation, and fights broke out continually with now one then the other gaining the upper hand, until the Philistines finally succumbed in the first years of David's reign. First Samuel, in particular, abounds with stories about the danger posed by the Philistines. The constant military engagement this involved was surely one of the reasons for the demand for kingship with its promise of a regular standing army and consistent military leadership. Kings, together with their appointed commanders and generals, were expected to go out with their armies. A warrior culture imbues the texts of Samuel, in which war heroes receive the highest praise, deeds of gory bloodshed receive no condemnation, and the writers felt the need to include at least one chapter focused solely on praise for the mighty men of the past and their deeds of daring and exploits in war (2 Sam 23:8-38). Some of the most difficult narratives for a modern reader are those that breathe the air of bloodlust and conquest in all their violent detail (e.g., 2 Sam 8). Such characteristics of the ancient stories should perhaps not surprise us, but they may hinder our engagement with the text.

Surprising, on the other hand, is the artful narration of events in these chapters. Beginning with chapter 1, many intricate scenes come to the fore in which not only political and military matters take pride of place, but also human relationships, family concerns and tensions, relations between parents and children, among friends, spouses—in sum all that human life generally involves. The narratives spin out these scenes with a wealth of detail that inevitably invokes interest. The following remark by Robert Alter puts it aptly:

> Lacking all but the scantiest extrahistorical evidence, we shall probably never know precisely what happened in Jerusalem and Judea and the high

> country of Benjamin around the turn of the first millennium B.C.E. when the Davidic dynasty was established. What matters is that the anonymous Hebrew writer, drawing on what he knew or thought he knew of the portentous historical events, has created this most searching story of men and women in the rapid and dangerous current of history that still speaks to us, floundering in history and dilemmas of political life, three thousand years later. (Alter 1999, xxiv)

Writing and Editing of the Text

Most scholars assume that the books of Samuel were not written in the time when the events described in them took place. Issues concerning writing and editing are complicated for many biblical texts, and one can easily become lost in a maze of competing theories that do not bring the reader much closer to understanding the text. A vexing question concerns the cohesion of the material. First and Second Samuel may present a collage of discrete narrative units: one centered on the Ark of the Covenant, a second with a focus on prophecy and prophetic circles, a third with its main subject Saul and the rise of David to kingship, and another with an intimate look at David and his court. Each of these units would then have belonged to its own source, sources that were eventually woven together into the final documents by editors who combined the material. The major candidates for the final editing process are the so-called Deuteronomists, writers who combined material that now makes up the books Joshua, Judges, Samuel, and Kings and who in tone, style and perspective shared the outlook of the book of Deuteronomy. The deuteronomistic editorial work may have taken place in two stages, with one part of the process completed in the seventh century, shortly preceding or following the Assyrian destruction of the northern kingdom in 722. Presumably, the second and final part of the process took place in the sixth or fifth century following the Babylonian exile. In both stages, the loss of land and kingship, especially after the exile, heavily influenced the perspective of the editors.

It is also possible that the books of Samuel present us with a mainly cohesive unit, written not long after the events described in them, perhaps in the early years of Solomon's reign and eventually edited by the Deuteronomists (Alter 1999). On the other hand, the Deuteronomists may have composed these books as one cohesive narrative during the Babylonian exile. In their work, the Deuteronomists made use of older materials but were themselves great artists and writers who wrote a work of unrivaled beauty and power (Polzin 1980, 1989, and 1993). In this volume, I lean in the direction of the first position: a cohesive narrative from the years of the united monarchy, perhaps under King Solomon, that the Deuteronomists edited with a light hand after the Babylonian exile. I agree with others that it is difficult to detect pervasive influence in these texts of the main concerns of the Deuteronomists, such as a focus on centralization of worship, an emphasis on national and cultic purity, and a call for obedience to the Torah's strictures against idolatry that would bring its reward, or failure if unheeded. Neither is the distinctive language of the Deuteronomists with its accompanying hortatory and didactic tone readily apparent. What we do find in 1 and 2 Samuel are narratives that portray the human protagonists in all their complexity as human beings, warts and all. In the case of the prophet Samuel, for example, the writer clearly supports Samuel's God-given authority. Yet, as Alter observes: "The prophet Samuel may have God on his side, but he is also an implacable, irascible man, and often a palpably self-interested one as well" (Alter 1999, xv). This depiction prevents the narrative from functioning as a simple advocacy of the prophetic vocation and ideology. Similar observations can be made about all the characters who receive detailed attention in these stories. Whether God accepted or rejected them, the personages of 1 and 2 Samuel appear before the reader in all their human complexity.

Concerns surrounding kingship certainly occupied the writers, concerns that would be equally valid in the tenth as in the sixth century, although from a different vantage point. Was kingship a good or a bad thing for ancient Israel? Did it have divine sanction? If written in the tenth century, the answer to this question still hung in the balance: time would tell what would come of it. If the writing took place much later, it would be evident that, on the whole, kingship had not been of particular benefit and had not prevented the ultimate destruction of the people and the loss of the land. In either case, the text deals with questions regarding kingship in an ambiguous manner. If the people must have kings as they thought they did, then kings they will have, with all the consequences of their choice. On the positive side, the threat from outside, embodied by the Philistines at the time, is eventually subdued with the help of gifted royal military leaders and their generals. On the other hand, warfare can also arise from the inside as the rebellions during David's rule make clear. The signs that the unity of the kingdom will not hold in the long run already begin to appear in David's time. Hence, the attitude toward kingship expressed in Samuel is full of ambiguity. At times the narrative takes a negative stance, as is the case in 1 Samuel 8; on the other hand, the first kings, Saul and David, are emphatically chosen by God and anointed by God's prophet. If we expect to receive easy answers about the profit of kingship for ancient Israel, these books will disappoint. If, on the other hand, our interest lies in realistic storytelling that evokes complex human characters and communities in their relationship to one another and to their God, these tales will stoke our imagination and create lively engagement between reader and text.

The Subjects of the Narratives

Who or what are these stories about? On the face of it they present the events that took place in ancient Israel at the end of the second and the beginning of the first millennium. We consider 1 and 2 Samuel part of the historical books of the Bible. They do not, however, present history as we think of it. I have argued elsewhere that the stories we read in the Bible were composed in a culture for which "myth" was the primary category. In myth, the most important issue is not whether the story happened exactly as told in every detail but what kinds of truths the story aims to tell. As I wrote, "With myth we need to take facts into account and look beyond them to what truths the story addresses and to what end it is telling these truths" (Van Wijk-Bos 2005, 65–66).

A brief look at the first chapter of 1 Samuel may serve as an example. This chapter recounts the worship customs of one specific family as it makes annual pilgrimage to the central cultic shrine of the region. In few words, an elaborate introduction of the male head of the household, Elkanah, serves to frame both the family and the center of worship clearly in time and space. Soon, the attention shifts from Elkanah to his wives who are rivals, because one has children and the other has only Elkanah's affection. The story now appears to be about a family situation, fraught with tension, rather than about the worship customs of the central male character. The woman with the greatest power in the household, because she has offspring, Peninnah, taunts her co-wife, Hannah, because of her lack of children, which causes Hannah to become deeply depressed, a victim of her infertility and her rival's cruel behavior (1 Sam 1:1-8).

Once again, the story takes a turn and unexpectedly reports movement on the part of the character with the least power, victimized and paralyzed Hannah: "She arose. . ." (1:9). From this point on, the spotlight shines on Hannah, on her prayer to her God, and on her conversation with the priest Eli. In what follows, the priest turns out to be mistaken in his view of the distressed woman he sees before him, an error that Hannah herself sharply corrects. Hannah receives her heart's desire and eventually fulfills her vow to dedicate her first-born to the service of God at the shrine in Shiloh. This first-born is, of course, Samuel, the prophet-priest-judge whose leadership will form the bridge between judgeship and kingship.

If we ask what the story in this chapter is about, multiple answers are possible. It is about the last years of the judges in ancient Israel before there was a monarchy or a temple. It is about the most sacred shrine, the Ark of the Covenant at Shiloh where people may go up to make annual pilgrimage. It is about the priesthood serving at this shrine. It describes customs of worship and temple personnel. The story is also about families, about what causes tensions and dysfunction in them; it is about the overriding importance of male offspring in that ancient society; it is about relationships, between spouses and between women in a culture that sanctions polygynous marriage. It also portrays relations between God and humans, giving rise to issues concerning the question of who serves God appropriately, who reaches God's ear.

The story is also ostensibly about the weakest character in the plot, a woman at first in the background, then in the foreground in a passive, victimized role, who eventually "arises" to take control of her situation. Furthermore, she does so in a way that enables her to act as a petitioner, a wife, and a mother, until she finally opens her mouth in the great paean of praise that now forms part of the second chapter (1 Sam 2:1-10). The story is of course also about Eli, whose house will not continue by God's decree, a thread in the narrative that is picked up in a subsequent episode. Finally, it concerns present and future leadership, as it reveals a priestly leader whose view needs correction and contains embedded within it the promise of better times to come.

It should be evident that, in this material, we do not face familiar categories of historiography. The text reads more like a novel, stirring the imagination, opening up gaps that ask to be filled, demanding sympathy and antipathy, providing false leads and unexpected turns. It does so even as it places itself squarely within the frame of ancient Israel's history and also tells of the great political and religious developments in which it took part. Within the large canvas of the historical events, it paints on a small, intimate screen. Whoever the writers were, they gave the events what Robert Alter calls "fictional shaping." In Alter's opinion, "the known general contours of the historical events and of the principal players are not tampered with, but the writer brings to bear the resources of his literary art in order to imagine deeply, and critically, the concrete moral and emotional predicaments of living in history in the political realm" (Alter 1999, xvii–xviii).

That the stories may have undergone such "fictional shaping" does not take away the importance of historical context for understanding a biblical text. Although we do not know everything, or perhaps even much, we have general information about the different periods in ancient Israel's history that may explain the framing and shaping of the material and help us to understand the truths of which it tells. Such information will be brought to bear on specific texts when it is useful. In general, the subject of the two books is the transition from a tribal organization to a monarchy and the first periods of the monarchy, with all that accompanies this vast change: taxation, conscription, forced labor, building projects, centralized worship, and more.

Literary Features

Most of the material in Samuel consists of narrative. Not all the texts belong to the narrative category, however. At significant places we find poetry, first assigned to Hannah as she gives her prayer of thanksgiving and subsequently to King David, as he laments the deaths of Saul and Jonathan at the beginning of 2 Samuel and utters a prayer of thanksgiving over deliverance and his "last words" at the end. In addition, there are two parables, as well as prophetic speeches and lists.

Yet, narrative takes up the greatest part of these books. A few times in these stories the voice belongs clearly to the Deuteronomist. For example, in 1 Samuel 7, Samuel reappears after an absence of three chapters to speak to "the entire house of Israel" (1 Sam 7:3) about the need to "return" to God, to "put aside foreign gods," to "set" their "heart" on God, and to "serve" God. All of this is deuteronomistic language. More important, the notion that the sin of the people consisted mainly in not showing exclusive loyalty to the God of the covenant by practicing idol worship together with the dire consequences of this failure indicates deuteronomistic ideology. *If* the people are willing and able to serve the God of Israel alone, God will *deliver* them. Similar themes and language appear in 1 Samuel 12, which reports that, after the definitive election of Saul to kingship, Samuel gives a farewell speech as the days of judgeship now draw to a close. Especially in the section that reviews the history of the people, deuteronomistic style and tenor are evident: the people sinned by forsaking their God and "serving" the Baals and Astartes, so God "sold them into the hand of . . ." and the people "cried out" and God "delivered them" (1 Sam 12:10).

In most places this Deuteronomistic voice is not clearly present, as noted above, and the narrative employs themes and styles that cannot easily be assigned to a particular school of thought or writing. One element worthy of note is the use of detail in narratives that at the same time leaves much unsaid and open to speculation. For example, the story of Hannah,

Peninnah, and Elkanah in 1 Samuel 1 provides fine detail that affords insight into the family relations, a situation that leaves Hannah powerless and victimized. When the narrator notes that she "arose" in v. 9, this action follows on the (rhetorical) questions Elkanah asked her in v. 8. Detail is provided in the specifics of Elkanah's questions and in the specifics of Hannah's actions that follow, but much is also left unsaid. We do not know the tone of Elkanah's questions. Was he grieved, puzzled, irritated? We do not know how Hannah received them. The reader/listener knows only that she went into action immediately following the reported words of Elkanah. What propelled her so suddenly? The gap in the text gives rise to questions and pondering them brings us closer to what is going on in a given story.

Sometimes detail provides an opportunity for linkage between different blocks of material. First Samuel 6 reports that the Philistines return the Ark of the Covenant, which they had captured and the presence of which had become intolerable, to the tribes of Israel. For this purpose, they use a cart pulled by two milch cows whose calves are restrained and kept behind. The cows, drawn on by the power of God, head straight for Beth Shemesh, the closest town across the border between the domain of Philistia and the ancient Israelite tribes:

> They took two milch cows
> and tied them to a cart
> and their young they restrained at home. . . .
> Straight-off the cows went
> on the road to Beth-Shemesh;
> on one lane they went and went lowing. (1 Sam 6: 10, 12)

First, we note that the word translated "their young," both here and where the instructions are given in v. 7, is the Hebrew *beneyhem,* the word for "sons" or "children," rather than "calves" (Alter 1999, 33 n.12). The nursing cows, desperate for their young, must go away from them, and, the text observes with fine detail "on one lane they went and they went lowing." A miraculous progress is described here, for the beasts without cognizance of their burden and knowing only their need to feed their young draw the Ark in the opposite direction, straight to the place where it needs to go. The cows go in pain, "lowing," but on they go. They are nursing mothers and in using the word "children" for the calves the link is made with another nursing mother who delayed giving up her nursing child; chapter 1 reports that Hannah decides to stay home until the "child," Hebrew *ben,* is weaned (1:22). The story is about the return of the Ark to ancient Israel, but it is also about sacrifice as it relates to parents and children. The cows are offered up as a burnt offering once they have arrived at their destination and have fulfilled their role. Sacrifice is also a central feature in the first chapter where annual sacrifice is a regular part of the pilgrimage of Elkanah and his family. In truth, Hannah sacrifices the most in giving up her first-born child to the service of the Ark, symbol of the presence of God. There, the sons of Eli exercise their office by defiling sacrifices brought by worshipers. In the meantime, as reported in chapter 7, the sacrifices of the "children" of Israel have been offered to the wrong gods. They have served the Baals and Astartes instead of the Holy God of Israel. Sacrifice, the right sacrifice, the right way to bring sacrifice, and its linkage to parent-child relationships are certainly threads that run through these chapters of 1 Samuel.

Second Samuel 9–20, together with the first two chapters of 1 Kings, differs in some respects from the rest of the material and is often considered to be a separate source titled "The Court History of David." The narrative is more clearly interconnected, and the separate episodes take part in a large plot that ends with 2 Kings 2. The setting is for the most part Jerusalem and David's court; the focus is on David and his family, and the narratives provide a close-up of David as father as well as of sibling relationships in the royal household. The perspective on David is highly critical as he moves from what may be termed an "adulterous affair," at best, to murder by proxy, to turning a blind eye to the rape of his own daughter, to dealing inadequately with his rebellious son, Absalom, to a paralyzing outburst of grief over the loss of this son, into old age without having properly provided for an heir. Dealing only with the material as it occurs in Samuel, this narrative clearly presents neither a saintly figure nor an idealized portrait of a king who must have become an object of reverence in many ways, especially in later years. At times it is hard to recognize in this all too human figure the courageous, charismatic figure of the earlier stories, loved by everyone who encountered him. If we take all the narratives about David together, he appears as the most complex of the characters. Talented musician, brave young shepherd, calculating and shrewd military leader, ruthless and murderous adulterer, loving and dysfunctional father; all these and more define David.

If this is not historiography as we know it, it is also not fiction as we ordinarily understand it. Commonplace details characteristic of contemporary writing are mostly absent in biblical narrative. The writer rarely provides information about a character's appearance, and as a consequence we do not know what people looked like or what they wore. We hear nothing about physical structures, houses, exterior or interior, field, and landscape. When descriptions of appearance occur, they serve a special purpose. Thus, Saul's description as handsome and tall stands out (1 Sam 9:2; 10:23), as does the description of young David as handsome with beautiful eyes (1 Sam 16:12). Similar observations are made about Abigail (1 Sam 25:3), Batsheba (2 Sam 11:2), Tamar, David's daughter (2 Sam 13:1), and Absalom (2 Sam 14:25-26). Even though these descriptions remain quite general, we pay attention to them because of their rarity. The effect of the overall lack of description is to make the stories move fast because descriptions of any kind slow the time-flow inside the story to a standstill, as is most cogently pointed out by Shimon Bar-Efrat (Bar-Efrat 1989, 146). The narratives frequently mention places, but the reader must decide where they are and what the features of the location may have been. A great deal of movement in narratives that lack detailed description lends them their dynamic quality. In the first two chapters of 1 Samuel alone, besides the annual movement from the homestead to the sanctuary, the family moves from Shiloh back home, back to Shiloh, and home again.

Descriptions of the inner life, motivations and intentions of characters are also missing for the most part. We must make decisions about such important elements based on the characters' speech and action. Characters may show emotion, but only anger and grief are clearly marked, with amusement or laughter quite absent. Humor is evident mostly in the use of irony, which may be bitter rather than a cause for laughter. For example, as Shimon Bar-Efrat points out, it is surely ironic that David's last words to his murderous and rebellious son Absalom are "Go in peace!" (2 Sam 15:9; Bar-Efrat 1989, 126). Of course, the king does not mean his words to his son to be ironic, but their effect is ironic when it becomes known that Absalom went to Hebron to have himself crowned king. This type of humor is not of the "ha-ha" variety, but it makes the reader wonder. Was King David really so obtuse and so blind about his nefarious son that he had no idea of his real purpose? David's feet of clay are abundantly apparent, of course, in the Court History, but in his dealings with Absalom he appears at his most inept. Or, is the mighty King David no different in his interactions with his children than any parent who is blind to the misdeeds of children and colludes unwittingly in their wrongdoing?

Other significant features of the stories, such as plot, key words and repetitions, use of time and space, and other distinctive stylistic elements, will surface as we begin reading these narratives. Enough has been said here to introduce us to the idea that the "fictional shaping" of these stories is complex and filled with potential for new levels of understanding if we have the patience and take the time to read with care.

Perspectives

The texts of 1 and 2 Samuel were written from certain social, religious, and political perspectives. They were the perspectives of a people now long gone, situated in a specific time and place. We may know a few things about their outlook on human beings, on God, and on life in general, and may surmise more from the stories. When the Deuteronomists' hand is evident, it is certain that there will be an emphasis on the religious responsibilities of a people who understood themselves to live in a covenant relationship with their God and consequently to be at risk of jeopardizing the benefits of this relationship if they did not act in accordance with the demands laid on them. In the Deuteronomists' view, this people owed their exclusive loyalty to the God of Israel, and when they failed in this loyalty, especially by adopting the worship of other gods, they could expect punishment.

As noted above, the Deuteronomists' assessment of kingship is not so easy to characterize. When all was said and done, kingship had not benefited the ancient Israelites in the way they had expected. As Everett Fox observes:

> The final editors of this part of the Bible, sitting in exile in sixth-century B.C.E. Babylonia, looked back on the entire history of Israelite monarchy and, as they mourned their losses, understood that there was something about that early request for a king that was intimately related to their present plight. (Fox 1999, xxiii)

According to the instructions for kingship set forth in Deuteronomy 17, the most serious danger for a king would be to place himself above *torah* (Deut 17:18-20). Certainly, both Saul and David were guilty of doing precisely this.

Yet, the Davidic house remains an ideal of kingship even for the Deuteronomists, and they judge the promises God made to David and his house to be enduring. On the other hand, although King David was approved by God and anointed by God's prophet, his actions, especially toward the end of his reign, undermine his credibility as God's chosen one. His rule falters and big cracks appear in the unity of the new nation. As a person, he clearly had many failings, failings elaborately described by the writer of these narratives and woven into the total fabric by the editors. In addition, a larger question may be whether the institution of kingship itself put at risk the people's exclusive allegiance to God. First Samuel 8 raises this question, and it underlies much of Samuel's speech in chapter 12.

In addition to an ambiguous portrayal of kinship, the texts present a complex picture of God. Initially, God appears as the one who hears the cry of a lonely, bereft, and distraught woman, the one who lifts the poor from the dust (1 Sam 2:8). This God is not open to manipulation, as made clear by the story of the Ark of the Covenant (1 Sam 4–7)—a God of might and awe who strikes the unbelieving Philistines and demands sacrifice to honor God's holiness. God is also depicted as displaying almost human feelings of rejection when the people demand a king. Most unsettling is the fact that God's first choice of a king, Saul, is retracted by a Deity who regrets that choice and who ultimately rejects Saul to choose another in his stead (1 Sam 15:11, 23). We overhear God voicing this regret to Samuel: "And the word of the Holy One came to Samuel: / I rue having made Saul king . . ." (1 Sam 15:10-11a).

A few verses later, however, Samuel tells Saul that his repentance is useless, for

> the Eternal of Israel
> will not deal falsely or rue
> for he is not a human to rue. (1 Sam 15:29)

The narrative first recounts that God has a change of mind and then God's prophet declares that God never has a change of mind. In subsequent episodes God is on the side of David, who engages in acts of incredible and needless bloodthirstiness (2 Sam 8:6, 14), but God disapproves of the murder of Uriah, the Hittite, the husband of Bathsheba (2 Sam 11:27). A complicated picture of God unfolds: a picture of a God who at once is near to the brokenhearted and is also distant and powerful; a God who punishes those who dishonor the Holy Name and all those who belong to their house (1 Sam 2:27-36); a God who chooses a king for Israel only to reject him later and send him a spirit that torments him, and a rival to replace him; a God whose holiness is so great that anyone who comes too close to it dies (1 Sam 6:19; 2 Sam 6:7). Extremely puzzling is the tale of God inciting David (1 Sam 24:1) to take a census for which not he but the people are severely punished, painting a picture of an inscrutable, cruel, and capricious deity. For the storytellers and writers, of course, Saul clearly did not turn out to be the one to found a royal house or to put an end to the Philistine threat. They concluded, therefore, that God had rejected Saul. Similarly, an outbreak of a serious contagious disease may have followed a census leading them to conclude that this was an ill-omened enterprise; since David was not punished for it, the impulse for it must have been from God.

Together with the rise of kingship, the prophet appeared in ancient Israel as God's mouthpiece and therefore as representative of God's presence. Samuel still combines in himself the offices of priest, prophet/seer, and judge. In his time, the prophetic task may have been viewed more traditionally as that of seer or forecaster, yet he also serves as critic of God's anointed king, Saul. With the foundation of David's rule, the prophet Nathan becomes the one who interprets the will of God to David in a critical fashion. Later, the prophet Gad will fulfill a similar function. These characters resemble more closely the prophet as critical voice to the central administrations of the kingdoms, the role played by the prophets of subsequent centuries. The prophetic power that resided in being God's representative and interpreter of God's intentions provided a balance to the power of kingship and its potential abuses in the era that followed. This course is already set at the time of the first monarch. So the voice of Samuel takes Saul to task for not acting according to God's will (1 Sam 13:13-14; 15:22-23), and Nathan rebukes David for his sin with Batsheba (2 Sam 12:1-4, 7-14).

A consistent thread in the narratives is the insistence that kings are not above God's law. This is surely the point of Samuel's harshness toward Saul. While the guidelines in Deuteronomy 17:14-20 warn against excessive possessions and polygyny, the longest section is reserved for heeding *torah*:

> . . . he shall write for himself a copy of this Instruction on a scroll . . . and he shall read in it all the days of his life, in order to learn to be in awe of the Holy One his God to keep all the words of this Instruction and these statutes to do them. Lest his heart lifts itself above his brothers, and lest he turn aside from the commandment to right or left . . . . (Deut 17:18-20)

Precisely what the guidelines in Deuteronomy 17 warn against is what happens when Saul decides to go ahead with the sacrifice before Samuel arrives (1 Sam 13:9, 13) and later not to follow through on the instructions concerning the battle with Amalek (1 Sam 15:17-23). In a similar vein, David puts himself above God's *torah* in his sexual encounter with Batsheba and the murder of Uriah.

This theme already appears in Hannah's thanksgiving prayer, where the main thought is that all power derives from God, including the king's power. This premise coheres with the reference to the king at the end of Hannah's prayer (1 Sam 2:9), which is often noted as being anachronistic. According to Dutch scholar Jan Fokkelman, this reference deliberately places royal power under God's power (Fokkelman 2003, 24–26). Fokkelman also points out the similarity of the last words of Hannah's poem (1 Sam 2:10e) to the last line of David's poem (2 Sam 22:51), a sign of the overarching idea in these books that God lends the king strength, "lifts high his horn" (Hannah) and provides him with "saving deeds" (David).

The State of the Text

The Hebrew text of 1 and 2 Samuel appears corrupt at times and occasionally needs emendation. The testimony of the Qumran scrolls of Samuel, which are of course far older than the extant manuscripts of the Masoretic Text, and of the Septuagint is significant in the case of obscure readings. In principle, I only emend the Masoretic reading when the Hebrew is incomprehensible and in such cases have leaned on the Qumran or the Septuagint versions or both. Together with other scholars, I do not have strong attachments to "an original" version of the Hebrew and accept the existence of texts in differing versions from earliest times. I give preference to the Masoretic Text as the version with the most consistent tradition in the transmission of Hebrew manuscripts and as the accepted authoritative version of the Hebrew Bible.

In translating, I found few places where the meaning is entirely unclear. In my translations, I have used the principles of Martin Buber, followed in the U.S. by Everett Fox, who also translated the books of Samuel (Fox 1999). Simply put, translators who follow in Buber's footsteps focus on rendering as faithfully as possible the structure and word choice of the Hebrew original and less on the accessibility of the translation in the receiving language. In Fox's words: "The purpose . . . is to draw the reader into the world of the Hebrew Bible" (Fox 1995, ix). For example, when a word comes first in the Hebrew sentence, where word order is far more flexible than in English, we pay attention because its placement puts a special focus on the word. As far as is reasonable, Hebrew vocabulary is translated with the same words in English to convey the importance of repetition, key words, and wordplay in the material. Furthermore, the text is set on the page in shorter lines than is usual in English translations, to emphasize the oral quality of the text and provide insight into its structure. As Fox points out, the line divisions are somewhat arbitrary, and mine differ from those of both Fox and Buber. Throughout, I have also consulted Robert Alter's translation and Jan Fokkelman's line divisions (Alter 1999, Fokkelman 1981, 1986, 1992, and 1993), both offering a close reading of the biblical text.

Good Reading (Fokkelman 2003, 11)

Although recognition of the cultural, religious, and political worlds in which the books of Samuel originated and were edited is indispensable, the text itself will be the center of my analysis. In this regard, I follow many contemporary scholars, such as Robert Polzin, Robert Alter, and especially J. Fokkelman. More than most of these, however, I consider the historical context essential to an understanding of the text, because without it interpretation is open to the winds of every conviction brought to the study of the Hebrew Bible. Within a postmodern framework, where multiple levels of truth in regard to text are considered acceptable, knowledge about the historical context sets one of the appropriate boundaries around the interpretation of any story, including the biblical story. With biblical scholar Joseph Blenkinsopp, I hold that the historical-critical reading acts as a type of constraint on tendencies to let our own agendas be the sole guide of interpretation. Together with language, thematic consistency, and current concerns and questions put to the text, historical context forms one of the "boundaries of truth" (Van Wijk-Bos 2005, 66–68). The problem with the historical-critical study of the past century was that so often it became an end in itself without bringing readers and students of the Bible closer to the text.

Three qualities are essential to achieving "good reading" of the Bible. They are patience, attention, and openness. "Good reading" requires patience because the meaning may not be laid open immediately; it may take time to figure out what precisely the narrator is trying to convey. It requires attention because not everything here may be what it seems at first. Gaps are left for us to fill in, links can be made that we had not seen before, and there is so much more here than meets the eye. It requires openness because of all the barriers to productive reading of the biblical text, the attitude that we already know what is available in it stands in the way of engaging with the text productively. Of these three, patience, attention, and openness, the last may be the most difficult, for it is often the very familiarity of the Bible that prevents good reading. Familiarity may of course be reassuring and comforting, two reasons perhaps that children insist on the story always being told in the same way. Yet, familiarity also breeds complacency (if not contempt) in the case of the Bible, and it prevents curiosity and playfulness; it covers the subject of the story and the way it is told, making it more opaque rather than clear. In order to read the Bible productively so that it holds our interest and remains or becomes meaningful for our own lives, we need to be open to the unfamiliar. Martin Buber wrote that in order to experience the power of the Bible we must read the Bible "as though it were entirely unfamiliar," as though we had not been faced all our lives with "sham concepts and sham statements that cited the Bible as their authority" (Buber 1982, 5). Similarly, Fokkelman (2003, 14) comments: "The text is otherwise than we thought we knew, otherwise than we expected, other than we have learned. In this aspect the text is no different from the other speaking totality: the human neighbor." Ellen Davis (2000, 85) speaks to this same issue when she counsels "willingness to enter into a new imaginative world whose presuppositions we do not initially share, some of which are startling and offensive to us." To be open to the unfamiliar is not always comfortable; indeed, it may be unsettling, even upsetting, especially if it overturns previously held cherished notions. This discomfort may be a small price to pay for the gain obtained when we approach the biblical text with this attitude. Once open to surprises and unexpected turns, there may be no end to the discoveries to be made. To put the obstacle of familiarity aside, we need to begin with questions, starting with the simple questions of "who?" "what?" "where?" and "how?". Exploring these questions may not always produce clear answers, but it will always render engagement with the text more profound and will provide new insights into the material.

A second major obstacle that needs to be overcome is the very need for clear answers. Perhaps as the world has become more baffling and disturbing, the need for direct responses to our perplexities has risen with new acuity and produced impatience with ambiguity and complexity. The biblical text is certainly complex and may also be ambiguous. Polzin, in considering more deeply Eli's impression of Hannah's drunkenness in 1 Samuel 1, observes that although on the face of it Eli was wrong, in some ways the request itself may represent a "drunken desire." Polzin views Hannah's plea as a foreshadowing of the people's request for a king and asks:

> Is kingship a matter of drunken desire, a mistake, or is it a proper matter of the heart? On one hand, Hannah appears drunk but is not; kingship appears ungodly but is not. . . . Was it a wise thing to have asked for? Which is more real in this detail of 1 Samuel's initial event, the literal drunkenness of Hannah that is not, or her metaphorical drunkenness that very well might be? . . . It only appears a drunken deed to ask for a king. What is it really? (Polzin 1989, 27)

Polzin's insight and questions bring out exactly the complicated issues that surround kingship in ancient Israel and the steps that led to it.

In terms of God's role in this affair, God seems to be taking God's sweet time in terms of establishing anything that resembles a stable royal house.

Once a candidate is chosen, there are prevarications and hesitations and finally a clear-cut rejection before one arises who seems to carry the burden justifiably. Very soon the flaws appear in this king too, until they become fissures, and the break-up of the fragile union of tribes is not very far away. Finally, from the vantage point of the ones who eventually wove together the narratives in Samuel, what did it all come down to? A conquered nation, with a king who ate his food at the table of the Babylonian overlord. Was kingship a good or a bad thing? Did it help or did it hinder? Was it a sober desire or a request arising from a moment of drunkenness? Perhaps, no clear answers to these vexing issues are found here, but the raising of the questions themselves brings to mind notions of good and bad government that need to be pondered in our own time and context. In place of straightforward answers, we read rather a reflection of the complex and often harrowing context of biblical Israel that in many ways mirrors our own, both on the micro and macro levels.

Good reading for Christians involves also laying claim to texts that were not written primarily for them but by and for a people with a different history, whose direct descendants are the Jewish people. Insofar as these stories reflect the universal human condition, it is of course not difficult to recognize ourselves as individuals and communities. The question, however, is how we as latecomers to the story engage these texts as God's word and how we find in them a word of God for our time and our perplexities. It is not just a matter of recognizing ourselves but of recognizing ourselves and our relationship to God. Let us begin with the acknowledgement that these are first of all stories about the way of the ancestors of the Jewish people, and about the way of God with them. This acknowledgment does not mean that we then write off the stories as relevant only to the failures and shortcomings of another people that have nothing to do with us. How these may by the grace of God also become *our* stories is the second step, a step that can be taken only after distance has been established. If we walk our way toward the stories with patience, attention, and openness, our reading may become an engagement with the work of God in our time.

Text Divisions

I have grouped the material of the two books of Samuel into three main blocks: the story of Samuel (1 Sam 1-12), the story of Saul (1 Sam 13–31), and the story of David (2 Sam 1–24). One could make a case for arguing that all of the material is there to support the story of David, who comes on the scene in 1 Samuel 16. The divisions are only there to help us grasp the contours and content of a specific set of chapters. The story of Samuel is not about Samuel alone, and there is much overlap between the story of Samuel and Saul, on the one hand, and that of Saul and David, on the other. We keep in mind at all times that the stories are about far more than just the central characters. They touch on subjects as vastly diverse as royal and military leadership, religious objects of veneration and worship practices, parental yearning for their young, spousal and sibling relationships, master and mistress to servant relations, friendship, military campaigns, occult practices, and many other subjects that make up the rich fabric of human life anywhere, also in the ancient Israel of the days of Samuel, Saul, and David.

Part 1

The Story of Samuel

(1 Samuel 1–12)

Introduction

Twelve chapters set the stage for the accounts of the monarchy that follow. The first chapters tell of the birth of Samuel to his mother, Hannah, who requests him from God and who eventually delivers him for service at the sanctuary in Shiloh. There a priestly house filled with corruption presides over the sacrificial cult, and there young Samuel receives his first revelation from the Holy God of Israel, constituting a forecast of doom over Eli's house. Then follow three chapters with a focus on the adventures of the Ark of the Covenant, the most holy object of ancient Israel. The Ark, taken into battle by the Israelites, is eventually captured by the Philistines, who take it to their own region and suffer dire consequences as a result. Lively depictions follow of the Philistine attempt to return the religious object, obviously filled with divine potency, to Israelite territory, and the successful execution of their plan. Leaving the Ark behind, the story turns its attention to Samuel, who moves to the center of the picture in chapter 7 and stays there for the most part until the end of chapter 12. Although Samuel appears to exercise an effective judgeship, his sons do not follow in his footsteps. The people demand a king, and both God and his servant Samuel allow it with misgivings. Chapter 9 introduces Saul, and the three subsequent chapters relate his becoming the first king of Israel on three separate occasions. The concluding chapter presents a speech by Samuel, who alerts the people once again to their apostasy in demanding a king and warns them of future tragedy if they continue "to do evil."

Stories alternate between quick descriptions of a time flow of months or years with pauses to provide detail of distinct moments or days within the longer time span. Thus, chapter 1 initially recounts events that occur annually, and then stands still at the moment when Hannah first prays in the sanctuary. The activities of Hofni and Pinhas are described as habitual and longstanding over an unspecified period, while the story of God's revelation to Samuel takes place in one night. The Ark of the Covenant stays in Philistia for one year, followed by an episode devoted to a minute description of the deliberations and machinations that take place in the effort to return the Ark. Much of the narrative's dynamism derives from this artful alternation of the flow of time. Vividly depicted human characters are for the most part male. The notable exception in the opening chapters is Hannah. In addition to her, there are also Hannah's co-wife Peninnah, the unnamed wife of Pinhas at the end of chapter 4, and the girls who play a role in Saul's quest in chapter 9. These females are not "full-fledged characters," however, and the overwhelming impression is that, with few exceptions, these tales deal with men and male affairs, the life of the cult, politics, and war (Berlin 1983, 23–24). The storytellers delineate characters in subtle and interesting ways, revealing a good deal about them but also holding back and leaving gaps to be filled by the readers' imagination. Hannah, once she moves out of her position of lethargy and grief, becomes a strong spokesperson for herself and for God. As a major character, Samuel comes on the scene as a devout interpreter of God's word and undergoes change as the story moves on. In his older age, he frequently comes across as a cantankerous and resentful figure who suffers rejection with ill humor. Saul, the first to be anointed as Israel's king, takes on his office with apparent reluctance and only adopts the mantle of deliverer under the constraint of God's spirit. He leaves an initial impression of uncertainty and diffidence, thus implicitly raising questions about his leadership.

God intervenes directly in human affairs: through granting pregnancy to Hannah (ch. 1), causing sickness and death related to the Ark (chs. 5–6), handing defeat to the Philistines (ch. 7), sending Saul into the path of Samuel (ch. 9), and giving Saul a new heart and overpowering him with the divine spirit (chs. 10–11). Frequently, God's engagement with people takes place via God's messengers and announcements, as the man of God in chapter 2 and thereafter as Samuel, God's spokesperson (chs. 7, 8–12). Although Hannah is said to "pray" twice and Samuel both "prays" and promises to "pray" for the people, most communication between God and humanity, usually through the agency of Samuel, is reported as direct speech: "God said . . . ."

The theme that runs through the chapters is loyalty to the God of Israel who has the power to change the fate of human lives and reverse situations of distress. This power is celebrated in Hannah's song, which she ends with an expression of trust that God will guard the feet of God's "devoted ones" (1 Sam 2:9). Hannah, who opens the tale with her strong presence, trusts that God will help her in her predicament and puts herself within the sphere where God's power is exercised on her behalf. Others in the story, notably the people who carry the Ark into battle and those who demand they must have a king, do not trust in God's power to intervene for them. Yet another group, represented by Hofni, Pinhas, and all of Eli's house, abuses its God-granted privileges and is therefore rejected from priestly office.

A related theme treats good leadership in all spheres of life. Hofni and Pinhas, later mirrored by Samuel's sons, provide examples of corrupt leadership while Eli is the model of a weak leader. Samuel leads the people in exemplary ways in the religious and political sphere and functions as God's devoted servant in the narrative, interpreting to the people God's will for them. Saul's leadership has not yet come fully into focus, but its beginning is not entirely promising. Although as an individual he makes a sympathetic impression—concerned for the feelings of others, modest to a fault, and later refusing to needlessly kill those who initially opposed him—his kingship begins with a fruitless search for his father's cattle, and one can hardly say he embraces his new role wholeheartedly. In addition, none of his own words or actions articulate his relationship with God; instead, only God's initiative expresses it. The entire setup in these chapters creates a mood of excitement and anticipation of the future, whether for good or ill, although Samuel's last words to the people (1 Sam 12:25) may lead one to fear the worst.

Hannah (1 Sam 1:1–2:11)

This first section, ostensibly about intimate family matters in ancient Israel, presents an opening story that sets much of the tone, introduces major themes, and prepares the way for what is to follow. Briefly, the narrative tells of a successful plea for male offspring made to God by a woman named Hannah at the central sanctuary of the time, where her family made annual pilgrimage. In her prayer, Hannah promises her firstborn to God, and at the end of the episode she brings her young son to Shiloh, where he remains in service at the shrine: "the boy served the Holy One in the presence of Eli the priest" (1 Sam 2:11). With this last line, the cycle of coming and going that began in the opening verses of chapter 1 is completed, and Samuel's service starts.

A Request in the Sanctuary (1 Sam 1:1-28)

Hannah is one of the less likely characters to receive prominence in the story, as her lack of children is mentioned almost immediately after she is introduced as Elkanah's wife. In addition, the first eight verses put Elkanah in the center; most of the active verbs belong to him, and he is the only one who speaks. The chapter opens with the words, "There was a man . . .," subsequently providing his place of origin, his name, and four male ancestors to continue with his wives and children. Hannah, who has no children, receives the love of her husband and his special portion at the time of sacrifice, but remains entirely passive in the face of this devotion. She receives, in addition, the scorn and hateful treatment of Peninnah, Elkanah's other wife and the mother of his children. Not once, but every time the family goes up for the annual sacrifice, "as often as she went up to the house of the Holy One, she [Peninnah] harassed her" (v. 7). Hannah is the subject of only two verbs, "to weep" and "not eat" (v. 7), and does not respond to Elkanah's avowal of love (v. 8). Until v. 9, Elkanah has the first and the last word, and there is no reason to assume that he will not continue to be at the center of attention.

Then time comes almost to a standstill compared to the setup in the first eight verses, where Elkanah and his family come annually, "year in year out," to the shrine at Shiloh. Verse 9 begins with the words "she arose," placing the verb in Hebrew first, drawing attention to it and creating a sense of disjunction and shock following Hannah's motionless, speechless appearance until this point. As time stops, Hannah gets in motion, and once in the center, she will stay there. The story that appeared to be about a man and his family, his habits, and his faithfulness in worship now turns its attention to a woman. Hannah arises to pray. We learn the location of her prayer through the appearance of Eli, the priest at Shiloh, who is sitting on a chair at the door of the shrine where Hannah's prayer takes place. Before she speaks, her state of mind receives emphasis once again through the description of her condition of bitterness and her continued weeping:

> She was bitter in her soul
> and prayed to the Holy God,
> and wept and wept. (1 Sam 1:10)

When she opens her mouth, she asks God in stereotypical lament fashion to "regard her," to "pay attention to her," to "remember/not forget her," and to "give" her male offspring. The last request, of course, carries the greatest weight, containing the core of her plea (v. 11), and the verb "to give" is the climactic verb in the series (Fokkelman 1993, 37). She follows the request for this gift straightaway with a promise of her own: "then I will give . . . ." The response to giving will not be "getting," but giving in return. In addition, her vow to God is more extensive than the usual temporary Nazirite dedication demanded (cf. Num 6:1-21). Her willingness to return

God's potential gift is extreme, thus underlining the extremity of her feelings and the lengths to which she will go to escape her predicament.

Before a word can come from God in reply to Hannah's prayer, the priest Eli, who has been observing her, steps in with his rebuke. Eli is looking on the outside of Hannah, an important thread that continues in the material, rather than on her "heart," her state of mind, and decides that she must be drunk. There is irony in Eli's conclusion, for Hannah vowed by implication that her son would not touch alcohol, even though this aspect is not explicit in the traditional Hebrew reading. (NRSV follows Qumran here, reading, "then I will set him before you as a Nazirite, until the day of his death; he shall drink neither wine nor intoxicants and no razor shall touch his head.") It is also most unlikely that Hannah would have indulged in drinking in view of her twice-mentioned abstinence (vv. 7-8). In her desperation, Hannah has bypassed male authority to reach out directly to God; now the man Eli, who represents God's presence, comes between her and God. Briefly, the question arises as to how Hannah will cope in the face of this negative priestly authority. For a moment her agency, no doubt hard won, hangs in the balance, but her first word takes away any doubt as to whether she will be able to continue on the road toward independence and agency. "No, my lord," she says, and then goes on to define her state of mind and heart. Rather than pouring wine, she has "poured out her soul" before God, to whom she spoke out of her great "anxiety and vexation" (v. 16). "No, my lord, do not take me for a worthless woman." She does not spell out the cause of her "vexation" or the nature of her request to God. Eli apparently does not need to know, for he sends her off with the prayer that God may grant her request (the Hebrew here is ambiguous, and it could be that he assures her God *will* grant her request). His phrasing is interesting, for he says literally, "May the God of Israel give your *asking* that you *asked.*" For the first time the verb "to ask" (Hebrew *sha'al*) occurs. It is a verb with strong resonance that will be taken up by Hannah at a later point in the story. Eli's reassurance, whether pious wish or announcement, is sufficient for Hannah, who responds politely and is on her way, her sadness and abstinence left behind.

The last two verses of the episode once more increase the tempo: A few sentences tell of the family's return to Ramah, Hannah's subsequent pregnancy, and the birth of Samuel (vv. 19-20). Verse 20 is phrased as a report from the narrator rather than as direct speech: "She called him Samuel, for [she said] from the Holy One I asked him." While the name Samuel can be variously linked to God's name, Hebrew *'el,* and to listening, Hebrew *shama'* it is not obviously connected to the verb *sha'al*, "to ask." For the second time the verb "to ask" occurs at a significant place in the story.

Time moves on and the season arrives again for Elkanah to make the annual pilgrimage to Shiloh. Hannah, however, refuses to go and tells her husband in clear terms that she will go up with him only when her son is off the breast: "As soon as the boy is weaned I will bring him." The root "to wean" occurs three times in this brief interlude of three verses (vv. 21-23), with "nursing" added in v. 23, an emphatic reference to the sacrifice Hannah was making in giving her child back to God. The bond as well as tensions between parents and children will be a continued theme throughout the books of Samuel.

In v. 24 Hannah is in charge of all the action: "she took him," "she had weaned him," "she brought him." She is the one who speaks to the priest Eli about the son she prayed for, whom she is now leaving at the sanctuary. In vv. 27-28, the key verb "ask" occurs repeatedly:

> The Holy One gave me the "asking" that I "asked" of him.
> Even I myself "lend him as asked" to the Holy One,
> all the days of his life he is "lent as asked" to God. (1:27-28)

Hannah's relatively lengthy speech ends in a clever wordplay on the verb "to ask." In Hebrew, the meaning "to lend him as asked" is produced by a manipulation of the verb "ask," a wordplay that is difficult to render in English so that we are "forced to walk around an elegant pun in Hebrew" (Alter 1999, 8 n. 28). In v. 27 Hannah echoes Eli's words to her in the earlier episode, when she "stood" there with him and he told her that God would give her the "asking that she asked" (v. 17). Then she goes on emphatically to reaffirm her vow of dedicating her son to God's service with her final words that this one is "lent as asked to the Holy One." In Hebrew the entire phrase takes only two words: *sha'ul ladonai*. Finally the verb "to ask" has come to rest on "the asked one," *Sha'ul*, the name of ancient Israel's first king.

Central to the story are the notions of asking and getting, of asking and giving back what has been asked. The people's "asking" for a king is just over the horizon, and the repeated use of a verb that so clearly connotes the name of the first anointed king of Israel is therefore not accidental. While one may be tempted to assign clumsiness to writers or editors who presumably got mixed up in their stories relating to Samuel and Saul, it may be that we should take the hint from the repetitive use of words for asking. The true thing, kingship, has not been asked yet, but it will eventually be asked. Then the *asking* will entail sacrifices from the one who is here "lent on the asking,"

Samuel, as well as from those who are doing the asking, the people. Samuel will have to step aside for one who will carry final authority in the land. The people will have to give up a good deal of their financial means and relative independence to support the king and his household, his armies, and various building enterprises. When Samuel later warns the people regarding the doings of kings, the key word is that this king will "take" (ch. 8). Finally, the asking for a king will demand also a sacrifice on God's part. From then on, leadership will not arise in Israel through direct intervention of God's overpowering spirit. Hereditary kingship will take the place of God-driven, God-inspired leadership. "For not you they have rejected, but me they have rejected from being king over them," God replies to Samuel when he consults the deity about the people's request (1 Sam 8:7). The desire for kingship affects all—leaders, people, and God—and its cost will demand sacrifice from all involved in the development of ancient Israel as a nation.

Family Relations (1 Sam 1:1-8)

The tale tells of a central sanctuary in Shiloh where, as we shall find out, the most sacred object of the tribes, the Ark of the Covenant, resides. The Ark will continue to play a significant part in subsequent narratives, while the issue of a sanctuary to house it will arise as well. In terms of human characters, the spotlight shines first on Elkanah, a man who lives in Ramah. Next to Elkanah, the priests who serve in Shiloh appear: Eli and his two sons, Hofni and Pinhas. While Elkanah's occupation is not reported, we may assume that he was a fairly well-to-do farmer because he had two wives, a sign of some affluence in a society where polygyny with the resulting expanded family was reserved for those who could afford it. In addition, Elkanah has the resources to travel annually to Shiloh and bring the necessities for sacrifice. Finally, when at the end of the story Hannah brings young Samuel to the sanctuary, she takes with her substantial contributions, "a three-year-old bull, half a bushel of flour and a skin of wine" (1 Sam 1:24). In Hebrew, the man's name, Elkanah, connects the deity, El, with acquisition, *qanah,* and may be a pointer to his economic standing.

In the background of this prominent male are his two wives, Peninnah and Hannah, "Pearl" and "Grace." The women receive an introduction only as Elkanah's wives, without ancestry or locations in contrast to the naming of their husband. These are *his* women, and he doles out portions to them, to each appropriate to her standing in the household:

> . . . he gave to Peninnah, his wife,
> and all her sons and daughters portions.

And to Hannah he gave one special portion,
for he loved Hannah,
and the Holy One had shut her womb. (1 Sam 1:4-5)

We note that Peninnah is called "his wife" and that these short lines pack a lot of information. Previously we knew she had "children," and now that she has both sons and daughters. Peninnah gets her due from her husband. Or does she? In the next breath, it sounds as if Hannah has a special place in the household, despite her lack of children, because she receives beside her special portion the love of Elkanah. Is it so surprising that Peninnah resents Hannah, who has a prize that she, Peninnah, would perhaps like to have? The description of Peninnah's harassment follows on the heels of the statement about Elkanah's love for Hannah. Although the text does not state this explicitly, it raises the question of whether Peninnah is loved at all. Is she in the household only for the sake of producing children? Her behavior, while not in any way admirable, can become more understandable.

The first dysfunctional family in the Samuel narratives has appeared on the scene, and it will not be the last. Eli and his two sons are at odds, as Samuel and his sons will also be. Saul and his son Jonathan are deeply divided over the presence of David at the court. Michal, Saul's daughter who becomes David's wife, ends up in an unhappy relationship with both her father and her husband. Above all, David's family, with its large group of wives as well as concubines, suffers fissures and deep tragedy, with three of his children dying a premature death and one daughter raped by her half-brother. Elkanah's family presages these family relations that still lie in the future.

The names of the priests together with their father Eli occur following the location of the sanctuary. The priests receive no further qualifications, but they will become more prominent in the sequel. The effect of the naming in these initial verses is that the names of the women are surrounded by those of powerful males, the householder Elkanah, and the priests who serve at the sanctuary, Hofni and Pinhas, with their father, Eli. Of the two women, Hannah clearly has less standing than Peninnah. Not only does Hannah receive the scorn of her rival "year in year out" but her wound is also rubbed raw by what she receives from Elkanah's hand each year, which though special is only a fraction of what the others get. Only Elkanah speaks in the opening verses, and he addresses Hannah as follows:

And Elkanah, her husband, said to her:
 Hannah, why do you weep?

And why do you not eat,
and why are you downhearted?
Am I not better to you than ten sons? (1:8)

That Elkanah's questions are not a true inquiry into Hannah's mental state becomes clear in his last question, which reveals that he knows the solution to Hannah's problem: his own presence. As David Jobling observes, "If you wish to assure someone of your love, the line 'Are *you* not more to *me* than . . . ?' seems much more promising than 'Am I not more to you . . . ?'!" (Jobling 1998, 131). The three "why's" may be a sign of Elkanah's impatience with Hannah's depression, with his final question in truth a statement that he, Elkanah, is indeed worth more than ten sons (Fokkelman 1993, 29). Alternatively, Elkanah may be asking for affirmation. "He does what most people do when confronted with great affliction: drift off into their own history of distress and traumas . . . and from this position try to stave off the negative by manipulative means. In the end what is hurtful in the contact between Elkanah and Hannah is that he invokes the mother figure in a woman who has been stricken with childlessness" (Fokkelman 1993, 30). Whatever Elkanah's exact intentions may have been, the result is that Hannah gets on her feet and makes a move toward her liberation from the oppressive forces of culture and family.

Childlessness was a serious disability in the culture of ancient Israel, as it is in large parts of the world today. It could amount to a sentence of isolation and economic deprivation if the husband were not able or willing to tolerate a childless wife in his household. Psychologically, the lack of children, especially sons, would have created a condition of despair and hopelessness, as Hannah experiences. The presence of a husband, even a loving husband, would not fill the yawning abyss of a life without offspring in a setting where offspring was the guarantee of people's ongoing existence. The presence of a loving husband would not create a sense of productivity and agency in a woman deprived of being a productive contributor to her family. Hannah lived in a time when the family was the only location for her to be productive and contribute to the well-being of society.

Elkanah, the man of substance, is at best obtuse in his questions. They must have been the final straw for Hannah, for in the next breath she appeals for help to an authority higher than Elkanah or the local priests. Henceforth, Elkanah moves to the margin of the story while Hannah takes his place in the center. Even though Hannah will gradually fade out to make room for her son as the central character, her appearance in the opening scenes of 1 and 2 Samuel is of great significance, pointing to issues on a far larger scale than that of one family, be it a faithful and religiously responsible one. She personifies the unlikely person who catches God's attention and receives God's benefits and favor. In addition, Hannah, on par with other women such as Yael, Ruth, and Esther, is an unexpected hero in the Bible who steps forward from the shadows cast by powerful men and her own grief to take a lead role. Moreover, like other biblical women, her role breaks through the private and domestic sphere into one of significance in a national framework. As Carol Meyers observes, "the national purview of this tale transposes it beyond the sexual politics of domestic life and into the realm of national service" (Meyers 1994, 103).

God appears first in the story as the one thought to be responsible for Hannah's infertility. Twice in the opening lines the phrase, "the Holy One had shut her womb," occurs (vv. 5 and 6), both times in connection with family members and their behavior toward her. Elkanah's posture toward Hannah is loving, *even though*, as we might say, God had prevented Hannah from having children. The Hebrew of v. 5 connects the phrase about Elkanah's love for Hannah to her infertility with the simple conjunction "and," while Peninnah's harassment of Hannah is followed by the conjunction "because." Peninnah bases her treatment on the fact that God has apparently singled out Hannah for punishment. There is no ambiguity in Peninnah's posture and behavior. Elkanah's action in v. 5 is less obvious. Did he give Hannah a single portion, albeit a special one, or was it a double portion? Was his action based on the fact that he thought God had caused her not to have children? The Hebrew text about the portion given to Hannah is difficult, and translators go in different directions. Clearly and emphatically, the text records that Hannah had no children and that both her husband and her co-wife ascribe this fact to an action of God. Hannah's lack of children, referred to three times in a short span, creates a sharp portrait of a desolate woman, eliciting sympathy for her plight from the listener.

Hannah, in a surprise move, bypasses all male authority to claim direct access to God. To make this more explicit, the text describes the priest Eli as seated on a chair at the doorpost, implying that she must have passed him. Like Elkanah, Eli is sidelined during Hannah's prayer, a hint of the doom that will eventually befall him and his house. Eli's house, as foretold in a double announcement, will eventually fail, and he himself will fall to his death, as he sits on his chair excluded from the main events of the day (1 Sam 4:18). Perhaps as an anticipatory sign of Eli's inadequacy, he mistakes Hannah's desperate and silent cries for inebriation (1:13, ". . . Hannah was speaking to herself, only her lips were moving and her voice was not heard").

When Hannah corrects him about his misapprehension of her state, she admonishes him not to take her for "a worthless woman" (Hebrew *bat beliya'al*). This very expression, "worthless men" (*beney beliya'al*, 2:12), will later describe the sons of Eli, Hofni and Pinhas. On account of the "worthless" sons of Eli, his house is doomed, as will be reiterated in the following episodes. Instead of paying attention to the worthlessness of his own sons, Eli is ready to judge a woman who, far from worthless, will become the mother of a true servant of God. Eli may exhibit misplaced rage. He knows about his own sons, he does not know what to do about them, and he takes his anger out on an innocent person. In any case, the word "worthless" casts an ominous shadow forward.

Hannah's direct plea to God, the "Holy One of Hosts," succeeds, but even before the result of her prayer is announced, she rebounds from her depression: "the woman went on her way and she ate and her face was no longer sad" (1:18). The act of taking her case directly to God achieved for her the ability to throw off the cloak of victimization and reclaim her status as a family member. In this episode, God is the one who hears the voice of the weak and disempowered woman and provides the ultimate solution to her predicament:

> Elkanah knew Hannah, his wife,
> and the Holy One remembered her.
> In due time Hannah became pregnant,
> and gave birth to a son. (1:19b-20a)

For the first time, Hannah is called Elkanah's "wife," and she calls him "her husband" for the first time in the subsequent lines when she refuses to go up for the annual sacrifice. She will bring her son when he is ready and when she is ready, perhaps after three to five years. Three years would be a minimum, but she may have stretched the period of weaning so she could keep him with her (Alter 1999, 8 n. 25).

The theme of leadership so central to the books of Samuel is clearly present in this narrative. At the time of Elkanah, the man from Ramah, and Eli, the priest at Shiloh, their leaders do not serve the tribes of Israel well as will become evident in the second part of chapter 2. In addition, the narrative serves to introduce Samuel, the leader who will combine in himself the offices of prophet, priest, and judge. This Samuel was "asked for," Hebrew *sha'ul*, by his mother. Behind Samuel looms the figure of Saul, *Sha'ul*, the one "asked for" by the people, and beyond him arises the boy-shepherd, silver-tongued, enchanting David, the one on whom God's favor will come to rest. It will turn out to be a work of trial and error, this choice of leadership, and even in King David the people and God will be faced with a far-from-ideal leader. It is all set in motion by an infertile woman and her refusal to accept her bereft state any longer. What she *asked*, God *gave*, and she *gave* back in return. What the people will ask, God will also give, albeit not without demurring. As much as Eli was wrong about his perception of Hannah, essentially the entire desire for such centralized leadership may have arisen from drunkenness.

Perceptions of God

We pause to consider the perceptions of God in this episode. The Elkanah family is clearly devout, trekking every year to the central sanctuary to make annual sacrifice. Only later (3:3) is it revealed that the sanctuary housed the Ark of God, the most sacred object of the ancient Israelite tribes last heard of in Judges 20, when it was located in Bethel (Judg 20:28). The Ark will eventually play a significant role in the events, but as yet is ignored. The place where the worshipers go is simply called the "house of the Holy One," and once the "sanctuary" or "temple" (1:9). There, as the text notes, priestly personnel oversee the orderly proceedings of sacrificial worship, although as it turns out the present servants of the sanctuary fall far short of their calling. The sanctuary is located in Shiloh, which has both a positive and negative history (Josh 2:9, 12; 18:1, 8-10; 19:51; 21:2; Judg 18:31; 21:12, 19, 21), perhaps begging the question as to the way worship is conducted there (Fokkelman 1993, 20). Be that as it may, the God present here is approached through sacrifice handled by the appropriate personnel. The family who goes to Shiloh comes from Ramah. Ramah is closely associated with Samuel and is mentioned only in connection with him. Zuph, twice mentioned in the first verse, will occur again when Saul first appears on the scene (9:5) during the search for his father's straying donkeys. The geography of chapter 1 points in this way to future events.

Against this backdrop, the family of one man and two women comes to the fore, one of whom suffers deeply from her lack of offspring. This lack merits mention three times and is twice ascribed to an act of God (see "Family Relations" above). If the text implies that both Elkanah and Peninnah held God to be the author of Hannah's infertility (see "Family Relations" above), the question arises as to whether Hannah also lays her bereft state at God's door. It is worth noting that she seeks recourse directly from God, putting herself in God's path rather than in the path of the official who serves the sanctuary. Hannah lays a claim on God's attention because in her view God is withholding her deepest desire from her and only

God can remedy this state. The narrator most likely shares this point of view since the phrase "the Holy One remembered her" appears between the occurrence of sexual intercourse and Hannah's pregnancy (1:19). God is portrayed as the one with the power to withhold and give life. In addition, the view of God is of one prepared to intervene directly in the life of an individual, to accede to her "drunken desire." In some ways, of course, the episode is parabolic for what will take place eventually when the request for intervention will come not from an individual but from the community. Yet the view of God as the one who bends down to aid the destitute woman who feels forsaken and forgotten is one that deserves attention by itself. The God of the Bible is the one who hears the cries of the lowly and powerless. This fact may also be what Hannah counts on as she implores the God of her faith to intercede on her behalf. The perception of God as the one with the power to give life, to "raise from the dust the poor," prevails in the prayer assigned to her at the end of this part of the story.

All about Power (1 Sam 2:1-11)

For a relatively brief passage handed down with little evidence of textual corruption, couched in evocative lyrical language, Hannah's prayer has raised a chorus of discordant voices as to its genre, cohesion, and subject. Is this a typical thanksgiving or victory prayer, or is it impossible to assign this poem to a specific type? Is the poem a unity or a collection of fragments? Finally, what is the main concern voiced in this prayer? Is it about kingship, or is viewing the song from the perspective of kingship a distortion of Hannah's voice? (Fokkelman 1993, 86, 108; Polzin 1989, 30–39; Jobling 1998, 168)

First, since the writer puts the prayer in Hannah's mouth, it is important to keep Hannah's context in mind. This is Hannah's second prayer, and she is the only one to resort to prayer as a solution for a problem in the opening chapters. In addition, her first prayer has proved successful. She was the one who, in Eli's hearing, "stood there praying to the Holy God" (1:26-27), and God granted her request. The fact that Hannah does the praying on this second occasion is significant in itself. It should not come as a surprise that in later times the rabbis considered Hannah to provide the model for prayer (Bronner 1994, 94–95). Second, the poem opens up more clearly to an understanding of its theme when approached as a cohesive prayer rather than as a collage of fragments gathered together for the occasion by an editor. There is nothing surprising about the similarity of certain phrases to those found in some of the psalms, since biblical poetry in general relies on stock phrases and expressions.

Returning to Hannah and her story, we have already learned that she was a woman without power in her situation, perceiving herself as someone without personhood, a victim of circumstances over which she had no control. Her lack of offspring spelled lack of agency and ultimately lack of life. No person in her context could move her from this situation into a different position: not her husband, who represented economic and emotional sustenance; not her rival, who represented fecundity and who faced her daily with the abundance she missed; and not the priest who represented God. Hannah propelled herself out of this situation by taking a vital initial step, maybe on the basis of the conviction that only one had the power to change her lot, the one who, in the words of the poem, could "raise from the dust the poor" (v. 8), the Holy One of Israel, the incomparable God (v. 2). She opened her mouth with intense prolonged prayer in supplication only to this one, with no human being hearing her plea (1:13).

Once Hannah's conviction has been vindicated that God is the one with the power to give life, her mouth naturally opens again in prayer, this time in praise. She, who "wept and wept" (1:10) before God, now sings her rejoicing:

> My heart exults in the Holy One
> Lifted high is my horn in the Holy God. (2:1)

The heart that was once "down" (1:8), squeezed in anguish, now "swells," the literal Hebrew root used here. She who had no power now "*lifts* her horn *high*." The verb "to lift" (Hebrew *rum*), key to the entire poem, is also connected to the town of her origin, later Samuel's home, Ramah. The horn, raised by the victorious animal, clearly symbolizes power. It will recur at the end of the poem to symbolize the power of the king, reflecting at the same time the utensil used to anoint the royal candidate with oil (Alter 1999, 9–10): "[God] will give strength to his king / lift high the horn of his anointed" (2:10).

While there seems little doubt that there is a deliberate proleptic reference to kingship in v. 10, it may be helpful to consider the reference to royalty not only as a portent of things to come but also as reflecting back on Hannah. Her strength, her newfound personhood and agency, are comparable to that of a king; her horn is raised as high and is as empowered by God as that of the legitimately anointed ruler.

The first lines of the prayer (vv. 1-2) put Hannah as the speaker directly in relation to God. The first person occurs only here in the poem, while God is referred to in the second person. Hannah's relationship with God is deeply personal; while others did not care, or put themselves in a position of animosity ("my enemies"), or showed a caring that was essentially ineffective, God rescued ("your deliverance"). Everything that follows flows from this source. She sings of a personal God who was the only one with the power to create a reversal in her situation. This reversal is, however, not only applicable to one individual but is typical of this God and may be applied to all who find themselves in like situations.

The main body of the prayer (vv. 4-8) concerns the nature and acts of God set against the background of God's incomparable nature: "for there is none beside you / there is no rock like our God" (v. 2). Hereafter, the language about God will turn to description preceded by the admonition, "Talk no more so high and mighty" (2:3). Hannah speaks here in the plural, and we may understand that she addresses her counsel to her community. Her rival, her husband, and the priest had all addressed her in mistaken ways, thinking they knew things that in reality they did not know. Only God knows in truth. The opening line of v. 3 uses the word "to multiply" and literally states, "do not multiply speaking high, high." Hannah herself had "multiplied" speaking to the only source of knowledge and power (1:12), while others spoke to her out of ignorance from an arrogant point of view. There is height and then there is height. There is the height of Hannah's horn and of God who is the rock (v. 2), and there is the false height of pride and arrogance, the origin of human perceptions and speech, in Hannah's context and by extension in many human contexts. In contrast, God is the one who "knows" ("a God of knowledge") and who weighs "human deeds" (v. 3).

In the initial description of God's actions (v. 4), Hannah uses a set of three vividly contrasting pictures. The first two contain masculine references in Hebrew: a hero's bow broken in pieces, while those (males) with faltering steps continue in strength; filled bellies of men needing to work for their food, while hungry ones, presumably once scrambling for food, now have the leisure to grow fat. Then, with the last picture, in stark contrast to the preceding plural masculine references, Hannah refers to a singular woman without offspring, the "barren one" who now bears seven, while the fecund one, "she with many sons," dries up (v. 5). The pictures of reversal thus culminate and find focus in the specific situation of Hannah herself.

The next lines (vv. 6-7) have God as the subject of the action with no explicit human recipient. God is in charge of such reversals, it appears, bringing death and causing life, taking down to Sheol and raising up, impoverishing and enriching, bringing low and exalting. Verse 8 then wraps up the subject by bringing God and human recipient into the picture together and making clear the subjects of God's attention: the poor and the needy. No other categories are mentioned. Hannah herself belonged once to this group and she knows what she is talking about:

> God raises from the dust the poor
> and from the ash-heap lifts high the needy,
> to seat them with nobles
> and a seat of honor bequeath them.
> For to God belong the pillars of the earth
> and he has set on them the world. (1 Sam 2:8)

To undergird her declarations, she emphasizes that it is God the creator, who fashioned the foundations of the world, who executes these acts of grace (Fokkelman 1993, 95).

God, in Hannah's view, is not a neutral party but is solidly on the side of those who need help and strengthening. That is where God's power goes. At the same time, God has the power to humble and bring down those who are in positions of false self-aggrandizement—the hero who believes in his own strength, the rich who has others working for his bread, the one with wealth of offspring who considers this her virtue. The final lines (vv. 9-10) reiterate and summarize this conviction once more: God guards the feet of those devoted to God while silencing those who once spewed arrogance (Alter 1999, 11 n. 9). God is the one who will open his mouth, thundering in heaven against God's adversaries, since God is the only one worthy to judge. The mighty man/hero/king is equally subject to God's power, for he too is under the guidance and control of this incomparable God. God alone can "lift high" the horn of God's anointed. For the last time, Hannah uses the verb "to lift," employing again the root that occurs in key places in the poem (vv. 1, 7, 8, 10).

Clearly, Hannah's prayer concerns issues of power, both in Hannah's own context and in the context of the events that follow (Fokkelman 1993, 105). The skill of the writer closely interweaves issues of individual and national importance. In the portrayal of Hannah, these are inseparable. What pertains to her personally pertains to the larger human context of her people. Lifting up and casting down have not only become evident in her own life but will also become evident in what follows. God's partiality for those in need and those who are devoted to God's service, with its uncomfortable concomitant of hostility to those who put themselves in an adversarial position to God, will become evident also. Those who follow their own guidance, who are heroes by "their own strength," will find out who is ultimately in control.

Besides the voices of Hannah and that of a triumphant king, Robert Polzin hears in Hannah's prayer also the voice of the Deuteronomist, "the author of the song in its present setting at least." This voice, in Polzin's opinion, ultimately casts a "melancholy tone" over the prayer. Referring to 2 Kings 25, where King Jehoiachin is said to eat bread before the Babylonian ruler, Polzin points out that from the Deuteronomist's point of view, the emphasis of the reversals falls on the ones once powerful and rich now having to beg for food to receive a portion at the foreign overlord's table (2 Kgs 25:30), with only the poor left in the land of the promise (2 Kgs 24:14). This voice "casts a final poignant shadow over Israel's high hopes for kingship as portrayed in the story of Hannah" (Polzin 1989, 30–39). From the Deuteronomist's perspective, neither king nor people had lived according to God's *torah*, and thus their fate overcame them on account of their own failure.

We may perhaps agree with Danna Nolan Fewell and David Gunn, who suggest that "Hannah's song is both her own and not her own," overdubbed as it may be by editors who used her words for their own political ends (Fewell and Gunn 1993, 139). There is no doubt that this story, ostensibly about a man, Elkanah, turned into the story of a woman, Hannah, in the course of which she gained both agency and voice. Hannah "arose," she said "no," and she "prayed." While Elkanah goes to bring annual sacrifice, Hannah brings the one true sacrifice. There is also no doubt that both her victimization and her gain of personhood take place "under the sign of patriarchy" (Fewell and Gunn 1993, 139). Under this sign, a woman's lack of children prevents her from being fully human; her becoming a person is located only in her reproductive capability and in her willingness to sacrifice what is most dear. It is not the "sign of patriarchy" that is so remarkable in ancient Israel's context, but rather that, when all is said and done, Hannah is a woman of "speech and action." She is valiant once she arises, contradicts the most powerful males in her surroundings, the priest Eli and her husband Elkanah, and finally articulates her strong convictions about the God of her faith in a voice no less eloquent than that of King David, the great singer of Israel.

There is also no doubt that Hannah's story is a part of the larger story of the beginning of kingship, of the roots of prophecy, and of the eventual fate of the nation under their kings. There is no need to see Hannah robbed of her authentic voice when we read her story and prayer in this larger context, no more than when we transpose it into our own context. The narratives of these texts face readers today with questions that arise out of contemporary situations. As David Hester observes, "Where, the narrative asks us, is the line between acting within covenant relationship and usurping the intentions of God? What is our role, what belongs to God?" (Hester 2000, 14). These texts speak of what makes for good and bad service under the guidance of God's *torah*, of good and poor leadership, and also raise anew the question as to what makes a person a human being in her context, "under the sign of patriarchy." Hannah's personhood resided perhaps not so much in her becoming a mother but in the fact that "she arose" (1:9) and took her fate to the one source of power she trusted. Hannah stood up for herself, for her family, and finally for her people. Far from being the "worthless woman" the priest Eli thought her to be, her character and behavior show her to be the woman of valor of Proverbs 31 (Prov 31:10), for which Ruth provides the exemplar (Ruth 3:11) in the Bible.

After the prayer, Elkanah and Samuel are the subjects of the action in the closing lines. Elkanah goes home, and Samuel stays in "service" to God at the sanctuary in the presence of Eli (2:11). A narrative that had a woman at the center closes with the mention of three male names. Hannah is almost gone from the story, and we say farewell to her reluctantly, for she is a sturdy sign of hope and human integrity at the beginning of tales in which such qualities will at times be rare enough.

Sanctuary Activities (1 Sam 2:12–4:1a)

Following Hannah's song, the second chapter provides information about the priestly house of Eli in telling and sordid detail (2:12-25). Against this background, it depicts Samuel as the bright counterpoint, with a description of his presence and service at the sanctuary twice interrupting the report on Eli's sons (2:18-21, 26). The notes on Samuel prepare for the shift of focus to his presence at Shiloh in chapter 3. The last part of chapter 2 has as the subject an oracle of doom on Eli's house brought by an anonymous "man of God" (2:27-36). Unlike chapter 1, there is no orderly flow of time and events; instead, this section paints a picture of habitual corrupt behavior over an extended period, while the boy Samuel was growing up at the sanctuary. The oracle from the man of God has no precise time indicator attached to it, so we assume it took place at some point during this period.

While the events of chapter 2 take place over unspecified stretches of time, chapter 3 slows the tempo to focus on one incident at the sanctuary concerning Samuel and Eli (3:1-10). The episode serves to provide a detailed portrait of faithful Samuel and to reiterate the pronouncement of doom on Eli's house (3:11-18). A coda summarizes the status of Samuel with God and people and ends the narratives of people and events at Shiloh on a positive note (3:19–4:1).

A Pack of Scoundrels (1 Sam 2:12-26)

Immediately following Hannah's song, the text provides a close-up portrayal of Eli's family, specifically of his sons, termed "worthless men" (Hebrew *beney beliya'al*, 2:12). The phrasing recalls Hannah's protest to Eli that she was not a "worthless woman," literally a "daughter of *beliya'al*" (1 Sam 1:16; see commentary at that section). In the section that follows, the picture of the sons of Eli, who legitimately officiate at the sanctuary and profane the service of God by abusing the sacrifices and the people who bring them, serves as the negative background to the positive portrait of Samuel, the one "asked" who was "lent as asked" to the service of the Holy One (2:20). The picture of Samuel puts the sordid actions of the priests in sharp relief; unlike Samuel, they do not serve God but only themselves (Goldingay 1988, 28).

The first verses of chapter 1 introduced Hofni and Pinhas, the sons of Eli, as priests of God (1:3); now the text reveals how they exercise their office. Three times, in escalating fashion, the narrator issues a note of condemnation:

> The sons of Eli were worthless men,
> they did not know the Holy One. (1 Sam 2:12)
>
> The sin of the boys was very great before the Holy One
> for the men treated contemptuously the offering of the Holy One. (1 Sam 2:17)
>
> But they did not listen to the words of their father,
> for it pleased the Holy One to kill them. (1 Sam 2:26)

Each time, the text relates the misdeeds of Hofni and Pinhas directly to the God they are expected to serve; as Eli points out, in such a case, there is no intercession possible (v. 25). The last indictment of the sons (v. 26) brings home the truth that indeed *beliya'al* is their father to whom they listen rather than Eli (Fokkelman 1993, 116, 128). A description of three ways of misbehaving supports the three indictments. These may be summarized as follows: Eli's "boys" take what does not belong to them. Their actions are identified by the word *mishpat* in v. 13, i.e., the practice but more accurately the behavior that accords with *justice*. First, they take what belongs to the people who bring sacrifice (vv. 13-14); second, they take from God the part of the sacrifice that belongs to God (vv. 15-16); and, third, they take the women who were on duty at the sanctuary in order to have illicit sex with them (v. 22). When Samuel later announces to the people who demand a king how royal rule will affect them, he uses the same word used here for the practice of the corrupt priests: *taking* will also characterize the king's *mishpat* (1 Sam 8:11-18).

While Hofni and Pinhas go unnamed in this part of the narrative, the word "boys" or "lads" (Hebrew *na'ar*) is used to excellent effect to designate them, their servants, and Samuel. Their immoral behavior is habitual (v. 17, "the sin of the boys was very great") and spreads to others: their servant, called "the priest's boy" (vv. 13 and 15), the people who forcibly give up their own and God's share, the women who were employed at the sanctuary, indeed "all Israel" (vv. 14 and 22). A spreading pool of misrule affects all who come in contact with them. In contrast to these bad "boys," both the priests and the servant who engage in corrupt behavior, Samuel is the "boy" who does true service (v. 18). In addition, the root *gadal* ("to be/grow great") refers to all the "boys," Eli's sons and Samuel, in contrastive ways. The sin of the priests is "very great," while Samuel continues to "grow," in Hebrew literally "to become great," in the presence and favor of the Holy One (2:21, 26).

The short section devoted to a description of Samuel and his parents, vv. 18-21, opens and closes with lines that put Samuel in direct relation to God, as do those concerning Eli's sons, except that in his case the relation is the right one:

> And Samuel served before the Holy One,
> And the boy Samuel grew up with the Holy One. (1 Sam 18, 21)

He is after all, this time in Eli's words, the *requested* one (v. 20), an echo of Hannah's own words to Eli when she brought Samuel to the sanctuary (1:28).

For the rest, one hears about Samuel only what he wore: "a linen ephod" and "a small coat" made and brought annually by his mother (vv. 18-19). Because these stories only occasionally remark on people's attire, this seemingly incongruous detail must point to a feature that is more significant than might seem at face value. Indeed, the ephod is the garment assigned solely to priests in the Samuel texts (1 Sam 2:18; 14:3; 21:10; 22:18; 23:6, 9; 30:7), with the exception of Samuel himself and King David (2 Sam 6:14). The wearing of the ephod thus points to Samuel's exercise of the priestly office. In addition, the touching detail of the "small coat" opens a window both into

Hannah's continuing care for her "boy" and into the continuing role of the coat or mantle in Samuel's life. Saul will grasp Samuel's mantle in vain in his effort to hold on to Samuel and thus to his kingship (1 Sam 15:27), and the medium at Endor will recognize Samuel by his mantle (1 Sam 28:14).

Hannah appears one last time in the story, at first nameless and in relation to the male members of her household—as Samuel's mother (v. 19) and Elkanah's wife (v. 20). Yet, she is the subject of three action verbs in the opening lines, where she is said "to make," "to bring up," and "to go up," and perhaps may be understood as the subject of the verb that refers to bringing sacrifice (Fokkelman 1993, 125):

> And a small coat *made* for him his mother,
> that *she brought up* for him yearly
> when *she went up* with her husband
> *to make yearly sacrifice* at Shiloh. (1 Sam 2:19)

According to Carol Meyers, it is telling that earlier in the story Hannah brings the sacrificial materials to Shiloh (1:25), a sign of the prominent role women could exercise in early Israel in making vows and bringing sacrifice. A reference to her making sacrifice at Shiloh at this juncture would also point to this possibility (Meyers 1994, 101). It is, in any case, a fact that Hannah has brought the ultimate sacrifice, her firstborn son, to the service of God. In addition to young Samuel, she represents the positive to the negative picture provided by those who are the official "sacrificers." When her name occurs for the last time in the story, it is connected to God and birthgiving:

> The Holy One visited Hannah;
> she became pregnant and gave birth
> to three sons and two daughters. (1 Sam 2:21)

Eli's blessing has twice proven effective, and the "barren one" has now become fertile indeed (cf. 2:5)!

The story resumes with the account of the misdeeds of Eli's sons and their father's unsuccessful attempt at reining them in. This time, through reports that reach Eli's ears, we hear about sexual corruption and immoral actions that defile both the women with whom Eli's sons are having intercourse and the sanctuary at which these encounters take place. Eli finally finds his voice to speak in opposition to his sons. The information preceding his speech indicates that he is "very old." Indeed, the reproaches coming from his mouth sound as if they come from a weak old man at his wits' end as to what to do with these worthless creatures he has for sons. Unlike his question to Hannah earlier in the narrative, which implied a stern rebuke and was followed by the command to "put away her wine" (1:14), his tone is plaintive as he asks "why" they do "these things, . . . wicked things" that he hears about. His "no" comes only secondarily and in response to "bad reports" (v. 24). His reprimand takes the form of questions: "Why? . . . Who?" (vv. 23, 25). To their old father's reproaches the wicked sons do not bother to reply; they do not even listen to him. In contrast to these scoundrels who stand in an entirely negative relation to God, their family, and all around them, the "boy" Samuel is once again held up as the paragon of virtue who continues to grow "in favor with God and people" (v. 26).

A Doomed House (1 Sam 2:27-36)

The gloom that settled over the story with the report on Eli's sons' corrupt practices deepens with the announcement of the impending end of the Elide priesthood. The flow of time stops as a "man of God" (v. 27), a divinely inspired person, brings a message to Eli. "Man of God" will designate Samuel in a subsequent chapter (1 Sam 9:6-10), when he functions in a prophetic capacity. Furthermore, the discourse of this section uses terminology ordinarily employed in prophetic speech: "thus says the Holy One" (v. 27), "oracle of the Holy One" (v. 30, twice), "see the days are coming" (v. 31). Eli himself is clearly not in direct communication with God. To highlight this painful reality, the message begins with a reference to God's revelation that took place in the past: "Did I not reveal myself to your father's house?" Thus commences God's opening salvo.

The prophecy consists of three main parts: indictment (vv. 27-29), sentence (vv. 30-34), and promise (v. 35). The word *house* is key to the discourse. God chose Eli's *house* for service to God rather than to Pharaoh's *house* in the past. God made a promise to Eli's *house* for the future (vv. 27, 30). This *house* now falls under God's chastisement (vv. 31-33, 36). Opposite to this house stands the *true house* that God will establish for God's service:

> I will establish for me a true priest,
> who according to my heart and my soul will do,
> and I will build him a true house,
> and he will walk before my anointed all the days. (1 Sam 2:35)

The indictment in v. 29 takes the form of a question, a relatively common way for prophetic speech to confront the audience with its failures. Eli too had reproached his sons with questions, but unlike his vague questions about "things," which sound plaintive, the divine question is in reality a sharp rebuke that goes straight to the heart of the matter. Eli and his house, once chosen by God, act as despisers of God and people rather than as chosen servants. They "trample" on the sacrifices meant for God, and they rob the people of their gifts to God. In effect, Eli has given more "honor" to his sons than to God. Eli is clearly implicated in his sons' behavior according to this perspective. Just as once his entire house was chosen, his entire house will now suffer for these infractions.

Although Hebrew word usage and phrasing in this passage are difficult to make out in many places, and nowhere more so than in the particulars of the sentence pronounced in vv. 31-33, this sentence clearly lays down a dire future for Eli's descendants. They will die young and will become servants of the one chosen by God to replace the Elides. The sign for this impending doom will be the death of Eli's sons on one day (v. 34). Even embedded in the promise of the "true house" is an announcement of deprivation for the house of Eli, whose descendants will come begging for a piece of bread (v. 36).

Food has been a central concern in all episodes of these first chapters, beginning with the sacrificial portions doled out by Elkanah to his family, continuing with the mention of the "satisfied" and the "hungry" in Hannah's song (2:5) and the withholding of food from the sacrifice, and leading to this last reference to the remaining descendants of Eli's house begging for a bite of bread (v. 36). In the self-sustaining agricultural economy of ancient Israel, the presence and absence of food was naturally in the forefront of people's consciousness. The regular occurrence of famines could affect even those who were fairly prosperous by the standards of the time, such as Hannah and her family. If, as some scholars think, the eating of meat was reserved for times of sacrifice, the withholding of the rightful portions of the sacrificed animal by cultic personnel was an even more serious infraction than would have been the case if meat were a more regular part of the diet (Lev 17:3-4; Van Wijk-Bos 2005, 217). Hunger and poverty are, of course, also threatening realities in the modern world, but they were most likely more evident and more imminent in the lives of ordinary folk in biblical times (Cook 1999, 40). Naturally, at the time of the exile this double threat took on new life. Consequently, the vision of someone "begging for a bit of bread" would be near the consciousness of the final editors of these texts.

We may wonder about the identity of the "true priest" established by God for whom God will build a "true house" (v. 35). Some assume this figure of the future to be Zadok, who came to prominence in David's time and could be said to "walk before" God's "anointed," a term that refers to the monarch as it did in Hannah's song (cf. 2:10). The true house, in that case, would be the Zadokite priesthood (cf. 2 Sam 15:24-37; 1 Kgs 2:35). The expression "true priest" could also refer to Samuel, who has already donned priestly garb and who will exercise a priestly office later in the story. Yet Samuel's house excelled in virtue no more than did Eli's. Samuel's sons too were corrupt and unjust (1 Sam 8:3). The phrase "true house" also recalls promises the prophet Nathan will make to King David regarding his "house" (2 Sam 7:8-17). The text remains ambiguous, and we may need to leave it so. The ambiguity inherent in the question concerning the identity of the future true priest may also reflect the tension that would ensue once power was divided among the three functionaries—prophet, priest, and king—all in God's service. There is a promise here of future leadership, and for a while Samuel will indeed embody the three functions in his person, but it will not stay that way for long.

An unsettling question that hovers over this part of the chapter involves the reversal of God's decision. Once, God appointed Eli's ancestors to be in God's service forever (v. 30), but now the matter has changed. How is one to trust the promise of such a God? From a historical perspective, the Deuteronomistic editors, who may well have had a hand in the formulation of this speech, had witnessed the collapse of what seemed to have been divine promises of "forever," and their explanation for the dire turn of events put the burden on human responsibility. God's promises were not without the possibility of change insofar as they were connected to the way in which God's people lived up to their covenant commitments. According to this view, human failure may result in a divine failure to fulfill the promise of "forever" that once seemed secure. It was apparently so after the Babylonian exile with regard to David's house that had received the same pledge. Looking at the issue from God's perspective may shed a different light on the "forever" promise: human beings may fail, demanding a change of direction on God's part, with God always hopeful that this time the leadership will be trustworthy. Robert Polzin puts it this way: "It is as though hope must spring eternal in the divine breast. Given the dishonor, the burden, the heaviness that will characterize Israel and its kings to the very end, how can the Glory keep on promising all his 'forevers'?" (Polzin 1989, 48). At times, the God of the Bible rues the choices God made, beginning with the creation, and the historical texts of the Bible reflect this reality as ancient Israel experienced it. In any case, the house of Eli will not be the last one caught in the fallout of a reversal of divine decisions.

A Boy in the Sanctuary (1 Sam 3:1–4:1a)

The moment has come to shed light on the person of Samuel. His mother, who received so much attention in the early part of the story, has receded into the background, and the significance of his mentor Eli has faded under the weight of the announcement of its doom. Concerning the boy Samuel, we have so far heard only that he "served God and grew." One may wonder how his growing up could prosper in the environment of corruption described in the previous chapter. It is the right moment to hear more about him.

The episode of Samuel receiving a divine oracle in the sanctuary is told with great attention to detail, creating a vivid impression of the unfolding scene, which is probably familiar to many of us. Whose imagination is not stirred by the drama of young Samuel going to his sleeping master up to three times before Eli informs him that it must be God speaking to the boy? The period in the first section of the chapter (3:1-18), precisely delineated as one night, opens with the time for sleep and continues until morning when Samuel tells Eli what he has heard. Then time speeds up once more, and after the episode of revelation, the information about Samuel concludes with the statement about his maturation so that he is a grown man at the end of the chapter. Eli still has a role in the unfolding events. We note, however, that the word of God does not come to him and that his main function is to make Samuel aware of the possibility that it is God who calls to him (3:8-9). In the main, the chapter serves to set Samuel firmly on the scene as the leader who, for the time being, has taken Eli's place and speaks for God. Thereby, he also takes on a prophetic role. Later Samuel will in addition adopt the mantle of political leadership.

Beginning and ending units (3:1-3 and 3:19–4:1) are carefully crafted to provide the brackets that impart the most essential information about God, God's servants, and God's people. In the opening scene, Samuel, as God's servant, is still a boy, while God's servant, Eli, suffers from diminished eyesight. A boy and an old almost-blind man are hardly impressive figures to be in service of the Holy One of Israel. Not that it matters, perhaps, because this God is not actively engaged with God's people, as the narrator reports:

> the word of the Holy One was scarce in those days;
> visions had not broken through. (1 Sam 3:1)

In addition, both servants are portrayed asleep or at least "lying down," each in their place. No activity marks their service at this point. The text specifies the location of each, Eli in "his place" and Samuel in the sanctuary with the

Ark of God. This is the first mention of the Ark in the narratives, and it is startling to find this powerful symbol of God's presence and of the covenant between God and Israel here at the place of rest, of dimmed eyesight and guttering lamp. The juxtaposition of Eli's dimmed eyesight and the lamp of God "not yet gone out" (v. 3) is surely not coincidental. There is a lack of word/vision, of God's presence, in this place, where of all places the presence of God should be most powerfully present.

At the end of the story, Eli has disappeared from the picture and Samuel has taken the place of mediator and interpreter for God. Proper names and place names abound in four short verses (3:19–4:1). Samuel is once again said to "grow," but this time the statement is augmented to the effect that God is with him and makes his words come true (3:19). The boy is no longer a boy but is becoming God's "true prophet" to "all Israel," and the people recognize him as such (v. 20). In contrast to the opening situation, God continues "to be seen at Shiloh." The place of the sanctuary, Shiloh, once filled with corruption and scorn for God and God's people, has become a place of revelation through God's word. Sight and sound are once again potent vehicles of God's presence, which Samuel mediates to God's people. The scarcity of God's word, the dimness of sight, and the barriers to a breakthrough on God's part have been lifted by the end of the chapter.

The largest section of the chapter contains a great deal of activity in contrast to the "lying down" of the opening lines. Most of the activity is futile, however, until one of the two servants, Eli, recognizes what is going on. Ironically, Samuel once more assumes the prone position while God "stands." Until that point, Samuel breathlessly scurries to and fro to Eli's spot to declare himself at Eli's service. The two sleeping places cannot have been far apart; Eli, unable to take care of simple needs on account of his eyesight, probably often had reason to call for Samuel during the night. Samuel may thus have been accustomed to his master calling him frequently for something to drink or for help with relieving himself. It is night, Samuel is asleep, and he hears his name being called. Of course, it must be Eli! Samuel seems neither unduly dense nor naïve in his assumptions; in fact, he does what most of us would do if we had an elderly person depending on us. Only Eli knows that he is not the one calling, and in the end he realizes whose voice young Samuel may be hearing. Eli still has a function in the story, though a somewhat poignant one, since God bypasses him to speak to his young servant.

Then Samuel is ready to listen, as he invites God to speak, although he omits the sacred name (v. 10) that Eli instructed him to utter. This final note indicates that Samuel, who was said to serve the Holy God, has no more knowledge of God than anyone else in the sacred precincts (cf. 2:12). Indeed, earlier the text verified Samuel's ignorance in a statement that interrupts the flow of the account, underlining Samuel's lack of knowledge and making the general statement of v. 1 specific (v. 7). This situation is about to change as God's word comes to him for the first time:

> And the Holy One came and stood
> and called as at the other times:
> Samuel, Samuel!
> And Samuel said:
> Speak for your servant is listening. (1 Sam 3:10)

Many interpreters designate this passage "the call of Samuel," comparing it to the call of Moses, Isaiah, Jeremiah, and Ezekiel. It is, of course, possible to view the episode that way. After all, the verb "to call" occurs with great regularity (vv. 4, 5, 6, 8, 9, 10). Yet no specific appointment to a task occurs in God's speech to Samuel, nor does it mention a "sending." In fact, God does not commission Samuel to tell anyone the substance of God's message to him.

While announcements of chastisement are not unfamiliar as part of a prophetic commissioning, here no such task is laid on the new prophet. Nor does God command him to take any action. Instead, God is going into action according to the message. There is no self-identification of God, an element that certainly would have been appropriate in view of the reported ignorance of God that prevails. An introductory statement might have been fitting, for example, something like, "I am the God who responded to your mother's call when she appointed you from the womb to be my servant . . . ." Instead, the text launches abruptly into a promise of activity on God's part, action that will seal the fate of Eli and his house once and for all. The speech of vv. 11-14 serves to set up the specific events of chapter 4, in which God will bring to pass what had already been foretold to Eli. Samuel will play no role in those events. Samuel does not reply to God's words but reacts in fear lest he will have to tell Eli what he heard. He only tells Eli after Eli pressures him to do so (vv. 15-18). It remains peculiar and uncomfortable, this seeming need to repeat the announcement of the demise of Eli and his house. Perhaps the speech of vv. 11-14 reflects the need of the Deuteronomists to issue once again a warning that God's choices may not be permanent and that scorning God will have consequences.

God has chosen Samuel as God's "true prophet," and gradually Samuel grows into the position accorded to him. As interpreter of God's words, he replaces Eli who has fallen under God's judgment. One could say that in this passage Samuel grows into his name. His name, up until this point associated with the verb "to ask," actually connects to "to listen." Listening, heeding, a key concept here, underlies Samuel's openness to hear God and his capacity to continue to listen to God's word so that he, Samuel, can speak the word to God's people. In contrast to Eli's sons who did not *listen* to their father, Samuel becomes ready to *listen* not only to the needs of Eli but to what God may have to say to him. Tellingly, v. 10 repeats the word "Samuel" three times, and it ends with the root "to listen." After all, the task of the prophet is to *listen* and to be God's spokesperson. With others, I regard the end of this episode to be the first phrase of chapter 4: "And Samuel's word was to all Israel" (4:1). This phrase rounds off the section centered on Samuel and on his maturation in his task as God's spokesperson. It makes little sense as the opening to chapter 4, in which "all Israel" pays no attention to Samuel as far as one can tell.

People in Distress (1 Sam 4:1b–7:17)

In the next set of chapters (4–6), the Ark of God, having made its first appearance in chapter 3 (v. 3), moves to the center of the story, while individual characters recede somewhat into the background. In addition, the scenes shift from the small scale to the large, from family to nation, from individuals to groups. Chapter 4 forms a bridge between the opening narratives in chapters 1–3 and the sequel in chapters 5–7, with part of the chapter focused on Eli and his family. It provides both an ending to the first chapters with the death of Eli and much of his family and an opening to the next episodes with the defeat of the Israelites at the hand of the Philistines and the capture of the Ark, which thereafter resides in Philistia. The Philistines as a group move to the foreground and will persist in the narratives as the most important threat to the ancient Israelite tribes until King David routs them once and for all (2 Sam 5:17-25). A large part of the action in these chapters takes place in Philistia proper where the Ark resides for a time to deadly effect (5:1–6:16). At the end of the tale of the Ark's adventures, the holy object with its destructive power returns to Israelite territory.

Samuel disappears from the scene until he reappears in full force in chapter 7, which forms a counterpart to chapter 4. Every chapter portrays a community in distress, with the focus in chapters 4 and 7 on Israel and in 5 and 6 on the Philistines. While these chapters continue to relate the downhill slide of people and leadership in the ancient Israelite community, already evident in the first section of the book, and are therefore literally deadly serious, a great deal of humor and even hilarity runs through them also. Tales recount Philistines mouthing pieties about the God of Israel, tell of an Eli who is not only literally blind but who never seems to know what is going on, detail the sojourn of the Ark among bewildered Philistines, at best afflicted with diarrhea and at worst with the plague, and finally bring into view the poor cows who head willy-nilly for an Israelite town though their calves are bawling at home. These stories mean to entertain as well as instruct and, as such, provide some relief from the somber tone of the preceding chapters while functioning as the prelude to the scene in which people issue the call for a monarch.

The Glory Departs (1 Sam 4:1b-22)

"While the arrival of the Ark may boost the morale of both parties, the Philistines galvanized by fear . . . fight even better." (Goldingay 2000, 33)

Other enemies endangered the fledgling nation in that time and place so permeated by wars and rumors of wars, but none put it in such serious jeopardy as the Philistines. Sea peoples who had migrated into the coastal regions of Canaan, perhaps at the same time as the ancient Israelites, the Philistines both occupied precious real estate and were a superior and aggressive military force in the region (see "People in Distress" above). They come on the scene for the first time in Samuel in chapter 4 and remain in the story for a long time, for they have an important role to play and are more evident in 1 Samuel than in any other biblical book.

The chapter readily divides into two parts, each attached to a different location: the first the battlefield at Ebenezer (vv. 1-11), literally "Stone of Help," and the second the town of Shiloh (vv. 12-22), familiar from the preceding episodes. The first part describes two Philistine victories over the Israelites, during battles apparently originally initiated by the Israelites (4:1). The first defeat is ascribed to God's action (v. 3) and has the result of bringing the Ark of the Covenant to the battlefield. Afterward, a second fight ensues in which the Philistines once again have the upper hand, many more of Israel's men are slain (v. 10), the Philistines capture the Ark, and Eli's sons, Hofni and Pinhas, die (v. 11).

After the first defeat at "Stone of Help," the elders gather to wonder why God handed them such a defeat; then, without further consultation or deliberation, they decide to bring the Ark of the Covenant into the picture. This first section almost universally identifies the Ark as the Ark of the Covenant of the Holy One (vv. 3, 4, 5 and 6), once with an augmentation (v. 4) that underlines both God's military and transcendental power:

So the people sent to Shiloh
and they brought from there
the Ark of the Covenant of the Holy God of Hosts,
who sits upon the Cherubim.
And there the two sons of Eli
were with the Ark of the Covenant of God,
Hofni and Pinchas. (1 Sam 4:4)

The label "covenant" no doubt intends to emphasize the connection of the holy casket with the covenant God made with the people when they were on their wilderness wanderings. The Ark had also accompanied the troops on military campaigns (Josh 3–4; 6). Perhaps the elders thought that God caused the defeat because God's presence represented by the Ark had not been with the troops. Their action, perhaps foolish to modern sensibilities, may have been logical from their point of view. Tellingly, no consultation occurs, neither with Eli nor the freshly minted prophet Samuel, a sign that Samuel has not yet reached the stature ascribed to him in 3:20. The names of Eli's sons conclude v. 4, thus in the closest proximity possible to the "Ark of the Covenant of God," an ominous sign in view of the fact that these two had mishandled the holy things of God and were destined to die by God's decree (cf. Eslinger 1985, 168). Either no leadership or doomed leadership bodes ill for the community.

The arrival of the Ark causes strong reactions in both camps with the Philistines overhearing the Israelite tumult and giving voice to their consternation. In a few swift strokes the writer takes the listener to the Philistine side where unbelievers declare the great deeds of the God of Israel, albeit in their own fashion referring to "gods" and "Hebrews," a term mostly reserved for outsiders' references to the ancient Israelites and which may have had negative connotations (vv. 6-9). The Philistines quake in their boots, as well they might, but their fear only serves to make them determined in their resolve to fight (v. 9). They have reason to fear the Ark, but that part of the tale is yet to unfold. Initially, they succeed and take the Ark home while leaving the Israelite dead, including Hofni and Pinhas, behind.

Tumult also marks the scene in Shiloh to which the action now turns, and a surviving Benjaminite brings the bad news, the disaster he comes to announce already visible on his person with its obvious signs of mourning (vv. 12-13). Poor Eli has no way to discern these signs; he is now entirely blind and is not able to make out the noise he hears. As once he asked young Samuel, Eli now inquires of the survivor about "the word" (v. 16; cf. 3:17). The messenger relays the news in stages, working up to the death of Eli's sons and leaving the fate of the Ark to last. Whether he heard the word "taken," the last word of the messenger's speech in the Hebrew phrase, or not, it is clear that this accumulation of disasters is the last straw for Eli (Eslinger 1985, 180). He falls from his seat and dies (v. 18).

It would seem appropriate for the death of Eli to end this part of the story, but in a surprise turn the attention shifts to a woman about to give birth. This life-bearer, the otherwise unnamed wife of Pinhas, goes into labor at the shock of hearing the news of the capture of the Ark and the deaths of her father-in-law and husband, and she gives birth to a son. She herself is near death and with her last breath embeds her interpretation of the events in the name of her newborn: Ikavod, that is to say "No Glory" or "Where Is the Glory?" Then the text repeats twice that, according to her dying eyes, dim like those of Eli's but full of insight unlike his, the glory has gone into exile:

> She called the boy: Ikavod/no-glory,
> saying: Gone into exile is glory from Israel—
> about the taking of the Ark of God
> and about her father-in-law and husband.
> She said: gone into exile is glory from Israel
> for taken is the Ark of God. (1 Sam 4:21-22)

The wife of Pinhas makes three declarations in a speech the narrator interrupts with a clarification after the second utterance, pointing out that her speech concerns "the Ark of God" and "her father-in-law and husband," with the human relatives coming almost as an afterthought. Her closest family, even before their deaths, had reflected an absence of glory, after all. The word "glory," Hebrew *kavod*, also occurs three times: once in the boy's name, attached to absence, and twice with the verb *galah*, which should be translated here as "gone into exile" rather than the colorless "departed." Twice she states that the Ark of God has been *taken*, employing the same verb used earlier when the elders decided to *take* the Ark for themselves (v. 3); after the defeat of the Israelites it occurs again for the *taking* of the Ark by the enemy (v. 11). It is also the last word uttered by the messenger to Eli in v. 17. "Taken," "taken," "taken"—the refrain resounds like a death knell throughout the entire text.

The Hebrew root from which the word glory/honor derives also means "to be heavy" in Hebrew and ironically describes Eli at the point of his death: "for the man was old and *heavy*." This is the only obituary notice for Eli before the note on the duration of his leadership that identifies him as "having judged Israel" (v. 18). This first reference to this role of Eli comes somewhat as a surprise. He may not have exercised his judgeship any more adequately than his priesthood. Earlier Hannah had sung of a God who bequeaths a "seat of *honor*" to the poor and needy (2:8); Eli was accused of *honoring* his sons more than God (2:29), and God has declared that those who give God *honor* would be *honored* by God (2:30). The house of Eli had instead scorned and despised God (2:30; 3:13). Now their corrupt leadership has caused the *glory/honor* of God to go into exile.

Here, at the end of the house of Eli and the opening of an entire new chapter in the history of the people, an anonymous woman pronounces a true saying. It is a bitter saying, one not ordinarily associated with the joy of giving birth. Pinhas's wife stands in counterpoint to joyful Hannah. Yet these two are part of the same story. Hannah, too, had uttered truths that may not have been welcome to all: God, in her words, not only *brings life* but also *causes death* (2:6), not only *enriches* but also *impoverishes.* For some interpreters, God's judgment in these chapters appears arbitrary and untrustworthy (Eslinger 1985, passim). It is, however, a bitter truth in human society that corrupt and venal leadership produces countless innocent victims. In the end, the perverted justice of the leadership (2:13) caused death on the battlefield and the suffering of a great many others in Israel. From this point of view, the deaths of Hofni and Pinhas may have come just in time.

The Ark among the Philistines (1 Sam 5–6:9)

This part of the narrative takes place in Philistine territory and, unlike the preceding events, features only group action without mentioning individual characters. As in the previous episode, both deadly and comic notes resound in the recital, and "details both bright and shadowy" permeate the story (Polzin 1989, 64). The verb "to take" is repeated emphatically in the initial description of the Philistines bringing the Ark as war booty to the city of Ashdod to place it in one of their temples (5:1-2), perhaps with the intent to humiliate the foreign god, to honor their god Dagon, or both. In the end, the Philistines will be "taken" to the brink of despair by the presence of this holy object among them. First, the repeated fall of the image of the god Dagon, the second time including Dagon's dismemberment, demonstrates which god is really in charge. Next, a deadly plague strikes the inhabitants of Ashdod, so that they send the Ark on to the next city, Gath, and then to Ekron (5:6-10). Since the Ark resides among the Philistines for seven months, according to the note of 6:1, it may have gone to the two other cities as well. The fact that the "tumors" that strike them are deadly probably indicates some form of bubonic plague, with the presence of mice or rats, which make an appearance at a later stage (6:4), also pointing to this possibility. The account of this first stage of the sojourn of the Ark in Philistia ends with the note that "the cry of the city rose to heaven" (v. 12).

The root for "glory/weight" once again dominates. The glory/honor, the weight, that had departed from Israel now resides with "a heavy hand" (5:6, 9, and 11) in Philistia, to destructive effect. Whereas Dagon's visible hands lay cut off on the threshold of his temple, the invisible hand of the God of Israel wreaks havoc among the Philistines. The Ark is designated "the Ark of the God of Israel" except in the narration about the Ark in the temple of Dagon where the narrator calls it "the Ark of the Holy One." Eventually and only once, the Holy Name will be connected to the Ark on the lips of the Philistines after they recognize that the Ark must go back and their priests instruct them to "take the Ark of the Holy One" (6:8).

The first part of chapter 6 consists mostly of speech by the Philistine priests and diviners consulted by an unspecified group of representatives who are convinced that they must indeed return the Ark, but who are not sure of how to do it. The incident is revealing, for it portrays both Philistines and their religious leaders as speaking and acting prudently. To the question "with what shall we send it to its place," the reply comes that whatever they do, it must not be sent back "empty" (vv. 2-3). Philistine religious leadership is interested in halting the disasters that have overcome them but also in finding out whether it was really the Ark that produced them. Gold images of the outward manifestations of the plague, five for the number of their city-states, symbolically represent homage to the God of Israel. As they point out,

> And you shall make images of your tumors
> and images of your mice that ravage the land
> and give to the God of Israel glory.
> Perhaps he will lighten his hand from upon you
> and your god and your lands.
> Why should you harden your hearts,
> as the Egyptians and Pharaoh hardened their hearts?
> When he made fools of them,
> did they not send the people off, and off they went? (1 Sam 6:5-6)

In this speech, the issue of God's *glory* resurfaces, laid as a burden of responsibility on the Philistines. It reoccurs twice in the rhetorical question of v. 6 because the root of "harden" is the same as that for glory. Here, as on the battlefield in chapter 4, the Philistines demonstrate knowledge of the history of the Israelites in Egypt and the role God played in these events. The upshot of the last lines is that the Ark will leave, whether the Philistines are willing to let it go or not, with the implication that it will wreak even greater havoc than it has already.

Some scholars observe the humoristic side of these tales of the sojourn of the Ark among the Philistines, mostly in the depiction of the frantic Philistines who may have been suffering from hemorrhoids. While we may allow for an Israelite audience receiving the suffering and manipulations of the Philistines with amusement, one recognizes that the laughter may have died on their lips on hearing the end of the story (6:19-20). The Ark evidently has no regard for persons in sowing a path of destruction. Humor and irony are located rather in the portrayal of the religious establishment of Philistia uttering pieties that would be worthy of an Israelite seer and of priests who know just how to go about calming the ferocious spirit that has been set loose among them. Such a picture offers an obvious contrast to an Israelite priesthood depicted as venal and corrupt.

The Ark Returns Home (1 Sam 6:10–7:1)

The inventive solution of using cows to prove that it was indeed because of the Ark that they suffered disaster (6:9) stands as a testimony to Philistine ingenuity. Instinct will urge the mother cows to return to their calves, so their going in the right direction will be the proof that something stronger than nature drives them on. And so it is. The poor mother cows, followed by Philistine chiefs rather than their young, go lowing to their destiny in Beth Shemesh, with their calves restrained at home, and fall victim to being sacrificed almost the instant the Israelites set eyes on them (6:12-14). The links between mothers, children, and sacrifice is made here via the word *beneyhem,* "their children," rather than the word for calves (6:7, 10), and recalls the story of Hannah's sacrifice (see "A Request in the Sanctuary" and Alter 1999, 33, n. 12).

In v. 13 the perspective switches to Beth Shemesh in Israelite territory, where the sight of the Ark's return causes joy and leads to the sacrifice of the cows (v. 14). Verses 14 and 15 are disjunctive, with the Levites taking down the Ark of God that still rests on a cart already split up in v. 14. It is not clear whether the disjunction between the two verses implies a criticism that the people of Beth Shemesh offered up the cows prematurely before the Levites, to whom this office is assigned, could reach the scene, thus opening themselves up to God's wrath. Certainly, sacrifice, including its proper handling, has so far been a subject of great interest to the story and will continue to remain so in its sequel. Sacrifice, inappropriately handled, inaugurated the doom of Eli's house, and untimely sacrifice, offered by the inappropriate person, will herald the beginning of the end for Saul's kingship. Here, the question arises at least as to both timing and appropriate personnel. In any event, the arrival of the Ark causes more destruction, this time among God's own people. As once God "struck" the Philistines, now God strikes the Beth Shemeshites. A far from cozy homecoming! The people of Beth Shemesh cry out as once the Philistines cried and, as the Philistines did, they decide to send the dangerous, all too holy object on to another city so that the final resting place becomes Kiryat-Ye'arim (7:1-2). There, the Ark is *taken,* the final use of this verb in this part of the story.

The Ark of these narratives is clearly not a comfortable item to have in one's neighborhood. A numinous power goes out from it that, far from bringing support to the beleaguered Israelites, sows death and destruction wherever it is *taken.* Up to three times it marks death for the people who come in contact with it, first for the Israelites on the battlefield, then for the Philistines in their cities, and finally again for the Israelites in Beth Shemesh. Evidently, the Ark is connected to God's presence, but it is not clear to what degree it should be identified with God. Some interpreters seem to take this identification for granted (Smelik 1980, 42–50; Brueggemann 2002, 26). Thus, for example, Brueggemann assumes that along with the taking of the Ark, the God of Israel is taken into captivity. For others, this tale is told from the perspective of the Babylonian exile, from which vantage point the Holy God had abandoned Israel with the devastation of the temple (Smelik 1980, 42).

Although the Ark is the object of being *taken, sent* from one city to the next, and *brought* back to Israelite territory, the Ark is also the subject of significant action—it *went round, came,* and *will go up* (5:8; 10; 6:8, 9, 20). In addition, in some lines it is not clear whether the subject of a verb refers to God or to the Ark. In 5:10, the Ekronites cry out that the Ark of the God of Israel was brought to them "to kill me and my people." In the next verse, the Philistines have made the decision to send the Ark back to "its place," for they think that thus "he/it will not kill me and my people" (5:11). In 5:7 and 9, the subject of the action moves smoothly from the Ark to God's hand, while in 6, 8, and 11 it is not always obvious whether the pronouns refer to God or the Ark. At times, what may be a deliberate blurring of the boundary between the Ark and God occurs, especially in the mouth of the Philistines, perhaps to indicate that from their perspective there was total identification between the object and its owner. For the Israelites of the story, it becomes apparent that the presence of the holy object does not guarantee the sustaining delivering presence of God. In addition, manipulation of the holy shrine in order to move God to action on behalf of God's people will plainly be of no benefit. One of the names of the Ark is after all the Ark of the Covenant, a covenant freely given by God in which the people had a responsibility and a role to play. Having fallen short of their sacred covenant task of living as God's people, carting around the sacred shrine will not guarantee them God's delivering presence; it may rather risk provoking God's anger to break out against them, very much as it broke out against the Philistines.

Considering the presence of the Ark from the vantage point of the exile, there may be some comfort in these accounts. The Ark now lost, the temple now lost, and the kingship lost, God-sanctioned though these may have been, were never guarantees of the people's presence with God or God's presence with them. In fact, the story of the travels of the Ark of the Covenant reveals the fatal flaw in that assumption.

Repentance and Deliverance (1 Sam 7:2-17)

The travels of the Ark have ended, but the distress of God's people remains unresolved. This part of the narrative opens with a time marker, twenty years, during which the people are said to "yearn" after the Holy God. The verb used here is one of mourning and lamenting, and it indicates the state of a community bereft. The Ark may be home, but God is apparently still absent. Into this situation of communal lament steps Samuel with a condition and a solution:

> And Samuel said to the entire house of Israel:
> If with all your heart you return to the Holy One,
> put aside the foreign gods from your midst and the Ashtaroth,
> and set your heart on the Holy One
> and serve him alone,
> he will deliver you from the hand of the Philistines. (1 Sam 7:3)

The condition is a complex set of demands. First there is the requirement to "return" to God with "all your heart"; then follows the necessity to cease worshiping "foreign gods"; after this the first demand is repeated in different and expanded wording: to "set your heart" on God and to "serve God alone." The emphasis on turning to God with the heart and on serving God only thus frames the abandonment of idol worship. The mention of idol worship is surprising. While the worship of God at Shiloh was portrayed as corrupt, there was no mention of worshiping the wrong gods; neither was such a practice a part of the prophecy of doom that Eli received. Phrasing and ideology at this juncture in the text appear to belong to the Deuteronomic perspective, and the hand of the Deuteronomistic editor is more clearly present in this chapter than we have seen so far. The phrasing highlighted above and the perspective that the worship of "foreign gods" was a sign of the people's most serious disloyalty to the God of the covenant, a disloyalty that would bring dire consequences on the community, as well as the conditional phrasing of the promised deliverance, all belong to the Deuteronomistic storehouse of language and theology. From the solution offered by Samuel, one may assume that the people's "yearning after God" basically meant that they wanted God to get them out from under the Philistine boot or, as the biblical text has it, "the hand."

The people's compliance with the demands made by Samuel consists of three stages. First, they turn away from false gods to the service of "God alone" (v. 4). Then they engage in a ritual of purification, fasting, and confession (vv. 5-6). Finally, under the pressure of renewed threats from the Philistines, they implore Samuel to continue to "cry out" to God. Samuel, in turn, engages with the people by instructing them regarding the conditions under which they might be freed from Philistine oppression, then by praying and offering sacrifice. Samuel has grown into his promise and is living out the statement made at the end of chapter 3 and the beginning of 4: all Israel now knows that Samuel is a "true prophet," and Samuel's word is indeed for "all Israel" (cf. 3:19–4:1a). In addition to these descriptions, Samuel is said to "judge" Israel once in v. 6 and three times in vv. 15-17. The verb "to judge," Hebrew *shafat,* indicates the role of a leader appropriate for the tribal confederacy. Samuel is the last of the judges that led the tribes during the early period of the settlement in the land of the promise. In some aspects, Samuel differs from the model of the judges as it is set up in the biblical book named after them. The text never portrays him as a military leader, for example, while in his prophetic and priestly capacities he exceeds the model. It was apparently important for the writers to depict him as one of the last leaders of the people named a "judge," dedicated by his mother and called directly by God, because in this way Samuel closes a chapter in the history of ancient Israel. The portrait of him offered in chapter 7 is of one who is in all respects successful, with the Philistines put to flight forever during Samuel's time and peace enduring with the indigenous peoples (cf. vv. 15-17). This statement, proven entirely inaccurate in what follows, offers a standard description of a successful judge.

Samuel "cries out" to God and God answers with thunder, sowing panic among the Philistine armies and putting them to flight. The thundering God brings to mind the image in Hannah's prayer (2:10). Here the adversary is indeed "broken into pieces." Here, as in the story of Hannah, the power of prayer moves God to action. The Israelites do not even have to engage in battle; it remains only for them to finish what God began. The situation of Israelite manipulation of the Holy Shrine recorded in chapter 4 is thus transformed into a reorientation of the heart, and prayer changes the earlier defeat into victory and conquest (Fokkelman 1993, 297). Ebenezer has now become a "stone of help" indeed (cf. v. 12). The people in distress have become the people at rest under an able and God-appointed leader. It is not clear whether the writers intend to hold up this idealized situation as the one to which the people should have aspired and to which they should have clung or whether they merely depict it as something that could have been, if only . . . . If the Deuteronomists indeed had a hand in the writing of this episode, are they pointing out that a good and God-blessed life could have been possible if only the people had not asked for a king?

The Beginnings of Kingship (1 Sam 8:1–12:25)

The end of the previous chapter could have been the end of the story, but of course it is only beginning. Samuel, although identified as the one "asked for" in the opening episodes (1:17, 27, 28; 2:20), is after all not the one "asked for," who will be Shaul/Saul, still to be chosen. According to the opening remarks of chapter 8, the ideal situation depicted in chapter 7 turns out to be far from ideal because the people are dissatisfied and demand that Samuel give them a king. After Samuel brings the request to God, and with both God and Samuel unhappy about the request, God commands Samuel twice to give the people what they want, but no act of compliance follows on Samuel's part. Chapters 9–11 serve to introduce Saul as the first candidate for the task, relating his appointment no less than three times, once by Samuel's anointing (10:1), once by lot (10:20-24), and once by acclamation after a successful military campaign (11:15). Chapter 12 presents a long speech from Samuel to the people with his final instructions and recriminations, so that two speeches by Samuel (chs. 7 and 12) bracket the appearance and election of Saul as first king. Following Fokkelman to a degree, I have divided the stories that serve to introduce Saul into three quests, the first of which is Saul's, the second Samuel's, and the third the people's (Fokkelman 1993, 364.) All are looking, but what or whom they are seeking is not always clear, and what they find may not be what they sought.

King Them a King! (1 Sam 8:1-22)

". . . the reader develops a picture of a judge whose words and inaction show him to be obstructive in a self-interested way." (Polzin 1989, 84)

The introduction to chapter 8 paints a different picture of the national situation than the one created at the end of the previous episode. There one hears only positive statements about Samuel as a national leader who combined in his person the offices of prophet, priest, and judge, offering leadership that resulted in a lasting peace. The last lines in that chapter constitute an emphatic report of Samuel's judgeship (7:15-17). The word "judge" immediately occurs again in the opening lines of chapter 8 with Samuel appointing his two sons as "judges." Before this notation, the narrator writes that Samuel had become "old." Anyone who has followed the story so far will now sit up and pay close and apprehensive attention, for this sounds all too familiar: an old man in charge of the people, with two sons! Postponing the most essential part of the information, the narrator lets the tension grow a bit by providing first the names of the sons; they are fine names, each including a part of the Holy Name of God. Then, with the next verse, the shoe drops. As was the case with Eli's sons, these two were not like their father:

> And when Samuel was old
> he set up his sons as judges over Israel.
> The name of the firstborn was Joel
> and the name of the second Abijah—
> judges in Beersheba.
> And his sons did not walk in his ways:
> they turned after profit, took bribes,
> and turned justice on its head. (1 Sam 8:1-3)

These lines set the scene in only a few strokes.

The Hebrew words for "judge" and "justice," related also in English, both derive from the root *shafat*. We encountered it for the first time in these texts in chapter 2 with the reference to the "justice" of the crooked priests (2:13). It occurred next in relation to Eli (4:18), somewhat as a surprise, because this role of Eli had not been mentioned before. Samuel, following in Eli's footsteps, also takes on the mantle of leadership identified with the word "judge," besides his roles of priest and prophet (7:15-17). As noted earlier, connections are thus made between the period in which charismatic individuals, directly called by God and overcome by God's spirit, led the fledgling nation, especially in military campaigns, and the new stage in national affairs that is about to begin. There are other verbs for ruling or leading in Hebrew, and the term "judge" for a military and political leader is peculiar to the early period. It dropped out of usage as a term for political rule during the monarchy. At this point, we are at the cusp of a new era. To indicate the ending of the old order, the root *shafat* dominates in this chapter. The people desire a new king who will be "judge" over them (8:5, 6). Hence, God commands Samuel to declare to the people what the "justice" of such a leader will be, and Samuel does so in the speech that takes up a large part of the chapter. In fact, after its introduction, the verb "to judge" or its related noun "justice" occurs five times, always in connection to the noun "king" (Fokkelman 1993, 328).

Justice, Hebrew *mishpat*, is a word that embraces a large complex of ideas. It certainly includes law and can sometimes be translated "practice." Above all, justice is an attribute of God (cf. Deut 10:18; Ps 146:7; Jer 9:23-24) and points to God's care for the disenfranchised, the poor, and the needy. Because God upholds "justice," God's people must do the same, and the leaders of the people are held responsible for executing justice, i.e., defending the cause of the orphan, the widow, and the stranger (cf. Jer 22:16). In the words of Stephen Mott, "justice is associated with the basic requirements of life in the community. Basic needs are basic rights." Furthermore, he says, "Justice is a deliverance, rectifying the gross social inequities of the disadvantaged . . ." (Mott 1985, 520). We saw earlier how Eli's sons abused justice exactly because they neglected the basic needs of the members of the community (2:13). In the same way, Samuel's sons, who are supposed to be judges, i.e., leaders under God's tutelage, are "turning justice on its head."

Samuel, who unlike Eli does not reprimand his sons, has "set his sons up" to be judges. He obviously intended them to be his heirs. Yet judges were not usually appointed but directly called by the Holy One of Israel to fulfill their task. From the start of this note, then, there are signs that something is awry. That the present situation is fragile and the future bodes ill is clear at least to the elders who come to Samuel with their request for a king (v. 5). The demand displeases Samuel (literally, "the word was evil in the eyes of Samuel") and, forgoing a response, he turns to God. What he said to God is not reported; we have only God's answer. The account does not spell out Samuel's replies either to God or the people, and the effect of this omission is an impression of a Samuel choked with rage. He speaks at length only to lay out in detail how bad things are going to become once they have a "king to be judge over them." The people twice demand a king (vv. 5, 19), and God commands Samuel three times to accede to their request (vv. 7, 9, 22), but at the end of the story Samuel sends everyone home without having taken any action.

God's words to Samuel (vv. 7-9) tap directly into Samuel's disgruntlement, while at the same time indicating that the Almighty is not very pleased either. God's counsel to Samuel is not entirely logical: "They did not reject you but me; just as they have done to me in the past so they are now doing to you." The last statement cancels out the first. Then God fills in the comment with the observation that the people "served foreign gods." In other words, they set God aside just as they are now setting Samuel aside. In comparing service to the king with idolatry, God surely is going too far. Yet both assertions are framed by the command to "listen to the voice of the people" (vv. 7, 9), finally exhorting Samuel to testify to the people about the "justice of the king" (v. 9). God's replies to Samuel evince a disturbance in the Deity also.

Samuel takes God's instruction to mean that the people should be clear about what they will lose if they have a king, presumably so that they may reconsider their desire. Who wants a ruler that only "takes," both offspring and property, and gives nothing in return? Such is the royal "justice" Samuel reviews in his speech, in which the verb "take" dominates, occurring in almost every line. Things will become so bad, he concludes, that you will "cry out" on account of your king. Yet God will not answer you, reversing the situation of the past when God habitually answered the people's cry through the appointed deliverer/judge (cf. Judg 3:9, 15; 4:3; 6:6-7; 10:10). The people are not to be dissuaded and merely renew their plea, adding that a king will lead them in war.

Has Samuel acquitted himself adequately of the God-given task to tell the people about the king's "justice"? Surely some idea of the king's responsibilities should have been included in this recital in view of the biblical understanding of justice. Instead, Samuel has emphasized only royal privileges with no mention of obligations. Is God's prophet accurately conveying what God said to him? Such questions lead to an increased sense of tension. God presents rueful acquiescence; from Samuel one only receives a sense of resistance, and at the end of the day he does nothing to act on God's directives and the people's demands. God suffers rejection of divine leadership and compares service of the king-to-be with idolatry. Rejection and idolatry are serious matters and lead one to think that everything may not go entirely smoothly from here on.

The chapter ends with a non sequitur that leaves everything open ended, thereby creating heightened anticipation for what is to follow:

And the Holy One said to Samuel:
"Listen to their voice,"
and king them a king.
And Samuel said to the men of Israel:
Go, everyone to their city. (1 Sam 8:22)

On God's word, Samuel should have at least searched for a suitable candidate for kingship. Instead, he sends everyone home. What will happen next?

Saul's Quest (9:1-27)

"Saul, therefore, is a seeker of answers as well as asses, a traveling question mark." (Polzin 1989, 103)

Through the end of chapter 11, the next chapters concern themselves with Saul and the manner of his becoming the first king. This process is not told in a straightforward way but with several twists and turns. Ultimately, the storyteller notes that "all the people went to Gilgal and they made Saul king there before the Holy One in Gilgal" (11:15). Three reports narrate Saul's appointment to kingship, once through anointing in secret (10:1), once through choice by lot (10:24), and a third time after proving himself in battle against the Ammonites (11:15). I shall not belabor the issue of a possible welding together of separate stories concerning the origin of Saul's kingship but approach the chapters as a unit, highlighting important facets of the complex beginning to what will turn out to be a troubled rule.

The anticipation left at the end of the previous episode may have led one to expect a search, on the part of either Samuel or the people or both, to find an appropriate individual to take on the role of monarch. When, therefore, the next lines open with the introduction of an important man from the tribe of Benjamin, he would appear to be a likely candidate. Soon, however, his son comes on the scene, and as soon as his name, Sha'ul/Saul, sounds in the text, all eyes and ears go in his direction because this surely must be the one! Sha'ul, "the asked one," has finally appeared! In addition to his name, it is noted that he was a handsome and tall young man; in fact, no one among the Israelites was as good-looking as Saul. In addition, the Hebrew word for "young man" occurs, a word that relates to the verb "to choose" and could literally be translated "chosen." Hence, older translations have "a choice young man." Based on this description, what could be more logical than to assume that this is the one? It will take some time, however, before Saul finally becomes "the one," and then the story tells it not one but three times.

Immediately following the introduction of Saul and his ancestry, the text announces the object of the first quest. Somewhat ironically, it concerns the pedestrian matter of his father's donkeys. These have wandered off, so Kish sends Saul to look for them, taking with him a boy. A few lines describe their extensive and fruitless search and end with the phrase, "and did not find them" (vv. 3-4). Saul then wants to go home, for he thinks his father will be worried, but the servant convinces him to keep looking—not for the donkeys but for a seer who can tell them the whereabouts of the animals. After some deliberation, the two set out to find the seer in his city (vv. 5-10). At the end of the segment, Saul and his "boy" are thus no longer looking for donkeys per se, but for a man of God/seer.

Saul appears to be not only good-looking but also sensitive, as revealed by the concern about his father's feelings. At the same time, he is a bit at a loss. Instead of issuing instructions to his servant, the boy gives information and provides solutions to the predicament that has arisen. He alerts Saul to the presence of a man of God/seer who can help them and, sounding resolute and optimistic, offers the resources to finance the seer's advice. Saul, on the other hand, is full of questions: "What shall we bring the man? . . . What have we?" (v. 7). In the end, the servant convinces him, and the two are on their way to find the anonymous man of God, neither apparently being acquainted with Samuel. On the way they encounter a group of girls who inform them that they are on the right track but that they must hurry, for the unnamed "seer" is on his way to a sacrificial feast. Again, it is the young people, this time the female equivalent of Saul's servant, who provide information needed to move things along (vv. 11-13).

In the next segment, the two from Benjamin enter the town and encounter Samuel, who is on a quest of his own. Saul asks him whether he knows where the seer lives. Upon revealing himself, Samuel tells Saul not to worry any longer about the donkeys that have been located, making at the same time a statement about Saul's significance, albeit in an oblique manner (vv. 19-20). Saul responds to this revelation with another question. Saul has not found his father's asses, but he has found his seer. We meet Saul next at a table with other guests from the town. The sacrifice, part of which must have been consumed on this occasion, has receded into the background. The meal serves as another delay, for although Saul receives a choice portion, Samuel does not mention to him that God had pointed him out as the future "leader" of God's people. Another night goes by and Samuel has still not made a clear declaration to Saul that he is God's choice (vv. 22-25). The anointing and the announcement take place in secret in the morning, while the servant is sent ahead, so that at this point only Samuel and Saul know of the matter (9:26–10:1). The quest that was first about donkeys, then about a seer, has now turned out to be about leadership.

Then follows a string of directives from Samuel to Saul, including meetings with anonymous men, first a pair who will give renewed reassurances about his father's donkeys, then three with provisions, and finally an encounter with a group of prophets whom he will join on the urging of God's spirit. At that point, Saul is to wait for Samuel, who will come down to offer the appropriate sacrifices and give him further instructions (10:2-8). All this happens more or less as Samuel foretells, but only the encounter with the prophets is recounted along with the saying that resulted from it: "Is Saul also among the prophets?" (10:11-12). According to Edwin Good, this saying constitutes an "ironic proverb, suggesting someone seriously out of place" (Good 1965, 62). Saul does not speak in this segment even though the narrative reports that he "ranted like a prophet" (10:10).

Saul's quest finally ends when, presumably on his way home, he meets an unnamed uncle to whom he reveals a part of his story, namely, that they met Samuel who told them the donkeys were found; he mentions nothing of kingship:

> And Saul's uncle said:
> "Tell me now what Samuel said to you."
> And Saul said to his uncle:
> "He certainly told us that the donkeys were found."
> And the matter of the kingship he did not tell him,
> of which Samuel had spoken. (1 Sam 10:15-16)

The story abounds with words for searching and finding. The root "to see," both contained in the verb "to look" and in the noun "seer," is prominent in the first half of the section. Yet there is little actual seeing going on, certainly not on the part of Saul who mostly speaks in questions. Saul does make a number of discoveries. Indeed, the verb "to find" echoes throughout the passage, but what he was sent to find escapes his grasp, while what he was not seeking, leadership over his people, is offered to him unsought. He has a number of significant encounters: with young women as if this were a betrothal scene (Alter 1999, 48 n. 11); with the seer who turns out to be Samuel; with a pair of men, then with three men; with a band of prophets; and, finally, with an uncle. Anne Marijke Spijkerboer concludes that Saul seems to be lost in a maze searching for donkeys and that "secrets are revealed but not entirely and Saul's anointing takes place in secret" (Spijkerboer 1992, 35–42). She points to the sphere of mystery evoked by the root "three," which occurs in different forms, and the words for "search/look for/seek" and "find" that are key throughout. Little of the account proceeds in a straightforward way, a sign perhaps of the trouble to follow.

Sacrifice again becomes prominent, first as a celebratory occasion and the second time with a reference to a future opportunity for Saul "to wait seven days" for Samuel, an ominous announcement in a tale that will turn on the failure of Saul to wait for Samuel (10:8; cf. 13:8-14). The story uses the word "heart" in significant ways. The servant declared that Samuel would tell them "their way" (9:6, 8), but Samuel announces to Saul that he will tell him "all that is in [his] heart" (9:19). Subsequently, the statement that God gave Saul "another heart" makes use of a powerful verb meaning "to overturn" (10:9). This statement together with the pronouncement that God's spirit rushed upon him (10:10) portrays a man set in a new direction by the power of God. Meanwhile the phrasing provides a link to past leadership, since the power of the spirit of God moved the judges of old to deliver their people. Even the reference to the spirit includes a somber note, however, as we descry in Saul's future the "evil spirit" sent by God to torment him (16:14). All in all, Saul's agency seems uncertain, questioning, following rather than leading, overcome rather than in charge. In no way does Saul give any verbal signs that he understands what is happening to him.

Samuel's Quest (1 Sam 9:14–10:27)

"Samuel exhibits his prophetic clairvoyance like a strong man publicly flexing his muscles in an excessive or unseemly fashion." (Polzin 1989, 105)

Samuel appears on the scene at the moment when Saul and his servant enter the town. The narrator then reports that it had been revealed to Samuel the day before that God would send a man from Benjamin for Samuel to anoint as "leader" over God's people (9:15-16). We do not know how hard Samuel had been looking for a candidate to be king, but one may assume that after this announcement he was on the lookout for a man that would fit the description. In this section, vv. 14-21, initially only the voices of God and Samuel are heard, while Saul chimes in belatedly with his diffident response (v. 21). Samuel's quest for a king is ostensibly over, as soon as God tells him the identity of the stranger he meets in the street. As before, he delays executing the task God has set for him, this time the anointing of Saul, alluding to Saul's important task only obliquely with his words: "And whose is the treasure of Israel/if not your father's house?" (v. 20).

God's announcement to Samuel in v. 16 makes it clear that Saul had not been randomly wandering in search of donkeys but had been "sent" by God:

And the Holy One had revealed
to Samuel's ear one day before Saul came:
At this time tomorrow
I will send you a man from the region of Benjamin
whom you will anoint
as leader over my people Israel
and who will deliver my people
from the hand of the Philistines.
For I have seen my people
for their cry has come to me. (1 Sam 9:15-16)

God is doing the sending, and both Samuel and Saul face a task in response: "you will anoint . . . a man . . . who will deliver." Only Saul, David, and Jehu are anointed to kingship in the texts of Samuel and Kings, a practice that is known from the wider cultural context (Lehnhart 2003, 148). The scarcity of references to this presumably common practice may highlight instances of a shift in dynastic leadership; the momentousness of the occasion warrants the reference. Samuel will anoint the man from Benjamin, sent by God, for a specific task: to be a leader who delivers the people from the Philistines. We note that the title for the anointed-one-to-be is not "king" but "leader" (Hebrew *nagid*), a word used only rarely for monarchs. The text goes to some length to avoid the word "king," here and in chapter 10, hinting at the ostensible reluctance with which both God and Samuel approach the transformation of Israel's leadership. A king is a leader, but a leader is not necessarily a king. In addition, the military purpose of this leadership is clearly stated: the goal is the deliverance of God's people from Philistine power. The language used at the end of v. 16 recalls God's opening words during the encounter between God and Moses in Exodus (Exod 3:7). On Samuel's meeting Saul, God assures Samuel that this is indeed the man "who will control my people" (v. 17). The verb used here meaning "to control" or "to restrain" may have positive or negative connotations. Polzin interprets the meaning here as negative in the sense that the new leader will constrain the people's liberties, "imprison" them in a way (Polzin 1989, 94). Even if we do not accept such an entirely negative reading, the verb points to a tension embedded in the leadership of Saul from the outset. If Saul was to be mainly a deliverer, then what accounts for this shift to the verb "control"?

As at the end of chapter 8, Samuel once again delays acting in conformity to God's instructions and instead speaks to Saul in hints and ambiguities that have the young man respond in a bewildered fashion. Samuel assures Saul that he will tell him "all that is in his heart," intimating that he knows all about him and that his father's donkeys have been found, and he finishes with a rhetorical question: "And whose is all the treasure of Israel / if not yours and your father's household's?" As Alter observes, "This is a deliberately oblique reference to kingship: if all the choice possessions of Israel are to be yours, why worry about a few asses?" (Alter 1993, 50 n. 20). Saul then utters his last words to Samuel in a testimony to his bewilderment: "why do you speak to me like this?" (v. 21). He only speaks once more, at the end of the episode, to his uncle about mundane matters, keeping mum about his impending role out of either diffidence or a lack of understanding (10:16).

When Samuel eventually anoints Saul, in secret with his servant out of eyesight and earshot, it is as "leader," the same word used earlier, again avoiding the title "king" (10:1; cf. 9:16). Samuel makes clear that God actually performs the anointing and once again puts his statement in the form of a rhetorical question. Then follows a series of precise predictions about what will happen next: Saul will *find* a number of individuals and groups, and others will *find* him, while the donkeys *have been found*. All the instructions end with a reference to the sacrifice at Gilgal, a sacrifice that Samuel will bring. Therefore, Samuel instructs Saul to wait for him. This final statement is especially troublesome in view of what we know will happen at Gilgal. If kings had the prerogative to execute sacrifice, as they seem to have had in ancient Israel as well as in its wider context, Samuel's claim reserving this office for himself is certainly interesting. According to Lehnhart, Samuel infringes drastically on the rights and privileges of kingship here (Lehnhart 2003, 152).

In these episodes Samuel speaks and acts hesitantly and with hints of resentment toward the notion of kingship and the individual God has chosen for the task. It looks as though he will accept this person only on his terms and under his guidance and control. Polzin interprets the picture of Samuel in these chapters in almost entirely negative colors. He argues that Samuel only bows to the notion of kingship if he can have a king who is under his control. "Personal control appears to be what Samuel is after; Saul as both king and prophet offers a double warrant for royal dependence on Samuel who himself leads the prophets" (Polzin 1989, 106). Lehnhart also considers Saul a weak king whose only significant function is that of military leader under the control of Samuel as the voice of God (Lehnhart 2003, 160). It is indeed difficult to escape the conclusion that Samuel acts here in a manipulative and not entirely sympathetic fashion. Consider, for example, the manner in which a public acknowledgment of Saul's kingship takes place. Once again, Samuel calls the people together at Mizpah (cf. 7:5), a place where Samuel first proved himself as the voice of God to the people. Not surprisingly, his opening words are, "Thus says the Holy One, the God of Israel," words stereotypically used by Israel's prophets. As before, he positions the people as a sinful crowd, with God as their rescuer (10:18-19; cf. 7:3-6). What Samuel had refrained from pointing out earlier in his speech about the "justice" of the king, he now reveals when he openly declares their demand a "rejection" of God (10:19; cf. 8:7). Subsequently, he organizes a casting of lots with the result that the lot falls on Saul. While lot casting does not have negative overtones by itself, it occurs elsewhere in these narratives in efforts to find a guilty party (1 Sam 14:38-44; cf. Josh 7), and it certainly adds another element of doubt concerning Samuel's handling of the king's appointment.

Samuel's last task in respect to his quest involves the establishment of the rights and privileges of kingship (10:25) in a document preserved in God's presence, that is, in the sanctuary, which at that time was probably at Mizpah. The reader does not learn of the contents of the document, and one can only wonder about them. It may have been a record in the vein of Deuteronomy 17:14-20, a text that provides *torah* for the practices of a king (see above, "King Them a King!"; also Fokkelman 1993, 451). We will hear more from Samuel on the issue of kingship and his own relationship to the king and the people in chapter 12.

The People's Quest (1 Sam 9:1–11:15)

While the people are not active participants until the last part of chapter 10, there are hints of their presence throughout the narrative. First, there is a much larger cast of secondary characters in the opening part of the story than usual. Saul's boy, the young girls, the people at the sacrifice, the cook, the different individuals who come to meet Saul, the band of prophets, and Saul's uncle—all play a role alongside Saul and Samuel in the development of the plot (cf. Jacobs 2008, 495–509). Assigning so much space to secondary characters could serve the purpose of setting the king-to-be firmly in the midst of the circle of those who will eventually become his subjects. Notably missing are those who will form his most immediate circle, soldiers, but we recall that Samuel has chosen much of the company surrounding Saul. Last but not least, there are the donkeys, always in absentia, but repeatedly mentioned until the end of Saul's quest (10:16). Rudman suggests that the donkeys, far from insignificant in chapters 9 and 10, represent the stubborn, sinful, and rebellious people who have rejected God as king over them and who certainly need "restraint" and "control" (9:17). A contrastive picture can thus be drawn between Saul's donkeys and David's sheep (Rudman 2000, 519–530 *passim*).

Samuel certainly identifies the people as sinners and rejecters of God on the occasion of the gathering to make Saul's choice official. We may assume that the people have been waiting for Samuel to present them with someone suitable, but their quest has not yet been successful. They are simply present in the episode of the lot casting with only Samuel and the lot in active roles. Then, at the crucial moment, the chosen one goes missing and the people go into action, assuming their role in the quest. Saul may also have been ill at ease with this manner of being chosen; it may be that he only now fully realizes what it may mean to have been anointed as a "leader." In any case, the people now ask where their candidate may be found, putting the question directly to God (10:22), while Samuel disappears into the background (Fokkelman 1993, 446):

> And then was caught by lot Saul, the son of Kish
> and they looked for him but he was not found.
> And they asked further of the Holy One:
> Did a man come here?
> And God said: Look here he is
> hiding among the gear! (1 Sam 10:21-22)

These lines weave the key themes of looking and finding closely together. The people "look" for Saul, but "he was not found," so they "ask" God. Saul, *Sha'ul*/the "asked one," will now truly become the one the people ask for directly from the Holy One, bypassing Samuel. God responds directly to the people by revealing the hiding place of the "man" they want. In this way, the people's quest comes to a successful end with their recognition of what we knew all along, that Saul is "head and shoulders taller than the people," and with Samuel's declaration that the one initially introduced as "the chosen" is indeed chosen by the Holy God. We note that the people declare Saul king with their utterance "long live the king!" (v. 24), while Samuel has yet to let the word "king" cross his lips in reference to Saul.

Everyone now goes home, with Saul finally surrounded by those who will, for the most part, constitute his immediate circle in the future, the valiant ones/heroes, the soldiers who will make up his army (v. 26). Yet all may not be well that ends well, since a group of dissenters termed "worthless fellows" question the ability of their newly minted king (10:27). Already doubts arise in regard to the one who stands head and shoulders taller than the people he is to lead.

The people's quest for a leader/king takes an anxious turn in chapter 11. While everyone is at home, a crisis breaks out east of the Jordan, where the town Jabesh Gilead is under threat from the Ammonites, here personified by their king Nahash. When the Israelites sue for peace, the Ammonite ruler responds with threats of torture and humiliation. Instead of "cutting" a covenant (a traditional Hebrew term for making a covenant) with them, he will have everyone's right eye "cut out"! The leaders then negotiate for time in which they can go looking through "all the territory of Israel" for someone to come to their aid (1 Sam 11:1-3). Jabesh Gilead has a fraught history in the annals of ancient Israel; both it and Gibeah were involved in the violent events recorded in the last chapters of Judges, a book that tellingly closes with the line, "In those days there was no king in Israel; everyone did what was right in their own eyes" (Judg 21:25). The text in Judges reports, ironically, that the Israelites themselves destroyed Jabesh Gilead (Judg 21:8-12), while earlier Jephtah had delivered Gilead from the Ammonites (Judg 11:4-33). First Samuel 11 resonates with both episodes.

Rather than trekking throughout the entire territories, the messengers go to "Gibeah of Saul," where their report causes such a great outcry that it reaches the ears of Saul out in the field with the cattle. Once Saul finds out what is wrong, the spirit of God "rushes" upon him and he calls up an army, sending pieces of his cattle, cut up for the purpose, around "all the territory of Israel," threatening that everyone's cattle will meet the same fate if they do not come out "after Saul and Samuel" (1 Sam 11:4-7). This action has the desired effect, and Saul is able to muster an army at a place west of the Jordan about equidistant from the river as Jabesh Gilead on the other side. Saul then sends the messengers who had come to Gibeah back to their hometown with the good news that help is on the way. The inhabitants first rejoice and then inform the Ammonites that they will be at their disposal on the next day, to "do whatever is good in your eyes" (1 Sam 11:8-10). This information is obviously a ruse, for they now know that Saul will be there with his army and that, at least, they will not go to their fate as helpless victims. The subsequent battle takes almost no time in the telling. In the same breath, the account relates that the battle lines are drawn and that the Ammonites are defeated (11:11). Thus, the entire episode comes to the desired conclusion.

Chapter 11 presents a short story of Saul's first act of deliverance as king, an act that was altogether successful. We recall that God had earlier instructed Samuel concerning the one he should anoint who "would deliver" God's people from the power of the Philistines (9:16). In a surprise turn, the fledgling king encounters as the first threat not the Philistines but the

Ammonites. In the setup of the tale, the leaders of Jabesh Gilead announce that they will surrender only "if there is no one to deliver us" (11:3). When Saul sends the messengers back, he instructs them to tell their town folk: "tomorrow deliverance will be yours" (11:9).

Clearly, Saul's leadership as depicted here follows in some ways the patterns of a traditional judge of the earlier period. The spirit rushes upon him as it had earlier (10:10) and as it used to do upon the judges of old, and he sends pieces of a cut-up body around, reminiscent of the action of the Levite in Judges 19 (vv. 29-30). The "berserker spirit enters him and ignites him with eagerness to do battle" (Alter 1999, 61 n. 6). Like the judges, he successfully averts the threat from hostile forces. There are also differences. Saul musters an army from the entire territory of Israel, working less locally than the judges did (Alter 1999, 62 n. 7), and his campaign does not result in "rest for the land," as was typically the case in the time of the judges, but in the people's reaffirmation of their intention to make Saul their king (11:15).

Some questions remain: Were the messengers intentionally heading for "Gibeah of Saul," or was it only one of the towns they encountered in their search for a "deliverer"? In other words, were they deliberate in their search for Saul as a potential military leader? If so, then why does the news reach Saul indirectly? Why is Saul still in the field as a farmer? Did he not have a royal residence that could easily be found? All of these ambiguities are symbolic of the fits and starts that mark the beginning of kingship. The messengers may have been tentative in their search for this tentative king, and Saul apparently carries on his life much as before. Not until the events recounted here have taken place does he assume more of the trappings of kingship. Yet, even afterward with his kingship more firmly established, one finds Saul more often than not in the tent of a commander in the field rather than in a palace. The story makes clear that, under the influence of the spirit of God, Saul takes on the mantle of military leadership with fortitude and success and achieves a double victory with this campaign: he subdues an outside aggressor and unites Israelite tribes settled on both sides of the Jordan who had a history of hostility between them (Fokkelman 1993, 472).

The events told here lead to another avowal of kingship after Saul refuses to do away with the naysayers that had questioned his ability to be king. Saul emerges as not only valiant and skillful in military matters but also as a shrewd politician who realizes that at this point he needs to keep the goodwill of everyone. Moreover, he attributes the victory, the "deliverance," to God rather than taking credit for himself (11:13). Perhaps this diffident, hesitant, indecisive candidate has the makings of a king after all! The people who rejoice with Saul when he is once more declared king certainly think so:

> And all the people went to Gilgal
> and they made Saul king there
> before the Holy One in Gilgal;
> and they sacrificed peace offerings there
> before the Holy One.
> And there rejoiced Saul
> and all the men of Israel greatly. (1 Sam 11:15)

Samuel suggests a renewal ceremony at Gilgal (11:14). Fokkelman assigns great significance to the fact that Samuel does not refer to Saul in this suggestion but rather urges "renewal of kingship." "Samuel believes that only God should be king but is charged by God to anoint a human king; he is therefore caught and speaks out of that dilemma" (Fokkelman 1993, 484). It is true that Samuel's name is notably absent in the lines that refer to the actual event of making Saul king. The people are in charge of the action, while Samuel is absent both from it and from the rejoicing that follows.

The Choice of a King (1 Sam 12:1-25)

"There is a leadership that does not 'take,' that does not seek its own." (Brueggemann 1990, 96)

Although 11:14-15 was already a part of the discussion above, I am inclined to agree with Fokkelman that these verses are the appropriate setting for Samuel's speech that follows and that the speech should be considered in the context of the people making Saul their king and rejoicing over the fact. There is no mention of Samuel during the rejoicing, and his absence may indicate that he is still brooding over the issue that there is only one true king in Israel, as well as over the fact that he himself has been set aside by the actions just taken. In a way, his speech in this chapter is a counterpart to the one of chapter 7. This time, however, his words are filled with dismay and warning with little comfort. "It does seem in character for Samuel that he would end up converting the coronation assembly into still another diatribe against the monarchy and an apologia for his own authority as prophet-judge" (Alter 1999, 65). As in chapter 7, the influence of the Deuteronomistic editor is more evident than in other places in these texts, as indicated by both the language and tenor of the speech.

The speech has an introduction (vv. 1-3), a main body (vv. 6-17), and a conclusion (vv. 20-25). The narrator intrudes only rarely to report on the reactions of the people (vv. 4-5, 18-19) and on the sign from God called for by Samuel (v. 18). In the introduction, the distress of the aged prophet is tangible: he has done everything the people asked ("I kinged you a king!" v. 1), and now they have their king while he is old and his sons—well, the less said about them the better, so wisely Samuel stays silent about his sons. He then launches into a self-defense depicting his own actions as the opposite of the king they have requested. He did not "take" anything from anyone, a fact indeed verified by the people.

The main body of the speech takes the form of a legal case, rehearsing the history of God with the people in summary fashion from Moses to Samuel himself. The first part ends in the words "you dwelt securely" (v. 11). The review then moves to the present and the situation involving King Nahash, which Samuel falsely portrays as the occasion for the people's demand for a king. At this point, his language hammers out in staccato manner the situation they have created with their demands:

> You said to me:
> No, but a king will be king over us!
> And the Holy One your God is your king.
> And now,
> there is the king,
> whom you chose,
> for whom you asked,
> there,
> the Holy One has given you a king! (1 Sam 12:12-13)

The word "king" rains down like pellets of hail while the name Saul is only alluded to with the verb "asked" from the root *sha'al.* Following this hail of words, the Holy One sends the sound of thunder together with rain, out of season and potentially damaging to the harvest (vv. 16-18).

It is small wonder that the people are "greatly afraid" (v. 18) and ask Samuel to pray for them because they are aware that they have sinned by asking for a king. Oddly enough, Samuel does not then counsel the people to reverse their decision for a king, nor do the people draw this obvious conclusion. All appear caught in the inevitability of a choice made, with which they have to live. Rather, Samuel counsels them not to be afraid but to keep serving God with "all [their] heart" and not to follow "confusion," i.e., false deities. God will surely be loyal to them as will Samuel himself, who will not stop praying for the people (vv. 20-23). Deuteronomistic ideology and language permeate the text through the final conditional clause:

But if you continue to do evil
both you and your king will be swept away. (1 Sam 12:23)

Samuel is not yet gone from the story, but here his story ends. It is in its own way a story that partakes of tragedy. Begun in great promise and faithfulness, continued in integrity and devotion to God, it ends as a tale of a prophet grown old and following in the steps of his mentor Eli in the worst way, with sons who belie everything he represents. While Samuel can boast that he has not "taken" anything from the people, his sons, according to the text's report, are takers of the worst kind (cf. 8:1). He sees God's authority and his own undermined by a king in whose appointment he was forced to collaborate. Samuel has made little headway in his efforts to delay the inevitable, but he has made clear to the people the implications of what they have chosen. He now faces not just a retiring, bumbling young farmer but a victorious campaigner. Thus, he must abandon the fight, but he does not go easily, and his last words cast an ominous echo into the future: "Swept away, swept away, swept away . . . ."

Part 2

The Story of Saul

(1 Samuel 13–31)

Introduction

Although Saul is present throughout 1 Samuel 13–31, the narrative presents his kingship as troubled almost from the beginning. Three chapters (13:1–15:35) recount a series of military exploits under Saul's leadership, two of them involving a condemnation of his kingship. In chapter 16 David appears on the scene, and thereafter Saul's story becomes intertwined with that of David, with Saul's character as king and commander more and more defined by his adversarial relationship to David. Only a short review at the end of chapter 14 affords a glimpse into Saul's role of able military leader, valiant and victorious in many undertakings. Over against this short positive report stand the chapters in which Samuel condemns his actions twice, declaring him rejected by God from his kingship (13:13-14 and 15:23). On the first occasion for condemnation, Saul offers sacrifice prematurely on the eve of a battle with the Philistines without waiting for the arrival of Samuel (13:9-10), and on the second he fails in executing a complete ban on defeated Amalek (15:8-9). While on the second occasion Saul transgressed a divine command, it is far less clear how he fell short the first time. Samuel's own reluctance to accept a monarchy may have influenced his bitter words to Saul in chapter 13 (vv. 13-14). As of chapter 15, the narrator makes clear that God has reversed course in regard to Saul, sending Samuel on an errand to secretly anoint another in his stead (16:1-13). It may have suited the purpose of the eventual editors of the material to highlight the instability of human rule, even when the ruler is a God-appointed one.

Between the two episodes of Saul's rejection, we find a story of the heroic exploits of Jonathan, Saul's son, who is out on the battlefield with him. This part of the narrative introduces Jonathan to the reader as a pious and brave man, while at the same time painting Saul in a less than flattering light (13:23–14:46).

The tale of David's appearance at the court of Saul is multilayered, presenting at least two versions: in one Saul invites young David to his side as musician to play a therapeutic role (16:14-23), and in another David volunteers to fight Goliath, the Philistine champion, who has thrown down the gauntlet to the Israelite armies (17:1-58). In braiding these myths of the young hero David together, the narrators manage to emphasize the multiple layers of David's character. On the one hand, he is the talented, handsome, well-spoken musician (16:18) who functions as therapist for Saul, now beset by an evil spirit sent from God (16:14-16). On the other hand, David is the clever, courageous fighter who slays a formidable adversary that nobody else dared to face (17:31). Although the narrator provides little insight into David's mind, in contrast to the revelations of the dark ruminations of Saul's psyche, David stands before us as the attractive, brave, young hero with whom everyone falls in love (18:1, 16, 20). Although David eventually becomes related to Saul by marriage, Saul nevertheless attempts to kill him a number of times, and at the end of chapter 19 David is on the run from Saul. David finds shelter with Samuel in Ramah, from where Saul attempts in vain to bring him forcibly back to his court (19:19-24).

The story of David's flight from Saul's presence takes a number of turns, involving an inexplicable reappearance at the court and intervention on the part of Jonathan, who has entered into a covenanted relationship with David (18:3; 20:16). When it becomes clear that his position with Saul is no longer tenable and actually fraught with danger, David leaves for good, finding refuge where he can, even making an unsuccessful attempt to hide out with the Philistine enemy (21:11-16). Saul descends ever further into a spiral of jealous hatred but, in spite of numerous spies who betray David's whereabouts, never catches his rival. Twice, Saul is close to David's rebel group, which has grown to considerable size, and both times David shames him into rueful admissions of mistreating David, while David escapes from the confrontations with laurels of honor and goodwill as the one who refused to kill the "anointed" of the Holy One, even when the opportunity presented itself (24:1-23 and 26:1-25). David avoids acting like a vengeful adversary who sheds blood needlessly not only in his confrontations with Saul but also in the course of an altercation with a local landowner. On that occasion, Abigail, the wife of the foolish landowner, intervenes successfully to avert bloodshed (25:1-44).

In the last set of chapters, scenes switch back and forth between David, in his various locations, and Saul, who faces a renewed Philistine assault (27:1–31:13). David has finally managed to hide from Saul with the Philistines in Gath, and from there he goes out to raid Israel's enemies under the guise of waging war on behalf of his Philistine overlord, Achish (27:1–28:2). Saul, faced with overwhelming Philistine forces gathered in the northeast of the country, resorts to consulting the ghost of Samuel via a medium at Endor. Samuel foretells his doom and the defeat of Israel. While David is out on a raid to retrieve families and goods from the Amalekites who have raided his place of residence in Philistia, Saul falls on Mount Gilboa, together with his sons, among whom is Jonathan.

First Samuel thus ends with the tragic fate of Saul, Israel's first king, while the star of David is still on the rise. Saul, unaware of the secret anointing of David by Samuel, proved himself to be keenly alert to the danger David presented to his person and his house. In the end he was unable to escape the spiral of hatred, fueled by jealousy and fear of young David, in spite of attempts at reconciliation from David's side. The narrator ascribes Saul's state of mind to an "evil spirit sent from God' (16:14; 18:10). On Saul's behalf it must be said that he, even though no longer in God's favor, did not go down without a prolonged struggle, and he died a valiant warrior in a fight against the Philistine enemy rather than against his kinsman David.

According to the narrator, God switches sides. After Saul's failure to execute a complete ban on Amalek (15:8-9), God's spirit, once inspiring Saul to perform heroic deeds (11:6), leaves Saul to stay with David. David never has trouble receiving God's counsel when he asks for it, while Saul fails to obtain divine guidance to the bitter end (28:6). Saul stumbles around in bewildered ignorance, yet aware of the threat to his throne in the presence of David. He is never able to slay his rival even though he makes several attempts on his life, twice unsuccessful in his aim with his spear, although David is in his immediate presence. Even as a failed king, having lost the all-important support of God, Saul stays in the story, perhaps as a crucial reminder that, for a people in exile who had lost their rulers, the presence of God is far more essential than human rule. Moreover, it is to God that the people owe their allegiance rather than to a monarch, even one who rules with God's support.

These chapters of 1 Samuel breathe a warrior culture where men play the important roles and male deeds of valor and courage are worthy of the admiration of the spectators. Women have only minor roles to play and often are pawns on the chessboard of male exercise of power. Three women appear in the narratives to influence the course of events. Michal, Saul's daughter, conspires on behalf of her husband David against her father but obtains no recognition for her intervention from David (19:11-17). Nor does David seek her presence on his unexpected reappearance at court, appealing instead for assistance to his friend Jonathan (20:1–21:1). Eventually, her father marries her off to another man as if David were dead (25:44). The second woman to receive attention is Abigail, the wife of the landowner in Maon. The narrator introduces her with praise for her beauty and sensible nature (25:3). Subsequently, Abigail acts on her own initiative to prevent the annihilation of her household, addressing David with prophetic words (25:28-31). Her appearance ends, however, with her as a member of David's harem, a position that ultimately may turn out to be less enviable than it appeared to her at the time (25:1-44). Finally, there is the "mistress of ghosts," the shaman at Eyn Dor, the well of generations past (28:3-25). She receives no name in the tale, but her role is significant as medium for Saul's agonized questioning and as provider of sustenance for the exhausted king and his retinue.

Character description is especially vivid when it comes to Saul, the tormented king, whose feelings of rage and jealousy, resulting in machinations to destroy David, regularly rise to the surface. David's character, on the other hand, is more opaque. It does not become clear what his anointing means to him or how he plans to fit into Saul's court in his position of claimant to the throne. Many love David, but we have no inkling of his returning any love. His feelings, even toward Saul, remain obscure. Love and grief will have their part to play for David, but those days still lie in the future.

A Kingship that Will Not Stand (1 Sam 13:1–15:35)

"At an early stage we become aware that this world is an arena of conflicting perceptions, rather than the scene of an unambiguous truth which can be stated in simple terms." (Fokkelman 1986, 83)

In this set of chapters, Saul suffers rejection as king by the God who chose him through the agency of Samuel. Following closely on the reaffirmation of Saul's kingship in chapter 12, with his leadership, as it seems, barely begun, Samuel meets him with condemnation in chapter 13. In actuality, Saul's kingship must have been well established by the time the events at Gilgal and Michmash occur, as his son Jonathan is fighting at his side. The note on the duration of Saul's reign up until the moment that he anxiously awaits Samuel's arrival at Gilgal is obscure, so that it appears as though events follow quickly on Samuel's instruction to Saul to wait for him at Gilgal

(10:8; cf. 13:1). All that happened until Gilgal now appears to have gone by in a blur until the moment of judgment.

To underscore the significance of Saul's dismissal, the text presents it twice with the effect that the narratives depict a double rejection. While it remains a question whether Samuel's harsh words in chapter 13 arise from a divine directive or from his own invention (13:13-14), the condemnation surely had its effect on Saul. The sequel to the events at Gilgal shows a man who is off-balance in all his dealings (13:23–14:46). He is in turns tardy in pursuing the enemy and overzealous, he imposes a prohibition on his army that saps his soldiers of energy, and, wittingly or unwittingly, he leads his own son into a trap that could have resulted in his death. After Samuel's criticism regarding a ritual transgression, he turns over-scrupulous and attempts to follow the rules to the letter. His son, Jonathan, in contrast to his father, shows cunning and daring in his military activities and exhibits a trust in God that does not have to rely on the trappings of religious ritual as motivation to action. Yet Jonathan's life is in immediate danger on account of his father's overzealous piety. In the aftermath of the defeat of Amalek, the situation comes to a head because of Saul's failure to comply to the letter with the command, issued by Samuel in God's name, for the total destruction of Amalek. In chapter 15, Saul receives the final blow to his kingship and the possibility of establishing a dynasty, with the narrator leaving no doubt that this time a divine initiative fuels the rejection. While the actual battles with Philistines or Amalekites receive little attention, the battlefield is a significant setting for Saul's dismissal. God's choice of Saul as king had its rationale, after all, in Saul's promise as military leader, and Saul established his kingship through military action.

Two large units make up the three chapters: one story is set in the context of a battle against the Philistines (13:2–14:46), and a second takes place against the background of a fight with Amalek (15:1-35). Notations concerning Saul and his reign frame the first unit (13:1 and 14:47). These records are generally positive in tone, without reference to Saul as a failed king (Fokkelman 1986, 82). The only negative note refers to continued fighting with the Philistines during his lifetime, thus pointing to a lack of success in subduing this enemy, a goal for which God specifically chose him (cf. 9:16). In the second unit, chapter 15, God returns as an active participant, and the story of Samuel and Saul's association comes to an end with Samuel in mourning, while the Holy One "rues" (1 Sam 15:35) the election begun with such high hopes.

A Failed "Appointment" (1 Sam 13:1-22)

"Who is to listen to (read: obey) whom? How sharply defined are the powers of the functions of the prophet and king, assuming that they are so defined? . . . has Saul kept to the agreement or not?" (Fokkelman 1986, 33)

As one could foresee, battle with the Philistines must eventually take place, for evidently these two peoples cannot live together in peace. In the prelude to the crucial episode, Saul musters his army, but on account of an act of provocation on the part of his son, Jonathan, and the delayed arrival of Samuel, he faces an overwhelming Philistine force with a dwindled contingent, while the Philistines go on a rampage in all directions (13:17-18). To make matters worse for Israel, Philistia had a monopoly on the most effective weaponry at the onset of the Iron Age (13:19-22). Once Saul sees his army melting away, he waits not a minute longer than the stipulated seven days for Samuel and makes the sacrifice when "Samuel did not come to Gilgal" (13:8). While the smoke from the burnt offering is still rising, Samuel appears without any explanation for his lateness (cf. 10:8). His first words to Saul, who perhaps unsuspecting has come out to greet him, are an accusing question: "What have you done?" (13:11). Naturally, they put Saul on the defensive. His army disappearing, Samuel not appearing, an overwhelming presence of enemy forces—all this without appropriate rites to seek the goodwill of the Almighty! Therefore, he got a grip, "took hold" (v. 12) of himself, and brought the required sacrifice.

Saul's perfectly logical explanation has no effect on Samuel:

> And Samuel said to Saul:
> You have acted like a fool
> and not kept the commandment of the Holy One your God,
> which he commanded you!
> For God had settled your kingship over Israel forever.
> And now, your kingship will not stand,
> and the Holy One will seek for himself
> a man after his heart.
> And God will command him
> as leader over his people
> for you have not kept what the Holy One commanded you.
> (1 Sam 13:14-15)

A play on the words "command" and "commandment" (from the same Hebrew root), used both for Saul's transgression and for the new "appointment" God will make as Saul's replacement, infuses Samuel's harsh and condemning speech (vv. 13-14). Samuel claims that Saul has not kept God's commandment, equating his own instruction with God's. Saul has no word in reply, as this judgment clearly dumbfounds him. So far in the text no mention has been made of a kingship that would last forever; to bring it up now as an established fact, if only Saul had been obedient to the divine directive, would destabilize anyone. Moreover, there has been no indication that God instructed Samuel about the duration of Saul's kingship or about the person in charge of bringing sacrifice. Nor did God announce a replacement for Saul. For a king to make sacrifice was certainly not out of place in that time and context. A number of interpreters view Samuel as overstepping his bounds, first playing what could be called a "cat-and-mouse" game with Saul by delaying his arrival until the last moment, and then making claims that are not borne out by the testimony of the text (Alter 1999, 73 nn. 10 and 14; Polzin 1989, 129; cf. Gunn 1980, 67ff; Brueggemann 1990, 107).

Certainly, the episode leaves the reader uneasy. If we review the options, it is possible that Samuel can only live with a king who is under his control, and thus the condemnation uttered here is his and not God's. It is also possible that Samuel, as God's spokesperson, knows more than we are told and condemns Saul rightly in God's name. It may even be that Saul misunderstood a condemnation that did not pertain to sacrificing but had to do with his delay in going to war with the Philistines. It was, after all, not necessary to make sacrifice before a fight, and Saul had not done so in his fight with the Ammonites. To go by Samuel's words, the issue is one of "keeping God's commandment," an indictment that both opens and closes Samuel's speech to Saul, and a topic that will return with emphasis in chapter 15. According to the criteria laid down in Deuteronomy, keeping God's commandments and studying God's *torah* are among the key standards for kingship (Deut 17:14-20). If we take into account the period of the Deuteronomistic editor, keeping God's commandments, with disastrous results following in case of failure to do so, would be of utmost concern. According to this view, both kings and people eventually failed in torah obedience, resulting in the loss of land and temple. Torah obedience has a basic foundation in the trust that the Holy One of Israel intends good for God's people, will be present with them, and will deliver them from distress. Saul, seeing his army melting away, aims at assuring himself of God's cooperation through sacrifice, and thereby exhibits ritual obedience that may not in itself testify to trust in God as the true deliverer of Israel. Saul acts as any responsible general would, but perhaps there are greater demands for a king leading a people dependent on God for their existence.

The truth about Samuel may lie somewhere between the picture of an imperious controlling prophet, jealous about keeping his prerogatives, and that of a perfect human being who always speaks the truth on behalf of God. Samuel, as we saw, was never enthusiastic about kingship; he may well have viewed Saul as a potential usurper of the duties that still remained to him, Samuel. He is also God's prophet, human being though he is and therefore not perfect (Fokkelman 1986, 34). When he speaks, he speaks both as God's prophet and as a human being, and at times he may become indignant either on God's or his own behalf, or a mixture of the two. What he says may still reflect truth in respect to Saul. We shall see how the theme of Saul's failure to be the king of God's choice plays out in the sequel.

Between "Twinkler" and "Thorn" (1 Samuel 13:23–14:23)

"Perhaps the Holy One will do it for us" (1 Sam 14:6).

Part of what took place in the previous episode was due to an exploit of Jonathan, Saul's son, who comes across in this part of the narrative as a counterpoint to his father. When Jonathan comes on the scene, some of the cloud that seems to hang over Saul lifts and a breath of fresh air enters the story. Jonathan earlier provoked the Philistines into action, as a boy poking a stick into a beehive may stir up the bees (13:3-7), and in what follows Jonathan takes the lead again with an aggressive move. The overwhelming force and superior weaponry of the Philistines clearly demanded stealth rather than direct confrontation. Jonathan and his weapon bearer, without telling Saul, creep up on the Philistines through a pass between two crags named Bozez and Senah, names one can roughly translate as "Twinkler and Thorn" (Fox 1999, 61; cf. Buber 1936/1956, 186). The naming of the two provides interesting detail in a scene already full of vivid description and dialogue. While Jonathan is on his risky adventure, Saul is said to "sit" near Gibeah, surrounded by what is left of his army and accompanied by a priest who is a descendant of Eli. The Elide house is apparently still functioning, at least by the side of Saul, a fact that casts some doubt on the legitimacy of Saul's religious practices in light of what has gone before and the curse pronounced on Eli's house earlier (see "A Doomed House"). In any case, a picture results of an inactive Saul in contrast to his daredevil son on the warpath.

A conversation follows between Jonathan and his servant that is revealing in what it says about the mindset of both. Unlike his father and without taking recourse to any religious ritual, Jonathan expresses hopeful confidence that God will fight with them and for them:

> Come, let us cross to the garrison of these foreskins!
> Perhaps the Holy One will do it for us,
> for God has no limit to deliver, whether with much or little.
> And his weapon bearer said to him:
> "Do all to which your heart inclines you;
> See, I am with you as your heart." (1 Sam 14:6-7)

Jonathan is aware that they will prevail only with God's help, and his "perhaps" indicates that he is willing to bank on this help. His weapon bearer is with him all the way, encouraging him to do as his "heart" tells him and assuring him of the loyalty of his own "heart," declaring that the two of them are of one mind in this adventure. Jonathan, proceeding on his hope, proposes a sign that God indeed will deliver the Philistines up to them and, when the sign is propitious, the two sneak up on their foe, one behind the other, to mow them down. The phrase "they fell before Jonathan" (v. 13) indicates that there is more at work here than human force, for no mention is made of Jonathan striking a blow. In addition, the phenomena of the "trembling" and the "shaking" of the earth, together with the "tremor" that befalls the camp, point to divine interference (Fokkelman 1986, 52).

Finally, on observing the panic in the Philistine camp, Saul joins the battle, although not until after a consultation with his priest, and the Philistines are on the retreat. The last line of the scene makes clear that the victory belongs to God: "The Holy One delivered Israel on that day . . ." (v. 23).

An Oath and Its Consequences (14:24-46)

"A general who withholds food from his army during the battle is not quite right in the head." (Fokkelman 1986, 64)

The next section leaves battle scenes behind to focus on a situation Saul created by subjecting an army in the midst of fighting to an oath not to eat anything on pain of death (14:24). Jonathan, in his absence from the main body of the army, takes some food, unaware of his father's command, and, when hearing of it, he condemns it in no uncertain terms, declaring that his father has "stirred up trouble" by this action (v. 29). He also observes that a well-fed army might have done more harm to the enemy than a starving one (v. 30). The people are still striking at the Philistine forces and in their famished state transgress the food laws by eating captured cattle with the blood. On hearing this, Saul decides to cleanse their offense by creating an altar for slaughtering the animals properly.

Saul's determination to repair ritual infractions highlights once again his punctiliousness in ritual matters in the aftermath of his own perceived transgression in this area. At the same time, it is not clear what will happen with Jonathan in view of his violation of the oath to which his father had committed the army. At this point, there is more mopping up to do in the aftermath of the victory, but uncertainty in the matter of pursuit of the Philistines causes Saul to question God, probably through oracular means (14:36-37), concerning its appropriateness. Ominously, the no-doubt anxious question receives no response: God "did not answer him on that day" (v. 37). Saul, convinced that the lack of answer must be due to someone's sin, declares that the culprit will die, even if it is his own son Jonathan (vv. 38-39). The lots cast fall first on Saul and Jonathan, until finally Jonathan is "caught" (v. 42). Jonathan declares his transgression, announcing that he is willing to die, and Saul assures him that this is what will happen (vv. 43-44). At this declaration, the soldiers intervene on Jonathan's behalf and the death sentence is lifted: "So the people saved Jonathan, and he did not die" (v. 45).

This baffling story raises a number of questions. Saul, by many accounts a capable military commander, is here a picture of passivity or hesitancy when it comes to engaging enemy forces. He repeatedly halts necessary action to engage in ritual niceties, and puts his army under an incomprehensible interdict that may result in the death of his son. He has stirred up "trouble" indeed. Is Saul aware that Jonathan could not have known of the prohibition and therefore might well violate it unwittingly? He knew, after all, that Jonathan was the one who had caused the turmoil in the Philistine camp (v. 17). Why are there descendants of Eli's house at his side as priests? Finally, what is the Ark doing in the field once again (v. 18)?

Various interpretations of Saul's actions are possible. First, even though it may not have been an effective move, Saul may have had sincere intentions in imposing a food prohibition on the army, with the thought that his own son would be liable to die because of it far from his mind. His insistence that, even if the culprit proves to be Jonathan, he must die may derive from a desire to be true to his word in front of his troops. In the end, he listens to his soldiers and complies with their wish. It is also possible that Saul, knowing of Jonathan's absence, is well aware that his son may be the one to transgress the interdict and purposefully plots the downfall of one he may perceive as a rival, even if it is his own son. Third, the story may essentially depict the actions and words of a son in rebellion against a father he perceived as ineffective and hesitant at a time that called for boldness and aggression. The truth of the matter may lie somewhere in between. Tension between Saul and Jonathan will occur in the sequel, but Jonathan never openly breaks with his father and dies together with him in battle. A young man may well have been chafing under too much restraint, so his acts of striking out against the enemy may have come from youthful zest for action. Evidently, Jonathan has the affection of his comrades, who intercede successfully on his behalf. Saul's motives are somewhat harder to unravel. There may have been a submerged desire in his destabilized mind for removing a loved and successful Jonathan. He may have interpreted Samuel's earlier words as pointing to his own son, the man "after God's heart" to be appointed after him. Certainly, at a later stage he throws a spear at his son in a rage over perceived betrayal and collusion with David (1 Sam 20:33). People rarely act based on only one motive, and Saul's reasoning, beclouded by the altercation with Samuel, was probably not the clearest. Whichever the case may be, the impression one gains is not that of a decisive commander with a firm grasp on his leadership. While not aiming directly for the death of Jonathan or deliberately setting a trap, he may have considered Jonathan's possible demise a not undesirable byproduct of the stricture he put on his army; such a desire may have existed only in the deepest recesses of his mind.

Fathers and sons have been at odds in previous episodes. Eli's sons were so wayward that they caused the demise of the Elide house; Samuel's sons were corrupt and did not walk in their father's ways; indeed, they became one of the motivating factors in the people's quest for kingship. Eventually, the most tragic father-son relationship will play itself out in David's family. Here we encounter another tension-filled relationship between a father and a son, but unlike other examples, the picture of the son shows more positives than that of the father. Jonathan challenges the enemy victoriously, without consulting any religious authorities or oracular devices, and demonstrates by word and action reliance on the hope that the God of Israel is able truly to deliver the people. He thus upstages his father in two respects: in his military skill and in his trust in the Holy One of Israel to do the work of deliverance "whether with much or little" (14:6).

Review of a Kingship (1 Sam 13:1; 14:47-52)

"He is just a fighter, really, is Saul." (Goldingay 2000, 102)

"An aura of dubiety surrounds Saul from the beginning." (Polzin 1989, 128)

The framework of the narrative contains observations about Saul as king, beginning with a note on his age and the period in his reign during which the episodes that follow take place. Unfortunately, the opening verse of chapter 13 is in poor condition so that we can no longer determine either how old Saul was or how long he had ruled before the events began. No solution is satisfactory; in fact, the Septuagint lacks the entire sentence. The confusion about the dating casts an air of uncertainty over all the proceedings; either it was no longer known at what age and in what period of Saul's reign the battle at Michmash pass took place, or the storytellers deliberately blurred the issue.

The final notations are a different matter. In them, Saul appears as an able military leader, victorious in many of his undertakings. Unlike the shaky behavior in the preceding narrative, he "catches hold" of his kingship (14:47). Just as Saul was previously "caught" by the lot as king (10:20-21), and later he and Jonathan were "caught" by the lot (14:41-42), now Saul catches, that is to say "takes hold," of his kingship. Subsequently, the narrator lists his many conquests, observing that Saul acted "valiantly." A brief list of family members contains the name of only one wife, pointing to Saul's lack of an extensive harem. Two of the family names will take up significant space in the sequel, his daughter Michal and his uncle Abner. The overview ends with a reference to lasting war with the Philistines. Nothing here reflects the tension-fraught events of the text that comes before. This overall positive picture of Saul has the effect of keeping one from "remaining locked in the naive position of a condemnatory attitude to Saul, taking Samuel's side" (Fokkelman 1986, 82).

A Failed Repentance (1 Sam 15)

"The question is not why Saul is rejected. That we know, regardless of whether we consider the rejection justified by Saul's actions. The question is why there is no forgiveness." (Exum 1992, 40)

Chapter 15 picks up and concludes the theme of the rejection of Saul as king over Israel, first by a divine word to God's prophet (15:10) and thereafter by Samuel's announcement to Saul (15:26). The ferocity of a type of war aimed at completely exterminating the vanquished enemy makes this a troublesome episode. Called by some "one of the cruelest practices of ancient Near Eastern warfare" (Alter 87, n. 3), war as the "ban" presents us with the gruesome picture of the violent death of every living thing. Such unsavory scenes as God's prophet butchering the life of a helpless victim who had survived the disaster (15:33) set up barriers to our insight into the passage (Good 1981, 65).

In the opening section, Samuel commands Saul in God's name to fight a war of total destruction on Amalek in retaliation for a bygone massacre of the ancestors of Israel at the time of the exodus (Deut 25:18 and Exod 17:8-16). The instruction is to put everyone and everything to the sword: "man and woman, child and babe, ox and sheep, camel and donkey" (15:3). In the ensuing battle, Saul defeats Amalek but spares the Amalekite king as well as the best of the sheep and the cattle (15:4-9). In the change of scene that follows this report, God reveals to Samuel repentance over the decision to make Saul king (15:10-11). Samuel sets out to meet Saul, again at Gilgal, questions Saul about the proceedings of the battle, and ends by declaring to him that God has rejected him from "being king over Israel" (15:26). Saul confesses his sin but receives no word of mercy; Samuel slaughters King Agag (15:33). This is the last report of an encounter between Samuel and Saul.

The theme of the chapter centers on the importance of listening to God's word as a criterion for faithfulness. Saul's transgression is that he did not listen to God's instruction, that he did not "maintain" it (13:11). When Saul greets Samuel on his arrival his first words about himself are that he "maintained the word of the Holy One" (13:13), a declaration Samuel immediately calls into question because he "hears" something entirely different, the bleating of sheep and the lowing of cattle, which are testimony to Saul's disobedience. This chapter pays close attention to the importance of Israel's king abiding by God's *torah* (see above, "King Them a King!"). First, Saul protests that the army saved the best of the animals for sacrifice, in other words as a special present to God:

> Saul said: From the Amalekites they brought them,
> for the people spared the best of the sheep and the cattle,
> in order to make sacrifice to the Holy One your God;
> the rest we put under the ban. (1 Sam 15:15)

When it comes to the wrongdoing, bringing the sheep and cattle along and sparing them for sacrifice, the subject is "they/the people." When it comes to following the command for destruction, it is "we," including Saul. When it comes to God, Saul uses the reference "the Holy One *your* God," establishing distance between himself and the Deity.

Samuel will have none of it and charges Saul with not "listening" to God's voice. When Saul protests that he did listen, Samuel declares in rhetorical question form that God takes more pleasure in "listening" than in sacrifice, for "listening is better than sacrifice, heeding than the fat of rams" (15:22). Finally, Samuel accuses Saul of practicing divination and utters the words that God has "rejected" Saul from being king because he "rejected the word of God" (15:23).

> For the sin of divination is rebellion,
> the transgression of idols—defiance. (Alter's translation, 1999, 91)

> Because you have rejected the word of the Holy One,
> God has rejected you from being king. (1 Sam 15:23)

Listening is of the essence rather than sacrificing, which after all can amount to little more than manipulation of the Deity—"divination." Sacrifice, its proper use; and its defilement, has received emphasis in these narratives at an early stage; the consequences of sacrifice were not always propitious (see above, "A Pack of Scoundrels"). Whether Saul's explanation for keeping the best of the cattle for sacrifice was merely an excuse invented on the spot or the truth, Samuel's words go to the heart of the matter: God has *rejected* Saul as king because Saul *rejected* the word of the Holy One.

With each of his responses to Samuel, Saul comes a little closer to admitting he did wrong. In his second reply, he takes responsibility for sparing the life of the Amalekite king, but he still accuses the people of taking the best of the loot in order to sacrifice (vv. 20-21). At Samuel's denunciation of sacrifice as divination, Saul finally stops making excuses. His next words are *I have sinned* (v. 24). As he explains, his transgression was in *fearing* the people and *listening* to their voice. Again, we cannot be sure that he is speaking the truth and that, indeed, he failed to execute the command for total extermination at the army's urging, for the text does not speak of it (vv. 8-9). Saul has dealt with "the voice of the people" in different ways, not heeding it when they demanded killing Saul's opponents (11:12) and complying with it when the soldiers intervened on behalf of Jonathan (14:45). Now he claims he assented wrongly. It is possibly true that a man, who so far has not acted as the despot described by Samuel at an earlier stage (8:11-18), would listen to the voice of the people. Truthful or not, Saul pleads for mercy: "Carry away my sin, go back with me and I will bow to the Holy One." Too late. There is, as David Hester observes, "no room for Saul to find a way back into the role of chosen king of Israel" (Hester 2000, 42). The Hebrew verb *shuv,* "to go back," also used for repentance and conversion, especially in prophetic texts, has become the keyword. There is apparently no "going back" on God's decision. Samuel denies Saul the opportunity for repentance and, for good measure, repeats the fact of Saul's rejection. When Saul will not let go and grabs Samuel's robe, tearing the symbolic cloak of his office, Samuel once more reiterates God's unchanging verdict to take away Saul's kingship and give it to a more appropriate candidate. Samuel's final words are that God is not a human to go back on God's word:

Samuel said to him:
The Holy One has torn the kingship of Israel from you today,
and will give it to a neighbor better than you.
And also the Eternal of Israel will not deal falsely or rue
for he is not a human to rue. (1 Sam 15:28-29)

Perspectives on God

". . . there is no necessary correlation within the History between the experiencing . . . of divine repentance as mercy and the human move toward repentance as precondition . . . for such mercy." (Polzin 1989, 114)

Samuel is obviously wrong in his statement, since the narrator puts the same verb used for "to rue" in God's mouth when speaking to Samuel about Saul's rejection (v. 11), a sentiment underlined by its repetition at the end of the episode (v. 35). Perhaps Samuel, at his wits' end in making clear the finality of God's decision, resorts to a platitude about God's nature more as a comfort to himself than anything else (Fokkelman 1986, 107). Coupled with Saul's confession and his plea for mercy, the statements about God having regrets give rise to a reflection on the notion of a God who may change course. In a number of instances in the Bible, God regrets an action or decision, beginning with repentance over having created humanity in Genesis (Gen 6:6). On other occasions in the Torah, God retreats from planned punishment (Exod 32:14; Num 14:20). Outside the Torah, the book of Jonah testifies to the possibility of God's change of mind over a projected disaster because of a community's repentance (Jonah 3:9-10; cf. Jer 18:7-8). There is also, however, a crucial notion of divine freedom that belongs to the nature of the God of Israel. This notion appears above all in the text of the revelation to Moses, where the name of God, "I will be who I will be," speaks to the dynamic nature of the Holy One of Israel (Exod 3:14). God is open to change, but this change is not predictable or under human control. A plea for mercy will not automatically elicit God's reversing a decision (Brueggemann 1990, 116). God may have a change of mind and refrain from planned punishment, but God's mercy does not depend on human repentance. Such reflections were especially important for the Deuteronomistic editors in the aftermath of the Babylonian exile, because they served as a warning for the remnant of Judah attempting to reestablish itself as a people living according to God's guidance. In any case, according to the perspectives present in these stories, God can evidently make mistakes or become involved in human mistakes to the degree that a change of course needs to happen.

Finally, Saul is not rejected from God's favor as a person but as a king. He was not the one God could sustain as ruler of God's people, even though to the listener Saul's shortcomings may seem much less serious than those of his successor David. Perhaps not only was he an inadequate king for Israel but kingship may not have been good for Saul himself. A certain instability in his nature, now leading to hesitancy and then to rash decisions, leaning on ritual rather than on trust in God, may have made him less and less able to guide and lead effectively. A diffident personality, having power thrust upon him, he carries power as a yoke he is unable to lay down. A family man, he ends up mistrusting those allied to him by bonds of kinship and service, and he squanders his gifts of leadership in squabbling with his presumed contender for the throne. These are speculations and may not diminish our sense of unfairness and feelings of sadness that what began, if in a somewhat tentative manner, with great promise has come to a moment of "mourning" on the part of Samuel and "regret" on the part of God (v. 35). Saul may have been, in Good's words, "a man not fitted for a job that should not have been opened" (Good 1981, 58).

Ways of Telling a Story

"The narrative is a reflection on the complicated entanglement of piety and policy, faith and reality. The tensions are so sharp for Saul, while the resolutions are so subtle and hidden." (Brueggemann 1990, 107)

Many biblical interpreters discern in these chapters a collage of narratives deriving from different sources. According to this view, one unit may go back to a source that provided a kind of annals of King Saul's reign; another may have been based on a fight with the Philistines at Michmash in which Jonathan played a major role; yet another may have focused on a conflict between prophet and king at a time when their roles were not yet clearly defined. All these theories are possible, but they do not bring us closer to the reason the writers tell the story of Saul's kingship in this particular way: a hesitant beginning told in great detail (chs. 9–11), on the heels of which follow a double rejection (chs. 13–15) and a drawn-out decline, so that the reader witnesses the spirit-filled hero of the fight against the Ammonites disappear into a fog of paranoia and depression, finally to die by his own hand in a losing battle against the Philistines (chs. 15–31).

To follow the frame that surrounds the text of chapters 13 and 14, Saul appears, in spite of it all, to have been an able king who acted "valiantly." Why then were the writers so hasty to take up his rejection, and why did they spend so much material on his slow decline? The writers must have had a reason to present the story of Saul just so and in no other way. For one thing, it could well be that they wanted to press on to the story of David, who is waiting in the wings to take over as the anointed "after God's heart." Soon the story of Saul will not be his alone but will become intertwined with David's. An elaborate account of Saul's kingship would only delay the urgent matter of presenting young David. Of course, as soon as David is on the scene the narrative becomes even more interesting, filled with new tensions and possibilities. In addition, from a point of view removed in time from the events told in these texts, it was known that Saul did not establish a dynasty. That privilege would fall to David, and the writers hasten to begin unfolding the tale of how he got to that point. *Sha'ul,* the "asked one," did not turn out to be the one "after God's heart" after all, and a kingship that began in uncertainty is in the end destined for demise; but the end is not yet, and Saul's decline has only just begun.

I Have Seen for Myself a King (1 Sam 16:1–17:58)

Immediately, the story records the anointing of Saul's replacement. God exhorts Samuel to cease grieving over Saul. Whether Samuel's grief arises out of resentment or regret because of personal attachment, the text does not say. When he receives his instructions from God to anoint one of the sons of Jesse, he balks at first, in real or pretended fear of what the king will do if he hears of Samuel's activities. Eventually he sets out to Bethlehem, provided by God with a ruse, and selects the Jesse family as instructed. Eliab, the eldest, catches his eye. Neither Eliab, however, nor any of Jesse's other sons will be the king "after God's heart," so Samuel ends up anointing David, the youngest, who is outside the family circle grazing the flock (16:11-14).

The scene subsequently changes to Saul, who is tormented by an evil spirit sent from God and who receives David at court on the recommendation of his servants to practice music as a healing device (16:14-23). This section ends with the observation that Saul loved David and that David became his weapon bearer (16:21), and notes the success David had in soothing the anguished Saul (16:23).

The next episode puts the spotlight on an impending battle between Philistines and Israelites and introduces a Philistine champion who challenges someone from the opposing army to a contest, the outcome of which will determine the victorious army (17:1-11). While Saul and his soldiers sit cowering in their tents at this provocation, Jesse sends David to bring provender to his brothers, who fight in Saul's army. Once arrived, David noses around to find out what sort of reward will be given to the one who takes on the challenger. David's bold speech reaches the ears of Saul, who summons David and in the end reluctantly sends him out to the contest (17:12-37). The account of the duel between David and Goliath follows, consisting mostly of speeches by the two champions and ending with a victorious David. A final note to the episode portrays Saul as ignorant of David's identity (17:55-58).

In these chapters, the writers weave different threads of David traditions together, without too much concern for apparent contradictions, so that a complex picture of David emerges. His good looks are emphatically noted (16:12) as were Saul's, but, unlike Saul's and David's brother Eliab's, his size goes unnoted. His first appearance in Saul's presence is as healer musician, although at the same time one of Saul's servants describes him as a "powerful man, a warrior and prudent in speech." "Love" seems to be the typical reaction of those who meet him. Saul, Jonathan, and Michal, as well as the people, all "love him." In the Goliath episode, David is the brave, foolhardy, but shrewd underdog who wins the day.

The Heart of the Matter (1 Sam 16:1-13)

". . . the heart of the matter is multilayered and relative, so that human looking upon the heart, however accurate or insightful it is, can turn out to be, from God's deeper point of view, mere appearance." (Polzin 1989, 158)

In the first episode of chapter 16 (vv. 1-13), Samuel stands at the center of the action while it records the anointing of David and all that leads up to it. The second episode (vv. 14-23) takes place at Saul's court and provides a rationale for David's presence at the court.

The first episode starts abruptly with God addressing the prophet:

> The Holy One said to Samuel:
> How long will you mourn Saul?
> I have rejected him from being king over Israel.
> Fill your horn with oil and go;
> I will send you to Jesse, the Bethlehemite,
> for I have seen among his sons for myself a king. (1 Sam 16:1)

The text does not reveal the reason for Samuel's grief, just as the motivations for his anger remained obscure earlier (15:11). Somewhat plaintively, the Holy One asks the prophet "how long," with words reminiscent of a human lament when a petitioner pleads with God to ease a situation of distress. The unraveling of Saul's kingship is painful to the prophet and painful to God.

The people have demanded a king, and, apparently, they must have a king. Therefore, God commands the prophet to get on with the business of king making. Only this time it will be a king to please God. Strikingly different from the former emphasis on the need of the people (cf. 9:16: "For I have seen my people/for their cry has come to me"), here the phrasing is "I have seen . . . for myself a king." This king will be primarily one anointed on God's behalf. Thus, the word *li,* "for me," recurs in v. 3: "you will anoint *me* the one that I say to you." Just as before "to listen" was key to the concern of the story, here the verb "to see" is central, with its fullest expression in v. 7. In addition, while the royal candidate in the earlier episodes found his way to Samuel and was only indicated by the words "a man from the region of Benjamin" (9:16), this time the prophet must go to find the one God has chosen. The instructions are more precise, with indication of family and town, but without clear information concerning which of Jesse's sons Samuel is to anoint, an uncertainty that will cause Samuel some problems.

God's prophet is reluctant to follow God's command for fear that Saul will find out and kill him; in a small country word would get around fast that Samuel was on his way with his anointing horn. To accommodate his anxiety God gives him a "cover story" (Alter 1999, 95) that will work for both Samuel and the Bethlehemites. The people of the town are as afraid as Samuel is and ask him if his arrival bodes well. They receive the assurance that he has come to make sacrifice. Indeed, Samuel gets on with the business of sacrificial preparation, singling out the Jesse family and purifying them. As Jesse and his sons come forward, the narration switches attention to the impending anointing, and the matter of the sacrifice falls by the wayside. The focus narrows more and more until young David stands before Samuel. Samuel anoints him and then leaves for Ramah (v. 13). The anointing does not proceed smoothly because at first, appearances deceive Samuel into thinking that the first of Jesse's sons is the chosen one. Apparently, like Saul, Eliab, Jesse's firstborn, is tall. God sets Samuel straight:

> The Holy One said to Samuel:
> Do not regard his appearance, and the height of his stature,
> for I have rejected him.
> For not as a human sees (does God see),
> for humans see in the eyes,
> and the Holy One sees in the heart. (1 Sam 16:7)

This time impressive height will not be the sign of royal material. The words "for I have rejected him" ominously echo God's words to Samuel in the opening phrase of the chapter (v. 1). God claims to "see" differently than human beings, for humans see either "with" or "in" the eyes, while the Holy One sees "with" or "in the heart." The Hebrew is somewhat ambiguous, but in light of the admonishment to Samuel "not to regard appearance," we should probably understand the "seeing" of God to concern the heart of a person rather than the outside, which may be impressive but misleading. We note that with this revelation Samuel is no closer to knowing the identity of the one he must anoint, but at least he is now on notice not to act hastily and to wait for instruction. Not receiving any signal, Samuel declares each of the next six sons of Jesse "not chosen." Samuel's heart may well have sunk in his shoes, as seemingly all the available young men parade by and God's mysterious actions seem bewildering.

Just to make sure, Samuel asks whether there are any other candidates, and when the one who was outside the family circle stands before him, once again Samuel sees the outside. According to the report, young David is "ruddy, with beautiful eyes, and of handsome appearance," even though not tall. It is hard to miss the irony of Samuel's view as compared to God's perspective. David's appearance is not what God sees, and even though his beauty will no doubt be a part of his charisma as he wins characters to his side, it will also be a liability in the long run for himself and his family, playing itself out to the bitter end in the life of his son Absalom. Now God gives the signal: "Arise, anoint him for he is it!" (v. 12), and Samuel can execute the action for which he came. Although still partly a clandestine act with the anointing taking place in the family circle only, there is less secrecy at work than with Saul's anointing, which was entirely private (cf. 1 Sam 10:1). As with Saul, the spirit of God overcomes David (cf. 1 Sam 10:10), but then the story shifts away from David, reporting no immediate effects on his behavior, while Samuel goes home without another word.

In this episode God's choice falls on the least likely, showing a penchant typical for the God of Israel, who frequently exhibits preference for the weak, the small, and the unimpressive (cf. Deut 7:7-8). David is the "youngest," in Hebrew the same word as "small." The word may hint both at David's stature and at his place in the family. Jesse only remembers his youngest when the prophet presses him on the issue. Sometimes the picture of David will be that of the youngest, the smallest, the underdog (cf. 17:33), and sometimes the emphasis will fall on his valor, courage, and strength as a warrior. From the beginning, the portrait of David is complex and multilayered.

See Me a Man (1 Sam 16:14-23)

"The Saul of the present does not see what our mind's eye perceives: the crown on the head of the lyre player." (Fokkelman 1986, 134)

". . . like medication, music soothes on the surface without dealing with the volcano beneath, which is thus left to erupt again and again." (Goldingay 2000, 122)

No sooner has the spirit of God descended on David than it departs from Saul, who in its stead receives an "evil spirit" from God to torment him (16:14). The contrasting ways in which the spirit affects David and Saul create an immediate link between the two episodes. Saul's servants observe that it is possible to soothe his type of trouble with music, so Saul asks them to find someone for him who can ease his agitated mind: "See me, please, a man / who plays well and bring him to me" (1 Sam 16:17) In similar terms as God's announcement to Samuel, "I have seen me a king" (v. 1), Saul intends to "see" a man to help him. Once again, a quest begins for which the verb "to see" is key, and once again the one to be found is David. Saul and his servants do not know about the anointing of David, but the servants know better than Saul does where to find "a man who plays well." The servants here remind us of Saul's servant, who turned out to be the guide who led him to Samuel in the earlier search for the lost donkeys. In braiding together different traditions about David and his appearance before Saul, the writers highlight Saul's ignorance and lack of knowledge. In the present case, this ignorance also connects to his doom, for, unbeknownst to him, Saul will bring into his presence the one who is to succeed him.

The servants speak in words that prefigure the arrival of the future king. Not only do the words of one echo the words of God to Samuel at the beginning of the chapter but this servant also refers to David as both a skilled musician and one with expertise in battle and prudence in speech, qualities that describe an efficient leader rather than a music therapist (v. 18). To cap it off, the last phrase the lad utters speaks of God's presence with this unknown candidate: "and the Holy One is with him." Since the narrator has just declared that God's Spirit is no longer with Saul, the servant's statements emphasize God's shift of allegiance to a more worthy candidate for kingship. The servants at Saul's court clearly know more than Saul; their insight and proleptic knowledge of David contrast sharply with their master's ignorance.

Verbs in the last paragraph of the chapter are highly symbolic and fraught with meaning. Saul "sends," and David "stands" before Saul as the one who will ultimately be the one to remain "standing." In contrast, Saul's fall, already begun, will gradually complete itself until he "falls" on his sword during the battle at Mt. Gilboa (1 Sam 31:4). Ironically, it is Saul who requires that David "stand" before him (v 22).

> David came to Saul,
> and stood before him
> and he loved him greatly
> and he became his weapon bearer. (1 Sam 16:21)

The most common reading of the third line is that Saul loved David, a fact that would make his later envious rage all the more tragic. Yet David is the subject of all the verbs in the sentence, and it is possible that as a young boy he felt a strong affectionate attachment for this physically imposing warrior-king, who nonetheless suffered from such debilitating instability. The fact that David is not said to love anyone until much later in his life argues against such a reading, although it is possible to have a change of subject in a sentence. The writer many also have left the matter deliberately ambiguous. Either way, tragedy is a part of this relationship that has begun at least on one side with warm affection (Good 2000, 73; Fokkelman 1986, 140).

David's therapy succeeds, and he manages, at least temporarily, to ease the torment of Saul. This optimistic note concludes the episode of David's first appearance in Saul's household. To this point, David has been a silent participant in the proceedings, and he remains therefore a somewhat enigmatic figure, combining in himself various qualities that may be in some tension with each other: poet/musician/skilled warrior/charmer. He has yet to speak his first word.

Perspectives on God

A difficult knot in the story involves the way God's presence torments Saul (vv. 14, 15, and 23). This is how the storyteller portrays the situation, both through narrative description and by the perspective of Saul's surroundings. Robert Alter describes this view as fitting for the "theopsychology of ancient Israel" that explained "extraordinary states as investments by a divine spirit" (Alter 1999, 98). Certainly, Saul's descent into depression is understandable after the abandonment by Samuel, the one who once forecast such high hopes on his behalf. The harsh words of the prophet may have eaten away at his already shaken equilibrium. More and more, Saul will go down into this pit until moments of blind rage will cause him to commit acts of violence against those in his household he most loves, first David and then his son Jonathan. Clearly, kingship holds less and less benefit for Saul as a person (see above, "Perspectives on God"), and from the perspective of the narrator, his paranoia and depression originate directly with God.

Perhaps the narratives may also reflect a divine distaste for kingship with its automatic conferral of authority and power. We recall that God had not been enthusiastic about the people's request for a king. Saul initially acts more like one of the judges of days gone by than like a royal figure. As he grows into his power, the divine spirit no longer supports him but turns to young David, who is yet powerless apart from what talent, courage, and youth lend him. Once David has gathered the power of kingship to himself, God's Spirit will not always support him. If we take into account the lines from Hannah's song concerning God lifting the poor from the dust while casting the mighty from their throne, God may not be acting out of character here. After the Babylonian exile, this insight may have provided some comfort to a community that found itself in a subordinate and lowly position, once again with no ruling royal house.

It is also possible to view Saul and his kingship more positively. During all the years of his kingship, when Saul fights off David's aspirations to the succession, he does not go down easily, in spite of seeing David's inevitable rise. Whether foolish or wise, blind or insightful, Saul confronts David with a thorny path to kingship far more difficult than his own had been. Unfortunately, Saul's tenacity sets him on a path in direct opposition to the demands of his God, a path that ultimately will lead to his doom.

Choose Yourselves a Man (1 Sam 17:1-58)

"Strong, tall and sure Goliath stood . . . only a stone's throw from disaster." (Max Brown Vestal, AD *[April 1982]: 7)*

A long chapter follows, with the well-known account of David's fight against Goliath as its climax. It divides neatly into seven units.

Setting (vv. 1-11). The first unit introduces the location of the battle, the war parties, and the champion. The story veers away from David to concentrate once again on Saul and his exploits against the Philistines. Thus, Saul and the men of Israel set themselves up for the fight in a specific location, the valley of Elah. At the end of the unit, however, Saul and his army are terrified rather than ready for battle. Between the preparations and this result, a champion has come forth who insultingly challenges the Israelites to choose a warrior to best him in a duel. Literally, this champion is called the "in-betweens-man" in the text, and indeed he would come between Saul and his zest for a fight. In a literal sense, the champion, Goliath from Gath, stands in the space between the armies where the duel would be fought. Notably, this section elaborately enumerates Goliath's equipment, a catalogue of weaponry that makes him appear to be a one-man army. This recital preludes the contrast between him and David, who in this part of the story is still mostly a shepherd boy.

David Arrives (vv. 12-16). David soon reappears, depicted in the context of his family rather than Saul's court, first in relation to his father Jesse and then to his three brothers—all of whom, it turns out, are fighting in Saul's army. As in chapter 16, the brothers appear by name, with David again specified as the youngest/smallest, still grazing the flock of his father, going back and forth to the battlefield to bring the necessary goods to his brothers. The notation concerning his age and the fact that his brothers are with the army, while David "only" shepherds the flock, add emphasis to the contrast between David and his brothers. The contrast between military might and the less obvious strength of the shepherd will reappear in the chapter (Fokkelman 1986, 172). The remark that he went "back and forth from Saul" (v. 15) is an attempt at harmonizing different tales circulating about David and his first appearance in Saul's presence.

A Challenge (vv. 17-24). The next scene takes place near the battlefield, where David has gone with foodstuffs for his brothers. Saul sits cowering in his tent, and the soldiers gossip about the benefits coming to the one who dares to take on the challenger. As did the introduction, this unit ends by noting the fear that befalls "all Israel," adding that they are in flight on account of the challenger. The reader still looks on at the activities: the opposing armies, the champion braying his insults in between the two, David scurrying back and forth, doing as his father asks and speaking with the soldiers about his brothers' welfare.

David Speaks (vv. 25-31). Now the reader is drawn into the story as, for the first time, David opens his mouth. The preceding chapter described him as a man who was "prudent" in his speech (16:18). We shall see whether he lives up to this description. His first words, in a fashion that fits the mode of a folktale, are a query about the advantages of taking on Goliath. Like the "little cabin boy" in "The Golden Vanity," David wants to know what is in it for him. Further, like the "little cabin boy," David reveals by his words that the speaker is clearly thinking about taking on the task. There is, however, more to his first words than his initial question, one he asked perhaps to make doubly sure after having overheard the soldier talking. He adds words that may sound a bit like bravado coming from this kid who still does his father's bidding, but they are telling words in view of the way they are repeated in the chapter. David accuses the Philistine—and who is this "foreskin" exactly?—of "insulting the ranks of the living God." It will not do to write off these words as a tactical diversion on David's part to deflect attention from his true objective (Alter 1999, 105). They are too significant and laden with meaning in the entire chapter. In the mouth of Goliath, they were insults to the "ranks of Israel" (v. 10), while David points to these same ranks as those of the "living God." He will use the phrase twice more: once when he stands before Saul (v. 36) and again facing Goliath, when he makes clear that by insulting the ranks of Israel that belong to God, Goliath has actually insulted God (v. 45). The line points to the opposition set up in the story between obvious military power and the power that arises from belonging to God, a power to which David may lay claim as God's anointed (Fokkelman 1986, 172). As David later confidently says to Saul, "the Holy One will rescue me from the hand of this Philistine" (v. 37). His speech resembles that of Jonathan when he is out on his foray against the Philistine camp (14:6). Two young men speak here out of trust both in themselves and in their God with the weight going to the power of God to deliver. Once again we are reminded of the assertion in Hannah's song that a man is not a hero by his strength but by what is given to him by the God who "brings low, (and) also exalts," the One who "breaks his adversaries into pieces" (2:7, 9-10).

David's brother, Eliab, not pleased with his little brother's trouble-making speech, upbraids him. In this way, the story not only sheds light on David's public persona and conversation but also reveals a glimpse of his family context and sibling rivalry. David will have none of it and claims that he spoke with good reason (v. 29). Yet David has not come on the scene for a family squabble, so he turns away and continues his exchange with the soldiers. In the end, the talk is public enough that it reaches Saul. When it does, Saul wants to meet the only one who is not shaking with fear at the sight and sound of the Philistine threat, one who in addition appears willing to face the threat himself.

David and Saul (vv. 32-40). David takes the lead in the conversation with his royal master with the encouraging words that no one should be afraid, for he will go and take on the champion! Although the text does not explicitly state that Saul laughed at this, a chuckle runs through his reply that a boy could not possibly fight someone who learned to fight from boyhood! David then launches into a speech that spells out more clearly the dangers he faces out in the field as a shepherd, protecting both his flock and himself from marauding wild animals. He ends with an eloquent flourish:

> Even the lion, even the bear
> your servant struck down.
> And this foreskinned Philistine will be like them,
> for he has insulted the ranks of the living God! (1 Sam 17:36)

By highlighting his own skill, David diminishes Goliath, to whom he once again refers as "this foreskinned Philistine," to the level of the wild animals that lurk to assault the helpless sheep of the flock, the current position in which the Israelite armies, the "ranks of the living God," find themselves. Saul has no reply to this, so David once again takes the floor and for the second time expresses faith in the power of God to deliver. In the end, then, not his own skill or courage but the Holy One will accomplish the rescue (v. 37). To such blind trust and faith Saul can only give his consent.

Convinced of the young man's determination to go out and face the "in-betweens-man," Saul makes an effort to give David at least some protection by dressing him in his personal armor. A short list of conventional weapons follows, in counterpoint to the armor that shielded the mighty Goliath, but it is in vain. Twice the narrator notes that David was not "used to it." There is no mention of the difference in size between the two men. Traditional weaponry will not defeat the threat, but rather the tools of the shepherd: pouch, sling, and stone.

The Contest (vv. 41-54). It is time for the fight. The actual duel in this climactic scene is reported in few words (vv. 48-51), while the greatest part is devoted to speech and insults. Probably such exchanges were just as important in this type of contest as the actual fighting, most likely with the intent of making one of the opponents lose his equilibrium, which the other party could turn to advantage. In this verbal duel, David gets the largest portion of speech. The Philistine, who after David has asked his question in v. 26 is never again referred to by his proper name, utters words of contempt and amazement at facing such a puny contestant, a "pretty boy," and, ironically, compares himself to an animal, a dog to be chased off with sticks (v. 43). Once within striking distance, he will make carrion of David. David's speech is loftier. He does not condescend to fling insulting words at his opponent but rather aims to teach a theological lesson. He begins by pointing out that they approach each other with different tools:

> You come to me
> with sword, spear and javelin.
> I come to you
> with the Name of the Holy One of Hosts
> the God of the ranks of Israel,
> that you insulted. (1 Sam 17:45)

To the three weapons Goliath carries, David opposes one, the Name, the only arms he needs. His own three weapons—the pouch, sling, and stone—

are as yet invisible to Goliath and will be revealed only at the last moment. The stick David carries is not a weapon, so Goliath is mistaken on all fronts. With this claim, David does no more than reiterate Hannah's statement that a man is not a hero by his own strength; rather, it is God who will deliver (1 Sam 2:9). Once God has delivered Israel from the Philistine threat by the hand of David, not only Goliath's corpse but the dead bodies of the Philistine army will become carrion. All this will not be for David's glory or Israel's glory, but so that the world may know there is indeed a God in Israel and so that Israel may know that victory in battle ultimately belongs to God; the lesson taught in Hannah's song is thus brought home (vv. 46-47).

The description of the actual fight (vv. 48-51) tells a tale of "great dexterity and speed versus cumbersome inertia" (Fokkelman 1986, 185). One can see the giant lumbering down the field, hindered by his heavy armor, toward the young man who even now wears what he always wears while grazing his flock, with the shepherd's pouch strung over his shoulder. In the text, two slow verbs with Goliath as subject ("he came and drew near") highlight the contrast with David's two fast actions ("he hurried and ran," v. 48). Four verbs follow in quick succession ("stretched," "took," "slung," and "struck," v. 48), with the result that the Philistine falls forward on his face (v. 49). To make the whole event accord with David's lesson about who ultimately wins the battle, the next verse notes that David killed Goliath without a sword (v. 50). Yet, depending on where it hit, the stone most likely only stunned the giant or caused him to stumble and fall, and he received the death-stroke by his own sword that David wrested from him. That takes care of David's heroic deed:

> David ran and stood over the Philistine
> and took his sword, drew it from its sheath
> and killed him and cut off his head with it.
> When the Philistines saw
> that their hero was dead, they fled. (1 Sam 17:51)

The deed is done, and the Israelite army has only to mop up while the Philistines are still in disarray from this unexpected turn of events. In his turn, David takes the spoils, including Goliath's head, which he will eventually bring to Jerusalem (v. 54). This latter anachronistic note seems entirely out of place. Could it be that the narrator, who has kept so much under wraps in terms of David's future in these stories, here gleefully lets it all show? Yes, this is the future king who will reign in Jerusalem, a city that was not yet on the historical horizon for ancient Israel at the time of the battle in the valley of Elah.

Coda (vv. 55-58). A coda to the story reintroduces David to Saul, who wants to know where he comes from. One may wonder why the narrator did not fuse the stories about David's introductions to Saul more seamlessly. Telling it just this way brings the two aspects of this closing to the David-Goliath story to the fore. Saul's question to Abner ("Whose son is the boy?" v. 55) once again reveals the ignorance in which Saul seems to stumble around much of the time, going back to the days he was looking for his father's donkeys. Second, he really does not know who "this boy" is, and his question aims at more than merely David's antecedents. Yet those antecedents are precisely what David reveals, and they are the only thing he reveals: "the son of Jesse, the Bethlehemite" (v. 58). These two indications point back to chapter 16, which narrates how this son of Jesse was anointed by Samuel to be God's chosen king, an event of which Saul remains ignorant (Alter 1999, 111). God has provided Godself with a new king, Saul has provided himself with a musician/therapist/weapon-bearer, and Goliath's challenge that the Israelites would choose themselves a man to fight him has been answered. Now the long unwinding of Saul's kingship and David's twisted road to the throne can begin.

The King's Son-in-Law (1 Sam 18:1–19:24)

"Manhood is about fighting. Womanhood is about being real estate . . . ." (Goldingay 2000, 124)

Two chapters describe both David's successes, in warfare as well as human relationships, and Saul's increasing distrust and jealousy, which occasionally turn into murderous rage. Chapter 18 relates how soon Saul's love for David turns to jealousy, escalating into hatred, while it recounts that two of Saul's children, Jonathan and Michal, love David. David outshines Saul in his ability to defeat the Philistine enemy according to public perception, so Saul descends ever deeper into paranoid envy until he attempts to kill David by throwing his spear at him. The writer puts David's success consistently in contrast with Saul's fear. While Saul's intentions remain hidden in chapter 18, they are entirely out in the open in the next chapter. By the end of it, David is permanently on the run from Saul, who has personally tried to kill him or have him killed a number of times.

David's prowess receives emphasis in chapter 18, turning Saul's previous affection into jealousy and hatred. Just as the story fast-forwarded earlier to tell of the rejection of the newly minted king, now it rapidly moves into describing a relationship begun in affection and trust deteriorating into murderous hatred. In the end, Saul attempts to kill his once-loved servant, music therapist, and gallant warrior, who is adored not only by his son Jonathan and daughter Michal but also by "all Israel and Judah" (18:16). Saul not only tries to kill David directly but plots to have him killed by the Philistine enemy, against whom David is portrayed as consistently victorious. By the end of these episodes, Saul fears David "greatly" and has become "his enemy all the time" (18:29).

Chapter 18, which contains an unusual amount of revelations about Saul's inner disposition, motivations, and thoughts, elaborates on Saul's anger-turned-fear of talented young David. The narrative retreats from the battlefield at Elah to inhabit not only the residence of Saul but also his psyche, a turn that lends a claustrophobic aura to the episodes. Over against these convoluted inner workings of the haunted king's mind, we hear of the openly affectionate attitudes of the people and of two of Saul's children, Jonathan and Michal. Of David's motivations and feelings one hears little. He acts, even on the battlefield, mostly in reaction to others: in chapter 18 he acts and attacks on Saul's appointments and orders; in chapter 19 he reacts to Jonathan's initiative and subsequently to Michal's. Only his setting out for Samuel and Ramah reveals a deliberate choice. Ironically, and tragically for Saul, the more intentional he is about eliminating the one he has begun to perceive as his rival, the more David's stature increases.

Love in a Cold Climate (1 Sam 18:1-16, 28-30)

"Jonathan gives everything to David—whereas David is not reported as giving anything in return." (Polzin 1989, 178)

"Women are not merely property passed from father to husband but devices in working out male fear and hostility." (Goldingay 2000, 130)

In the four opening verses, all the verbs have Jonathan as subject with one exception, the report of Saul keeping David by his side (v. 2). Twice the text reports that Jonathan loves David as "his own soul" (vv. 1 and 3), while noting in addition that Jonathan's soul is "bound" to David's. Jonathan shares with David his robe and his battledress, symbols of his princely and military power. What David once could not take from Saul he accepts from Jonathan, who appears here as a person in his own right, not in his relationship to Saul. Nothing is said of David's reaction to Jonathan's extravagant gesture; in fact, David is only present as recipient. The concluding lines, vv. 28-30, echo the opening ones and demonstrate a development. They also speak of love for David, this time on the part of Michal, Saul's daughter (v. 28). In contrast to the opening lines, Saul shows no desire to keep David close, but the narrator emphatically refers to Saul's fear and to his animosity toward David (v. 29). Thus, the story of Saul's evil machinations lies between the brackets of a love story.

Jonathan has been absent from the scene since his father's soldiers rescued him after the honey-eating episode in chapter 14. One may wonder why he, the brave and risk-taking fighter, earlier did not take on the challenge to combat Goliath, but brave and risk-taking David has taken the spotlight away from the son of Saul. Undeterred by rivalry, however, Jonathan attaches himself to David with a deep emotional bond, followed by extravagant actions of loyalty. In this chapter, so revealing of emotional states and feelings, Jonathan's inner motivations are the first to become evident. In the Hebrew Bible, however, love points not merely to depth of feeling but also to loyalty. Jonathan's loyalty to David, which will take more extreme forms after he makes his initial attachment, puts him on a thorny path in view of his father's murderous intentions. Jonathan is a good son who fights at his father's side and who will eventually die at his side; his loyalty to his father's rival makes him a tragic figure, just as a tragic fate will eventually befall his sister Michal. Saul's family is torn between the all-important loyalty to the family and emotional bonds to the newcomer and rival of the father. This situation is not made any less complicated by the fact that eventually David will also have family ties to both Jonathan and his sister Michal.

Jonathan affirms his bond to David by giving him his cloak and his soldier's gear. Hereby, Jonathan does not merely provide David with a nice set of clothes but lends him something of his own authority and princely power. Of course, at this stage, the two are not equal, with David occupying the lower position in terms of status, so Jonathan is raising David to a position of greater equality by his actions. To top it off, he gives David his battledress and weapons, thereby transferring to him the title of champion of the army, a position previously occupied by Jonathan himself. Finally, Jonathan enters into a covenant with David. In the Bible, people of unequal status often make a covenant when they have reason to seek protection from possible difficulties that may arise to disturb the bond between them (cf. Jacob and Laban in Gen 21). Through the covenant between Jonathan and David, clearly on Jonathan's initiative, he grants David certain rights and authorities and pledges to David his abiding loyalty. David's only role is being the recipient of Jonathan's benevolence.

With all the focus on Jonathan and his bond with David, it may almost escape attention that, from that moment on, Saul keeps David with him and does not let him return to his father's family (v. 2). This announcement, although made in a neutral fashion, has an ominous undertone in light of what follows. When David eventually leaves Saul's presence, he will be on the run, escaping his cage that has become a death trap.

The final lines of the chapter also speak of love, this time the love of Michal, Saul's daughter, who has in the meantime become David's wife:

> Saul saw and knew
> that the Holy One was with David.
> And Michal, Saul's daughter, loved him.
> Saul increasingly feared David,
> and Saul became David's enemy all the time. (1 Sam 18:28-29)

Here, Michal's love for David is framed by Saul's perception of David's success and by his fear of David and abiding animosity toward him. Michal, like Jonathan, is drawn to love David and has been used by her father as a trap. She does not engage in any activity, unlike her brother. Instead of engaging in giving, she *is* given by Saul to be David's wife (v. 27). Her loyalty to David has yet to spin itself out into a web of deceitful activity that will put her at odds with her father. At this point, love still surrounds David like a protecting cover, and the chapter ends with mention of the esteem that David's name attracts because of his success. All the love that comes David's way does so in the cold climate created by Saul's emotions and intentions.

The Marriage Trap (1 Sam 18:17-27)

"We all know from experience that in this world even the simplest context or the clearest words can be misunderstood; and that is what happens to Saul when he hears the poem." (Fokkelman 1986, 24)

"Someone in Saul's position does not have to be especially neurotic to find this a bit threatening . . . you have to be an especially secure kind of leader to be able to handle that kind of adulation of a member of your staff." (Goldingay 2000, 127)

After the defeat of Goliath, with Saul and David on their way back from the battlefield, the women come out to greet the victorious army and its leaders with a chant that has a negative effect on Saul. Their chant, "Saul struck down his thousands/David his tens of thousands" (v. 7), manifests correspondence of the second line to the first, typical of Hebrew poetry, and does not necessarily lift up David's accomplishments above those of Saul. Instead, the second line of such poetry also often intensifies and focuses the subject matter, and there is no doubt that this song celebrates David together with Saul on equal if not greater footing. In any case, the song throws Saul into a jealous rage. Suspicion, anger, and fear are from now on thick in the air between these two. Saul becomes so agitated that he falls once again into a prophetic trance and tries to kill his adjutant, David, as he plays his music. David's therapy is no longer effective. Fear has taken deep root in Saul, for the support of God has turned from him to David, so that all the young man does is successful and the people are said to love him. For the first time, Saul's fear of David matches others' love for David.

Continuing the flow of information about Saul's emotions, the narrator next reveals Saul's hopes that the Philistines will take care of the "David problem" (v. 17). If Saul sends David repeatedly into the fray, surely a day will come when they will kill David! In the course of encouraging David to fight, Saul dangles before him the prize of his daughter Merab. This turns out to be something of a tease, because when the time comes, he gives her to someone else. Saul may have had the idea that David would do his bidding more readily as his son-in-law, for when the next daughter appears to love David, the plan returns. This time Saul attaches a price to the bride that he hopes will be impossible to pay. Significantly, in plotting this second marriage proposal, Saul and David largely communicate indirectly (vv. 22-26). Apparently, the more Saul fears, the less he speaks directly to the object of his fear.

David takes up the challenge and comes back with not just one hundred but two hundred Philistine foreskins. The foreskins symbolize potency, and this trophy once again lends David the aura of invincibility (Fokkelman 1986, 245). The trap is closing not on David but on Saul, who now has no other choice but to give his daughter to David as wife. The prize, first mentioned when David appeared on the scene to witness Goliath issuing his challenge, has finally been bestowed.

A Tangled Web (1 Sam 18:1-30)

"The whole of 1 and 2 Samuel is an unhappy story." (Goldingay 2000, 130)

A tangled web of relationships is woven before our eyes. Parents, children, friends, and marriage partners all become involved in relationships that contain antagonisms and danger. For the first time since chapter 4, women play a role in advancing the plot, but the effect of their presence is to drive Saul deeper into the grip of his paranoia. The first character to appear is Jonathan. While other father-son relationships fall prey to the sons' failure to live according to the same standards as their fathers, Jonathan lives up to all expectations of what a son should be, although Saul will not always perceive Jonathan's behavior as such. Ironically, Jonathan, the good son, sets himself up for conflict by binding himself closely to the one who will eventually replace him as successor to the throne. Jonathan tries to hold together two impossible loyalties, one loyalty to his father to whom he is bound in the natural family covenant, and the other loyalty to the friend he loved as solemnized in a freely chosen covenant. The second loyalty will drive him to take actions that his father, not entirely unreasonably, will perceive as disloyal. Jonathan is caught between the hammer of his father's hatred and the anvil of David's aspirations.

Conjectures about the homoerotic nature of the relationship between Jonathan and David must remain speculative, but such emphatically stated love as Jonathan's, followed by the bonding ritual, at least leaves the impression of something more than the typical ties formed between brothers-in-arms. Jonathan's love, mentioned seven times in the material that refers to his relationship to David, the sharing of all his symbols of authority and power, and the lengths to which he goes to protect David from the murderous rage of his father all speak of a total devotion that appears to answer more closely to demands laid on a spouse rather than on a friend, even a very good friend. In addition, Jonathan's actions, when he deceives his father as to David's whereabouts (20:28), parallel Michal's in a subsequent episode. On Jonathan's part, at least, one may assume a deeper attachment than simple neighborly love.

What David feels the writers do not say, in any case not now. David speaks twice in the episode, both times in a self-deprecating way (vv. 18-23), describing himself as coming from nothing and being a nobody, a "poor man of little esteem." The statement flies in the face of the adulation he received from the home team on returning from the battlefield. Such statements cover up rather than reveal the speaker's true emotions. While the feelings of all others—Jonathan, Saul, the people, and Michal—are fully revealed, David remains somewhat nebulous, hiding what he thinks and feels, his aims and aspirations unclear. He remains the valiant warrior, never hesitant to enter a battlefield and bring home his bloody trophies to get his wife, the only context in which the narrator speaks of his feelings, observing that it "was right in the eyes of David to become son-in-law to the king" (v. 26). Why this would be so is not immediately obvious, unless David hoped that a closer family tie would prevent Saul from eliminating him. As we shall see, the family tie had no effect on Saul's intentions, but it may not have been an unreasonable expectation on David's part.

Saul's objectives are entirely clear in this chapter. Yet he too is caught between his need for David, the valiant fighter of the Philistines, and his jealous hatred of a potential rival. If we keep in mind the earlier statement about Saul's emotional attachment to David (16:21), it is clear that his feelings from now on will be conflicted. Affection will now and then reassert itself before Saul once again descends into the pit of his fear and anger. Saul is right to fear David, of course, for he is a true threat to Saul and his house. The fact that Saul does not know about the true state of affairs, Samuel having anointed David in secret, makes him all the more pitiable. John Goldingay observes that there seem to be no happy people in all the narratives of 1 and 2 Samuel. While one should make an exception for Hannah, this may be an accurate observation. Goldingay also directly addresses the apparent unfairness of the way God treats Saul versus the way God supports David. God's turning away from Saul cannot really be ascribed to any discernible faults, while God's support of David does not clearly rest on David's virtue. Of the two, Saul is certainly the more truthful character, and one could argue that "Saul dies a better death than David, and that may mean that in the end he had worked better with the hand he had been dealt, although it took him a long time to do so" (Goldingay 2000, 130–31).

Michal is, after Hannah, the first woman with a significant role in the narratives, one that will receive more attention in the next chapter. Like her brother Jonathan, she loved David and, like her brother, she will go to great lengths to protect him (19:11-18). Unlike her brother, she plays only a passive role in this part of the story, and in this episode the connection with her is at least potentially a connection with death, for Saul hopes that she will become a snare for David (Fokkelman 1986, 235).

The eventual editors of the story of King's Saul's descent versus David's rise wove the old stories together without giving them the gloss of romantic hindsight. After all is said and done, these are flesh-and-blood people, warts and all. This is what happens when the community desires kingship; these are the leaders they got. Perhaps one goal was for the post-exilic community to recognize that they may be better off without the leaders who often acted less than honorably with the hand dealt them.

Jonathan's Intervention (1 Sam 19:1-10)

"Where hate is gnawing and burrowing, communication becomes difficult . . . ." (Fokkelman 1986, 251)

The tensions raised by the ending of chapter 18 continue in the next section, with the change that King Saul now openly aims for David's death, where previously he plotted mostly in secret. The contrast between Saul and Jonathan could not be more starkly presented than in these opening lines:

> Saul spoke to Jonathan, his son,
> and to all his servants, to kill David.

And Jonathan, the son of Saul,
took great pleasure in David. (1 Sam 19:1)

Twice the text refers to Jonathan as Saul's son, emphasizing their relationship, which highlights the contrast between their different reactions to David. Saul intends to "kill," while Jonathan takes "great pleasure." Jonathan consistently appears in these verses in relationship to Saul, subsequently referred to as "his father/my father." His delight in David causes him to give his friend a warning and to try to persuade his father of the wrong he is contemplating. In speaking to the king, Jonathan reminds Saul of David's valiant deeds and three times uses the term "transgress": "Let not the king transgress/he did not transgress/why would you transgress?" (v. 4). When we first met Jonathan, he spoke as a person of faith, and he does so again, using words related to sin and ascribing the ultimate victory David achieved to the hand of God (v. 5). Jonathan persuades Saul to foreswear his desire to kill David, but we note that David returns to Saul's presence through Jonathan's agency rather than by direct invitation from Saul. The positive impression left by the line "he was in his presence as before" (v. 7) carries negative undertones, for we know what happened "before."

It takes only the fuse of another of David's victories to set Saul off, and he once again tries himself to kill David, as he had "before" (18:10; Fokkelman 1986, 59). Again, the two are together, one with the spear, the other with the lyre in "his hand." To make matters more precarious, the one with the spear is under the influence of an "evil spirit of God" (vv. 8-10). This time David not only eludes the spear but also flees the house, making his escape at night, a more ominous sequel to the attempt on his life. It must have become clear to David that no reconciliation would suffice and that being the king's son-in-law provided no protection. Jonathan's intervention only allowed for a short reprieve from the hostilities.

Michal's Intervention (1 Sam 19:11-18)

Getting away for the night is not sufficient for David, for Saul sends soldiers to guard his house with the intention of killing him in the morning, probably at the moment of his departure from his residence. It is time for Michal, the other of Saul's children who loved David, to intervene. By putting household gods in the bed, she helps him to make his escape through the window and fools the messengers, who have come to take her "sick" husband to Saul, bed and all. This ruse with the gods works only temporarily, but it gives David time to get out of the neighborhood. When her father reproaches her for her deception, she pretends David forced her with threats. Clever Michal lies on behalf of her husband, who three times is said to have "gotten away." She saved his life, but in so doing, she has ensured that he got away not only from Saul but also from her marriage bed. In addition, she will now be more dependent on her father than she was before.

Into this bed she puts the figures of the household gods, adorned with a braid to simulate a human being, ruse enough to mislead temporarily the ones who come looking for David. With this incident, the tale of Rachel and the stolen household gods comes to mind, another story of a daughter at odds with her father because of her husband. The household gods represented productivity and fertility. Putting these in the bed in David's place is both highly symbolic and ironic for a woman who was to remain childless.

The descending spiral resulting from her father's persecution of his rival will entangle Michal. Torn from her marriage to David by Saul, given to another man as wife, finally forcibly returned to David, all without her active participation, Michal will in the end resort to an anger reminiscent of her father's, her valor in defending the spouse she once loved turned to bitter condemnation. Unlike Hannah, she will die a childless woman. On the face of it, the offspring of King David and Michal could have brought about reconciliation between the two houses, but that is not the story. In Goldingay's words, it is not the hand that has been dealt.

> David fled and got away
> and came to Samuel in Ramah.
> And he told him all that Saul had done to him.
> So he and Samuel went
> and stayed at Nayot. (1 Sam 19:18)

From the arena of the two households at odds with one another, the story opens to Ramah, the place where David flees during his getaway and also Samuel's hometown. For the first time since his anointing, David puts himself in the presence of Samuel, who does not speak in the story but is clearly here in the role of protector. Together the two go to Nayot, perhaps the name of a prophetic center.

David and Saul among the Prophets (1 Sam 19:19-24)

"David's escapes from Saul are an escape from prophecy itself, from the evils that result from its illicit commingling with kingship." (Polzin 1989, 186)

David's hiding place is not so far away, nor is it difficult to find; indeed, Saul soon discovers where he has gone. Twice, Saul sends messengers with the intent, one assumes, not only of finding David but also of killing him.

Twice, the different groups of messengers fall into a prophetic trance. In the end Saul has to go himself, presumably resolved to execute the task of killing David. Instead, he too falls into a prophetic trance, removes his clothes, and lies naked, obviously in no state to kill anybody. No one speaks and no narrative comments lend clarity to the events, so we can only speculate about much of what happens. Three times the story of Saul refers to Saul's prophesying or "ranting like a prophet" (10:10; 18:10; 19:24). Both here and at the beginning of his career, events gave rise to the saying, "Is Saul also among the prophets?" In a way, the twice-mentioned saying brackets the rise and fall of Saul, who at this point lies helpless and humiliated before his former mentor. It is not easy to determine how to understand this question, since much depends on the tone in which it was asked. In the context of ancient Israel, prophets were considered to be endowed with special insight, with special powers lent them by the divine spirit; they could be leaders and interpreters of God's designs. In these stories, Saul has been open to God's spirit, for good or ill. His presence among those who represent God in a special way, joining them in extraordinary behavior, apparently caused enough astonishment that it gave rise to a question pointing to a certain incongruity. The storytellers saw fit to frame the beginning of Saul's rise and the beginning of his decline with the saying that calls into question the legitimacy of Saul's presence in this company. Perhaps, then, there is an implicit reference to the necessity of separating the office of prophet and king once the monarchy has been established.

Saul's current helpless state underscores his incapacity to do away with his rival, an inability he has displayed all along. In his own quarters and from close range, he managed, nonetheless, to miss David with his spear; he was too late in catching him exiting his house due to his daughter's deception; now, in his former mentor's presence, he has become incapable of lifting a hand against David, the shedding of his clothes symbolic of his lack of power to overcome his enemy. Both Jonathan and Saul disrobe, but they do so in contrasting ways. Jonathan delivers his authority and power to David willingly and out of love, and Saul takes off his clothes while not in charge of his faculties, a sign of his powerlessness.

David does not speak in this entire chapter. His presence is elusive, even as he eludes the threatening hand of Saul. Seemingly, he is the one acted upon by those around him, first Saul and his family, and then Samuel. His personality remains blurry, and his actions are not always logical. Surely, he must have been aware of Saul's intentions toward him, and yet one finds him returning repeatedly to a context fraught with deadly danger. He will only leave Saul's presence for good when there are no other options available. Was it his wish that Saul would finally recognize his worth, restore him to his good graces, and appoint him as successor to the throne? Was the prospect of living as an outlaw, with Saul constantly on his tail, too unappealing? We can only speculate, for at this stage the text does not mention his motivations, fears, or emotions, either directly by description or indirectly as revealed by his speech.

Open Season (1 Sam 20:1–23:29)

"The text invites us to reflect on the cost of loyalty and the terrible ambiguities within which loyalty must be practiced." (Brueggemann 1990, 153)

"Is Jonathan, knowingly or unintentionally, calling down divine wrath upon his own father?" (Exum 1992, 80)

As if to make up for the fact that he has not had voice in the preceding episodes, David speaks extensively in the following material. Three chapters initiate the story of David's flight and existence as a fugitive with King Saul in pursuit. The focus will shift back and forth between David and Saul, highlighting David's movements in greater detail. From now on David will be the protagonist, with Saul mostly reacting to David. David has become the number one enemy who needs to be eliminated at all costs. The story has already been moving toward this reality, but the decisive break does not happen until the events described in chapter 20. It is as though Saul faces a last chance here to make his peace with the fact that he will not found a dynasty. Once Saul has again declared his intentions to kill David, the split is final (20:30-31).

Jonathan's intervention comes to naught; it will be open season on David. Consequently, he leaves the court for good. From that time on, David must take refuge where he can find it, wherever someone is kindly disposed and courageous enough to take him in. The consequences of providing refuge to a man who is by royal decree fair game are many times disastrous, beginning with the priests of Nob who will perish at the command of Saul (22:18-19). It is therefore not surprising that people are not always inclined to protect David, and at times they even betray him to Saul (23:19-20). Only once in the next sequence does Saul break off his pursuit to turn to his task of warding off the Philistine threat, thereby saving David's life (23:27-28).

All these adventures bring to mind that the geographical scope of the country is limited with few places available for hiding, although the rugged terrain of the Judean wilderness may have offset this difficulty to a degree.

Yet David is never far away. Ironically, and as he is well aware, it will be among Israel's foremost enemies, the Philistines, that he will find the safest hiding place. In these episodes, he makes his first attempt to go underground with them (21:11-16). A successful effort on his part, however, must await another day. At the close of these chapters, David and his men are forced to remain constantly under cover. The last phrase of this part of the story emphasizes the breach: "Therefore they call this place 'the rock of separation'" (23:28).

David and Jonathan (1 Sam 20:1-23)

"Poor Jonathan . . . Poor Saul . . . Poor David . . . ." (Polzin 1986, 187)

The focus of chapter 20 is on the Jonathan-David relationship. Jonathan figures in each step of the unfolding events, first with David, then with Saul, then once again with David. The opening line, "David . . . came and said before Jonathan" (v. 1), does not make explicit where the exchange took place or the reason for David's return to court. It is perhaps natural to ascribe to different source material the presence of David once again at a place where his very life has proven to be in danger, and different traditions may underlie the stories of chapters 19 and 20. If we assume that the narrators intentionally placed the exchanges of chapter 20 in their current sequence, the narrators' purpose may have been twofold. On the one hand, it puts an end to the possibility of David's continued presence at court, with David shown as the victim of Saul's enmity, while nothing he has done can be construed as damaging to the king and his house. As he himself asks,

> What have I done?
> What is my guilt
> and what my trespass before your father
> that he seeks my life? (v. 1)

Second, the conversations reveal once and for all to Jonathan that reconciliation between his father and David is not possible. Jonathan has been a character of interest in the narratives. His presence with Saul always inserts a breath of fresh air, of goodness, into the dark space inhabited by his father. He is in some ways David's counterpart, a valiant warrior, a faithful companion who trusts in God. He is, on the other hand, more open than David; one learns of his motivations and affections. Moreover, he thinks he can bring about peace between his father and his covenanted friend. At times, he also sounds innocent and naïve, too innocent perhaps to serve David well. It could be that David's ruse and the way Jonathan interprets it in his father's presence also have the purpose of removing the scales from Jonathan's eyes. Consistent with this line of thinking, in the first exchange between David and Jonathan, David suggests that Saul wants to keep his intentions from Jonathan because he knows it will cause him pain (v. 3). Once Saul's intentions to kill David are clear also to Jonathan, it will be doubly important to know whom Jonathan supports.

The intense language of swearing and declaration in the opening lines underline the high stakes of the outcome. Fokkelman understands David's questions and statements to Jonathan, which consistently address Jonathan as his father's son, as subtle inquiries about his ultimate loyalty. Thus, in Fokkelman's view, David indirectly raises the question of Jonathan's willingness to side with such a father (Fokkelman 1986, 296–97). Once he has convinced Jonathan, David proposes a ruse to reveal what Saul really has in mind and whether there is still a possibility for his continuing in the good graces of the king. That there is little chance for the latter becomes clear from the fact that both friends lay elaborate plans for the event that Saul clearly intends evil, whereas the case for a positive outcome receives almost no attention (vv. 7-10).

To construct a plan, the friends go into an open space, the field, which creates the impression that until now they were inside, perhaps in Jonathan's quarters. There, a conversation might be overheard, so they go into the open. Before Jonathan proposes a plan to let David know of Saul's reaction, he makes a speech in which Jonathan is the supplicant and David the one who must grant a boon (vv. 12-14). Jonathan invokes God's name in almost every sentence, while on the one hand assuring David that he will indeed let him know the truth, and on the other imploring him to keep loyalty with Jonathan and with his house after him:

> Will you not, while I live,
> act with me according to the loyalty of God,
> so I will not die?
> And do not cut off your loyalty
> from my house for all time;
> not when the Holy One has cut off
> the enemies of David,
> each one from the face of the earth. (1 Sam 20:14-15)

In the long run, it is not David but Jonathan who must fear for his life and his house. It is worth noting that David does not reply to Jonathan's plea; in fact, David does not speak again in the entire episode, a feature of the narrative that directs all the attention to Jonathan.

The plan Jonathan devises is elaborate and in the end without a clear purpose. Few commentators make sense of it beyond declaring it irrelevant. This incident, in a narrative as intentional and focused as the one before us, deserves some attention. Arrows may indicate more than simply weapons; they may be used as a medium for an oracle or function in a symbolic act (cf. 2 Kgs 13:15-19; Ezek 21:26). Moreover, the words of both the formulation and the execution of the plan point to important truths about David. In the planning there is emphatic use of the root "send" attached to the shooting of the arrows, the boy who will go to retrieve them, and the departure of David (vv. 20, 21, and 22). This "sending" of arrows and a servant will issue in David's being "sent" away, a sending of which God is declared the author. The text executes wordplay on the notions "close" and "far," with proximity holding out the small possibility of David's survival at court, while distance points to the greater likelihood of flight from a place that no longer holds any guarantee for his well-being or, indeed, for his survival. The final episode will again employ words for distance and proximity, coming and going, to similar effect.

Saul and Jonathan (1 Sam 20:24-34)

"The rage is rage only a father can feel for a son." (Brueggemann 1990, 151)

As foreseen by both David and Jonathan, the next day is a day of ceremony and feasting, the first day of New Moon, and although Saul notes David's absence, he provides himself at the same time with a satisfactory explanation for it (v. 26). Nevertheless, temporary ritual impurity would not last beyond one day, so on the second day Saul asks his son why David is absent. Upon Jonathan's explanation, Saul's wrath explodes in a stream of invective against his son and an open declaration of his intent to kill David. David's earlier prediction that he was only a step away from death (v. 3) is borne out to be all too true. At Jonathan's protestations of David's innocence, it turns out that Jonathan also was only a step away from death.

Clearly, Jonathan's loyalty to David sends Saul into a tailspin of angry invective and action. That Saul is already inclined to think ill of David's absence appears from his asking the whereabouts of "the son of Jesse" (v. 27), a reference to David that distances his one-time protégé and current son-in-law. Jonathan, in pointed contrast, emphatically refers to David by name in his reply:

Jonathan answered Saul,
"David urgently requested me to go to Bethlehem.
He said, 'Let me go, please,
for we have a clan sacrifice in the city
and my brother ordered me;
and now, if I have found favor in your eyes,
let me get away, so I may see my brothers.'
Therefore he did not come to the king's table." (1 Sam 20:28-29)

The diction of v. 28 repeats the Hebrew root for asking three times in a row, beginning with Saul's name. A literal reading would render, "O Requested One, requested, yes requested David from me . . . ." The request concerned Bethlehem and specifically David's desire to be "let go" for a clan sacrifice on his brother's orders. In Jonathan's wording, David asked to be "let go," literally to be "sent," so he could "get away," a verb that was used three times in connection with David's "getting away" from Saul and his murderous intentions in the previous episode (19:10, 11, 18). Through his choice of words, Jonathan underlines the idea that David has gone to Bethlehem with his, Jonathan's, permission and on orders of David's brother; at no stage was King Saul involved in the matter. Jonathan's phrasing may hide a deliberate provocation, beginning with the utterance of the name of one to whom his father refers only by his patronymic. If this way of stating David's excuse will not provoke the old man into an angry outburst, then all must still be well!

Saul indeed lets go of all restraint. First, he calls Jonathan a son of a bitch, and then he chides him for foolishly siding with David, a man who will deprive the crown prince of his rightful succession. Finally, he declares the "son of Jesse" a "son of death" (v. 31). The only worthwhile "sending" in Saul's eyes will be that which fetches David to him. Jonathan, provoking his father even further, asks what David has done that he should die, implicitly refusing his father's order. This question results in a total loss of control for Saul, who throws his spear at his own son. Luckily for Jonathan, Saul is once again not effective at close range with his spear, and Jonathan escapes with his life. Grief at David's fate and anger at his father's treatment of him propel him away from Saul's presence.

While Saul's behavior can in no way be said to be admirable, it is also true that he is the one who sees the situation clearly and faces the fact that David's rise will mean the end not just of his kingship but of his house. To understand fully how devastating this insight would be, it is helpful to recall the significance of family in ancient Israel; ongoing life for the family and its individual members was guaranteed for the most part through offspring. The hope for survival centered on the family, and the end of the family line was equivalent to permanent death (Madigan-Levenson 2008, 115). This future devastation causes Saul to lash out at his son, who in his view refuses to face the danger to his family brought by "the son of Jesse." That Jonathan has at least similar concerns has not occurred to Saul.

Jonathan and David (1 Sam 20:35–21:1)

"Jonathan has proved his love for David. David bows and weeps." (Goldingay 2000, 145)

The plan with the arrows can only take place in daylight, so Jonathan waits until the morning before he goes out to the field where David is hidden. Then follows the act of shooting and calling out to the boy. His first word to the servant is "run" (v. 35). Then he shoots the arrow "past him" and calls out that the arrow is "farther," and for him to "hurry, be quick and not stand still." Fokkelman's interpretation of this section is that the words emphasizing haste and movement symbolize David's flight (Fokkelman 1986, 324). It is indeed difficult to see what other purpose the shooting of the arrow and Jonathan's instructions to the boy could have. On the surface, none of that was necessary, as in the end the two friends meet to say farewell, facing the fact that the door to David's presence at court has closed for good.

In this final section, which corresponds to the first, except that now Jonathan is fully cognizant of what lies ahead, Jonathan is clearly in charge of action and speech, while David relates to him as one who is stationed above him. The latter becomes clear from David's falling to the ground and his threefold bow, with his only sounds those of his weeping. "They wept together," the two friends, but David wept the more (v. 41). They kiss, the only time a kiss is exchanged in these stories besides Samuel's kiss for Saul as a seal of his anointing (10:1).

The question arises again as to the nature of Jonathan's love for David. After the events of chapter 19, one wonders why David sought refuge with Jonathan instead of with his wife, Michal. Michal also loved David and had shown herself loyal to him by helping him escape and lying to her father. In these episodes, there is no sign of Michal, but abundant presence of Jonathan. This chapter reinforces and extends the covenant bond between Jonathan and David into the future and in the life of Jonathan's descendants, reiterates the love between them, and depicts physical closeness at their parting. Jonathan plays the role here of covenant brother and loving spouse, provoking the anger of his father and risking his wrath as a spouse would, cognizant of the overriding loyalty of the marriage bond. Then they go their separate ways and will speak only once more in Jonathan's lifetime.

Sustenance in Nob (1 Sam 21:1-10)

"The source of Ahimelech's anxiety . . . is the shadow of Saul over the land, it is the terror side of the royal power." (Fokkelman 1986, 354)

The first of three episodes with David on the run depict him at a sanctuary in Nob, only a few miles from Gibeah, his point of departure. This first of three encounters in the sequel to David's flight from Saul's court consists almost entirely of dialogue and has a successful outcome for David. Initially, it does not look fortuitous, when the residing priest Ahimelek, a descendant of Eli's house, meets him in obvious fear and asks suspicious questions. What would David be doing all on his own without his usual retinue of soldiers? The rift with Saul can hardly have been a secret, and Ahimelek views the arrival of a weaponless David with trepidation, as well he might in view of the aftermath of the visit. It is David's task to convince the fearful priest, which he does effectively, declaring his mission from "the king" a secret one that even his soldiers do not know about, explaining his lack of armor, and immediately afterward demanding sustenance. When Ahimelek worries that holy bread should not be given to the men unless they have refrained from sexual intercourse, David assures him this is indeed so, and the priest hands over the consecrated bread. Once David acquires food, he addresses his second most urgent need, that of weaponry. It turns out that the only weapon available at the sanctuary, probably kept there as a trophy, is the sword of Goliath whom David himself defeated.

> The priest said,
> "The sword of Goliath, the Philistine,
> whom you struck down in the Oak Valley,
> see it is here, wrapped in a cloak,
> behind the Ephod.
> If you will take it, take it,
> for there is no other here except this one."
> David said, "Its like does not exist,
> give it to me." (1 Sam 21:10)

According to David, it does not matter that there is no other "here," for there is no other like it anywhere. An auspicious omen indeed! The need for explanation behind him, David's tone has become peremptory, where earlier it was far more circumspect. He has food; he has the sword; he is out of there!

The episode leaves some questions. Ahimelek may not have acted entirely according to the rules in the matter of the sacred bread. David lies to the priest and also shows no constraint when it comes to the matter of taking either the bread or the weapon, which was certainly kept in the sacred place next to a sacred object for a purpose. David's reference to the soldiers with him raises the issue of a possible retinue that fled with him. He probably had some loyal retainers, but one hears nothing about a following of any size until another day (22:2).

Striking is the introduction of a seemingly irrelevant character between David's two requests. There is an Edomite by the name of Doeg in the place, called "one of the servants of Saul" and "a chief herdsman of Saul" (v. 8). The narrator thus creates space in the story for a man with clear reasons to be loyal to Saul (note the double mention of Saul's name) as a witness to what has transpired at Nob. This proleptic reference portends Saul's eventual reaction when he finds out about the aid David has received. Doeg will yet have a devastating role to play.

A Madman in Gath (1 Sam 21:11-16)

"David is no fool." (Goldingay 2000, 154)

David's next stop is Gath, the Philistine city of the defeated champion Goliath, now ruled by king Achish. The text records that he "arose . . . fled . . . and came to Achish" (v. 10), implying that the king allowed him admittance. How long it was before the servants began to stir up trouble is not clear, but it may not have been long, for in the next breath they mention David's status. First they refer to him as "king of the land," a statement that, while not literally true, is intended to make their lord afraid of David's power among Israelites, Achish's enemies. They follow their observation with a quote, citing the fateful praise that came David's way from his own people that had caused Saul to first view him with jealous hatred (18:7-8), the one about Saul striking down his thousands and David his ten thousands! Then, for the first time, David is said to be very afraid. He has had reason to fear for his life before, but so far fear is not a word that occurred in relation to him. Fear overcomes him when it appears that with his move to Philistine territory he has taken his first wrong step. The decision to seek refuge with the Philistines was not as strange as it may seem. If he can fool the Philistine leader into believing that he has switched sides, as he will indeed do eventually (27:1-2), there may not be a safer place for him than with Saul's enemies. He does the first and only thing he can think of to get out of the trap he is in. He acts like a crazy man, scrabbling at the gate and drooling in his beard (v. 14). Achish is of the opinion that he already has crazy men enough in his entourage, and twice he asks his servants why they brought him another one. The implication, not clearly stated, is that he has David thrown out.

As Goldingay notes, David is no fool to act the fool. There may not have been much need for play-acting, and fear may indeed have driven him to play the part quite naturally. Although David's second attempt at securing aid meets with failure, he still escapes with his life, which at this point is all he may reasonably expect. For a while now, he will be an outlaw and will live life as a guerilla fighter, drawing to him those who are discontent with society or the government, and constantly chased by his sovereign who will never manage to face him and his men in open battle.

Between Adullam and Moab (1 Sam 22:1-5)

". . . the nadir of his existence as a refugee has already passed." (Fokkelman 1986, 372)

The next episode, recorded in a few words and of little interest to most interpreters, outlines the change in David from lone escapee to leader and protector, even if under constant threat of persecution and annihilation. While he hides in Adullam, border territory between Philistia and Judah in the west, David's family joins him and he manages to find protection for his family members in Moab. Although there is mention of only his parents in v. 3, we may assume that the entire "house of his father," as mentioned in v. 1, finds refuge in Moab, where David may have had relatives through his great-grandmother, Ruth. He certainly seems to be on friendly footing with the king, whom he addresses as an equal rather than a supplicant. His family, which once either ignored or upbraided him (16:11; 17:28), now runs to him for protection, aware no doubt that it has come to a final break between Saul and David.

The other group that attaches itself to David consists of men who lead lives on the margins of their communities, malcontents, so that at the end David manages to have a troop of 400 gathered to him. He is now the chieftain of a militia of poor men who have nothing to lose (Alter 1999, 135). Although this may not sound like an ideal situation, David is beginning to act as a leader in this short unit, and a change in his status is taking place. While he is still on the run, he now has some sort of militia surrounding him and is able to hide and to find refuge for his family elsewhere. For David himself, there is so far no safe resting place; most of the verbs connected with him relate to movement. While he hides in Adullam, he receives word from a prophet to go to Judah rather than stay in his hiding place. This means he goes to his own territory, but it puts him in greater danger. The prophet Gad, we may assume, speaks to David on behalf of God, so that in this seemingly irrelevant passage David not only grows into a leader and protector but also receives advice from the Deity (Fokkelman 1986, 376).

Saul and the Priests of Nob (1 Sam 22:6-19)

"Saul's story is one I keep coming back to, keep gnawing at, keep trying to understand the dynamics of." (Goldingay 2000, 169)

The focus of the scene changes from David to Saul, who appears seated in "Gibeah, under the tamarisk, with his spear in his hand" (v. 6). So far, a spear in Saul's hand has not been a good sign. Indeed, what follows constitutes one of the most ghastly episodes in the story of Saul, one we would as soon skip over, ending as it does in the massacre of a great number of innocents. While David gathers supporters and gets his family safely away to Moab, Saul engages in a bloodbath and wastes his time. This disastrous aftermath of David's visit to Nob also makes it clear that supporting David would incur the wrath of the king. In addition, the chapter discloses a good deal about Saul and other characters in his vicinity, especially as revealed through speech. Saul's opening words are mostly an accusation. First, he denounces his followers—his own clansmen!—as potentially benefiting unduly from the largesse of a Judean, referring to David as "the son of Jesse." Then he accuses them of conspiring against him by not telling him that Jonathan had not only made a covenant with "Jesse's son" but had actually incited David to rebellion against Saul. Such is the gist of vv. 7 and 8. Saul never mentions the names of either David or Jonathan, instead referring to them by their family ties, which, in Jonathan's case, means the ties that should bind him to allegiance. The phrase "all of you" recurs three times and contrasts with the repeated "against me" (also three times). In other words, this is a case of "all of you against me." Saul's paranoia may well be taking over, as he accuses all who surround him of being his enemy, even the ones who are obviously loyal to him. His words are not really a question, and yet they demand a response. As such, they may not be entirely pathological. It is possible that someone will respond with something useful regarding David's whereabouts. Additionally, his brute accusations may elicit protestations of innocence on the part of his followers, or they may flush out whether there are those among his retinue who have aided and abetted David in his flight.

What Saul may be hoping for indeed happens, and a reply comes forth that reveals information about David. While everyone is silent, perhaps baffled or embarrassed, one speaks up who has already surfaced in the story, while David was seeking help with Ahimelek (21:8; see "Sustenance in Nob"). Doeg, the Edomite, not a member of Saul's clan or indeed any Israelite tribe, is an outsider. He may be less affected by the accusations that Saul is making and may see a chance to better his position with the king. After all, he was there when David had his exchange with Ahimelek and saw the whole thing! Thus, he provides the facts, adding something not mentioned in the account of the episode between David and the priest at Nob, namely that Ahimelek had inquired of God on behalf of David. Whether or not Doeg the Edomite invented the provision of an oracle to David, he thinks it is important enough to mention it first, and Saul, on hearing it, may give it the greatest weight. Saul, after all, has not been able to receive an oracle from God. Why would one of his own priests perform this service for the rebel who is out to replace him on the throne if he was not in league with the traitor? Doeg's reply may have been deliberately aimed at provoking the king's anger further (Fokkelman 1986, 389).

Such is how it turns out, for immediately Saul summons Ahimelek to appear before him, not just by himself but together with all the priests. Consequently, "they all came before the king" (v. 11). First, there were "all of you, Benjaminites" (vv. 7 and 8), and now another group of "all" ominously appears before Saul, this time not clansmen but sanctuary personnel. Saul wastes no time and bluntly asks the priest, to whom he also refers by his patronymic ("Ahitub's son"), why he gave aid to David, "Jesse's son." As he had earlier with his followers, he uses the words "conspire against me." The party that is "against" him has now become less generalized and is focused on a specific person. Saul assumes that Doeg has spoken the truth, so he does not ask "whether," but rather wants to know "why." In his reply Ahimelek states the reason for his action, never denying that he had indeed helped David on his way.

> Ahimelek answered the king and said,
> "Who among all your servants is like David,
> trusted and son-in-law to the king,
> chief of your bodyguard,
> and honored in your house?
> Did I just now begin to inquire for him of God?
> Perish the thought!
> Let not the king impute anything
> to his servant, or all my father's house,
> for your servant knew nothing of all this,
> neither small nor great." (1 Sam 22:14-15)

His first words praise David, who is not only related to the king by family ties but who is also a trusted servant, military leader, and recipient of honor. Did Ahimelek not know that the last thing King Saul wanted to hear were words of praise for David? Either he is entirely naive, or he has decided to throw all caution to the wind and tell the king exactly what he thought when he encountered David in Nob. He helped David because he thought of him as one of the king's most trusted leaders and, moreover, as one of Saul's own family. On the manner of how he helped David, Ahimelek only mentions the possibility of David's request for an oracle. Wittingly, or unwittingly, he thus brings up the only thing that probably really irks Saul—that he consulted the Deity on David's behalf. His words do not make clear whether the encounter with David at Nob indeed involved such a consultation. Ahimelek says that it really does not matter, for he had often done so and would do so again if the occasion arose. Finally, he ends his defense by declaring his ignorance of what was actually going on. We have to infer that in the meantime Ahimelek has become aware of the true state of affairs between Saul and David. While some believe Ahimelek to be openly defiant, wanting to go down with all flags flying so to speak (so Fokkelman *passim*), and others attribute his behavior to naiveté, there is yet another possibility. Perhaps, desperately, somewhat like Jonathan, Ahimelek is trying to awaken Saul's better self, the self that loved David, the self that trusted him as his commander and loyal servant. It does not work; no matter the intentions of Ahimelek's reply, whether spoken bravely, naively, or in an attempt to assuage, his words seal his doom.

Saul's next words are an order: not only the culprit but all those with him must die. To highlight the gravity of the situation, his men refuse to execute the order. A second occasion has developed when Saul's orders for an execution are not immediately obeyed by his followers (cf. 1 Sam 14:45). Although this time there is no sound of protest, the narrator explains that they did not want to kill priests of the Holy One. It must fall to the hand of the outsider, Doeg, then, and Saul gives him the direct order. Doeg complies and, in so doing, extends the slaughter to the town, killing not only priests but also women, children, and cattle. Many commentators observe the irony of this execution of a total ban on an innocent crowd, while earlier Saul had been incapable of completing such an action on an enemy (1 Sam 15). Saul's rage against David has found its target; from now on he will have to hunt David across this sea of blood.

Aftermath (1 Sam 22:20-23)

"Saul eliminates the house of Eli, David rescues Abiathar and Solomon banishes Abiathar and establishes Zadok." (Brueggemann 1990, 161)

Thus the fate of Eli's house, foretold at an earlier stage in the text (1 Sam 2:27-36), is brought to semi-conclusion. Only one survivor remains—Eli's great-great-grandson, Abiathar, who flees to David and finds a welcome there. David blames himself indirectly for not taking care of Doeg while he had the chance and thereby causing the massacre (v. 22). At the same time, he extends protection to Abiathar (v. 23), guaranteeing himself the presence of a priest. In contrast to Saul, whose presence spells danger for just about everyone, David offers protection to the refugee. In contrast to Ahimelek, who knew nothing of what was really going on (v. 15), David confesses that he knew at the time (v. 22) that Doeg would bring trouble, and he did nothing about it.

In the next episode, it becomes clear that Abiathar has brought the oracular device called the *ephod* with him. This piece of news is withheld until David has cause to ask God's counsel twice (1 Sam 23:2, 4, 6). Unlike Saul, David will benefit from being able to ask counsel from the Deity. All in all, the balance is tipping at least slightly in David's favor. While Saul slaughtered his own people, including those who directly served the Holy One of Israel and thus legitimately provided access to God, David acts to protect the lone survivor of the massacre. This survivor, as it so happens, will be particularly helpful in divining the will of the Most High, a fact that will count heavily to David's advantage in what follows.

The Rescue of Ke'ilah (1 Sam 23:1-13)

"*One sends a town to its death, the other restores a town to life.*" *(Fokkelman 1986, 422)*

Chapter 23 records two episodes in David's life as a fugitive involving his relations with the local population (vv. 1-13 and vv. 19-28) and surrounding the last encounter of David and Jonathan (vv. 14-18). First, David, now with a growing band of followers (v. 16), rescues a town on the border of Philistine territory from marauding Philistines. His liberating act, however, does not bring the town's inhabitants firmly over to his side, as he may have hoped, but rather puts him in danger of being trapped in a city whose leaders will betray his location to Saul. That is how Saul sees it, anyway, concluding that God has "delivered" David into his "hand" (v. 7). The verb denoting God's deliverance of David to Saul literally means that God has "made a stranger of him." Whether wrongly perceived on Saul's part or not, the statement goes directly to the heart of the matter: at stake is the side God has taken. It now appears to Saul that David has lost God's support; alienated from God, Saul no longer is in God's confidence.

In direct contradiction to Saul's bravura statement stand the four consultations in which David engages to seek God's counsel, all successfully concluded. David and his men may appear to be close to disaster, both here and in the following episode. He is on the run, either trapped in a city behind closed gates or on the loose in the wilderness, with a relatively small band of followers and at constant risk of betrayal. Meanwhile Saul seems to have all the advantages, with his entire army at his disposal and the support of the local population with whom David sought to find refuge. Nevertheless, in the end, the deciding factor is the access to divine counsel provided to David, an avenue long since closed to Saul. To underscore the importance of divine support lent to David, the story presents the David-God communication in three ways. Previously, God's counsel came to David via a prophet (22:5). In this section, David seeks God's advice directly four times, twice without any intermediary and twice through using the ephod (23:1, 4, 10, 12). There appears to be a superabundance of methods for soliciting God's guidance available to David, all of them effective, while Saul is left without such help. The repeated consultation of vv. 1 and 4 is significant because it shows that David could successfully approach God without the ephod. The presence of the ephod, noted at the end of this episode, only strengthens his already strong hand (v. 13).

Fokkelman is most likely correct in concluding that while Saul was massacring servants of God among his own people, David was doing the work Saul was supposed to do, namely attacking the Philistine enemy and protecting a town from marauding invaders. It is thus Ke'ilah, where Abiathar has fled, bringing the ephod down with him. The concluding verses of chapter 22 anticipated the events taking place in the first section of chapter 23. The narrative wastes no time belaboring this detail but puts the two events side by side: one destructive and needlessly cruel toward the king's own people, the other liberating and protective, aggressive only toward Israel's enemy (Fokkelman 1986, 422).

A concluding note records that David continues the life of a wanted man on the run, while Saul no longer sees any reason to pursue him once he has eluded the Ke'ilah trap. It should be noted that a great deal of information flows between the two parties, often indicated by the phrase "they told" (vv. 1, 7). Both Saul and David have access to information from human beings, creating a background against which the importance of divine communication stands out all the more starkly (Polzin 1989, 203).

David and Jonathan in Zif (1 Sam 23:14-18)

"From now on we continually see that David wants to settle . . . he tries to take root, to establish a permanent power base in the region of his own tribe." (Fokkelman 1986, 438)

Jonathan seems to have no difficulty discovering David's hiding place, and the two friends meet for a last encounter. The story does not say whether David kept Jonathan informed of his location. Jonathan is not "told" anything, and he does not get to "know" anything. Yet this son, who attempts throughout to stay loyal to both his friend and his father, knows a great deal. In this short passage, only Jonathan speaks, but the names of all three characters concerned in the matter occur:

> And Jonathan, the son of Saul, arose,
> and went to David at Horesh
> and strengthened his hand in God.
> He said to him, "Do not fear
> for the hand of Saul, my father, shall not find you,
> it is you who shall be king over Israel,
> and I on my part will be your second;
> even Saul my father knows this."
> And the two of them cut a covenant before the Holy One;
> then David stayed in Horesh
> and Jonathan went to his house. (1 Sam 23:16-18)

Jonathan's movements envelop the unit, first with his coming toward David and at the end with his return home. Twice the text specifies David's location as Horesh (vv. 16, 18); Jonathan is called "the son of Saul," and he refers to Saul twice as "my father," underlining the relationship between the two. Jonathan has come for the purpose of reassuring David; his first words are "do not fear," the second time the narratives link fear with David (cf. 21:13). The expression "strengthened his hand in God" means to give encouragement. The word "hand" in its symbolic meaning of power, frequently repeated in the chapter, occurs also in reference to God and Saul. David's "hand" is strong because God supports him, while Saul's "hand" will remain empty.

The central lines of the unit refer to David's kingship as they establish the relationship to come between the two friends and set it on a new footing. The covenant that the two make before God is therefore not merely a reaffirmation of the bond they have already but also introduces more precisely what the content of the pact between them shall be: David as king, and Jonathan beside him as second-in-command. Jonathan speaks here in a predictive and prophetic voice, anticipating the speech of Abigail in a subsequent chapter. While Jonathan is generous to a fault and must have risked a great deal to seek David out, he is also prudent and wants to safeguard a role for himself, even if it is not that of first in the realm. He is in every way the good prince. Nor does he foreswear loyalty to his father. He does not say anything about Saul that is not to his credit, only allows that Saul knows what lies ahead, and then goes back home to put himself once more at his father's side. Jonathan may also have hoped for a change of heart on Saul's part, as Ahimelek may have done in the earlier episode. Since his father knows already what is going to happen, it is still possible that he will choose to ally himself with David as Jonathan has done. Covenants could be made also and especially between former enemies.

The Rock of Separation (1 Sam 23:19-28)

"All seems lost for David." (Brueggemann 1990, 165)

The sequel to his pact-making with David dashes whatever hopes of reconciliation Jonathan may have cherished. The Zifites, among whom David has been hiding, come to Saul and betray his hiding place with great precision. Saul only has to come to the region, and they will hand David over. Saul, in profound gratitude, blesses them and sends them off with a request for more information that will lead him to David:

> Saul said, "Blessed are you by the Holy One,
> because you took pity on me.
> Go now, and make very sure;
> get to know and see the place where he sets his foot and who saw him there,
> for they tell me that he is exceedingly crafty.
> See and get to know all the hiding places where he may hide;
> then return to me with certainty,
> and I will go with you and if he is in the land
> I will search for him among all the thousands of Judah!" (1 Sam 24:21-23)

This is a somewhat peculiar reply. Saul thanks the Zifites for "having pity" on him, as if he were a poor victim suffering persecution instead of being the pursuer. The verb "take pity/spare" appeared earlier in reference to Saul's "sparing" the Amalekite king from death (1 Sam 15:3, 9) and will later point to the evil of David's actions after the Bathsheba/Uriah affair (2 Sam 12:4, 6). It occurs in those narratives in a negative context. Here, its reference is both backward and forward. In the past, the act of sparing has brought negative consequences for Saul, while in the future for David the act of *not* sparing will be the problem. Furthermore, it is not clear why Saul would tell the Zifites to go back and make doubly certain of David's whereabouts. Surely, this going back and forth would cause a delay and risk the chance of David finding out that the king had discovered his hiding place!

Whether the Zifites were interested in "sparing" Saul or were simply acknowledging that Saul still had the power and that disastrous consequences could follow charges of harboring David does not become clear. They turn back home, presumably to act on Saul's request for information, but before they can do so the king himself has set out to catch his prey, perhaps aware that his instructions may cause unnecessary delays, or in mistrust that he can count on anyone to provide him with more accurate information than he possesses already.

Verses 26-27 provide a snapshot of both parties in movement on opposite sides of the mountain, but with David clearly within range of Saul's army. Then a miracle occurs to save David, who will never again come so close to capture. The king receives a message that the Philistines are on the rampage, so it is time that Saul turned his attention away from David to the enemy of Israel. An unnamed "messenger" brings the news (v. 26). The word can also indicate a divine messenger or angel; the ambiguity here may be deliberate, indicating that interference on behalf of David came from God. Saul's purpose is successfully thwarted, and the place name "the rock of separation" underscores the difference between the two protagonists. The Philistines unwittingly play the role of David's savior here. Later, they will offer David an unassailable hiding place where Saul's long arm cannot reach him. Therefore, Saul's pursuit of David has once again come to naught; the betrayals and machinations end with Saul retreating to engage the Philistines. As earlier his spear constantly missed its intended victim, now his sword turns away from David and instead turns against the true enemy of Israel.

The chapter exhibits a great deal of movement, putting different sets of characters on the stage as they relate to the protagonists. The Ke'ilites, whom David delivered from the marauding Philistines, would seem to belong on David's side, but divine counsel reveals that they are potentially traitors. The Zifites turn traitor on David and move over to Saul's side. The priest Abiathar, on David's side, represents God in the story. Each party, Saul and David, has his army, his "men." Jonathan is the only one who straddles the divide between David and Saul, making a pact for the future with David while staying loyal to his father. The Philistines, of course, are opponents of both Saul and David, but in this story they become unwitting assistants of David.

Viewed superficially, Saul has all the advantages. Even those who could be expected to be grateful to David, the Ke'ilites, are willing to betray him. Saul has his army, the Ke'ilites and the Zifites on his side, while David has only 600 men. Yet the crucial difference is the support God gives to David, with or without the priest and his ephod. It is an unfair contest, and Saul might have done better to reconcile himself to the truth and make a pact with his enemy as his son Jonathan has done.

Risky Encounters (1 Sam 24:1–26:25)

". . . the two figures recover their human, realistic dimensions. One is not a complete villain knowing nothing of humanity or contrition, and the other is not an angel of light . . . ." (Garsiel 1990, 124)

". . . a series of parallel episodes strung out along the storyline like a string of pearls." (Polzin 1989, 205)

The three chapters that follow concern themselves with episodes during the time that David, pursued by Saul, lives the life of an outlaw in the Judean wilderness. Two of them focus on encounters between Saul and David (chs. 24 and 26), both initiated by Saul with hostile purpose, while the middle chapter (25) recounts the narrow escape through a woman's agency from a potentially hostile encounter initiated by David. While the two surrounding chapters have familiar personages as the main actors, the middle chapter introduces new characters and stands out because it posits a female character as a main protagonist, a feature that is rare enough in 1 Samuel.

In the first episode, Saul, acting on information about David's whereabouts, is close on his heels in the rocky region near the Dead Sea. Yet, rather than hunter, Saul becomes the hunted when he is inadvertently at David's mercy while relieving himself in the same cave where David and his men are hiding. David refuses to kill Saul, in spite of his men pointing out that Saul is at his mercy through God's doing, and he later confronts Saul with the cut-off edge of his cloak. The two have a conversation during which Saul appears to be remorseful about his ill treatment of David, but the men go their separate ways at the end of the episode. In chapter 26, the third of the encounters, Saul again pursues David and again is the one found rather than the finder. David once more refuses to kill his enemy against the advice of one of his men, and another conversation ensues with Saul expressing regret over the wrong he has done David. In the middle chapter, David has to regret a decision made in anger and haste to destroy a man and his household. The speech and actions of a woman bring him to this point.

At the heart of the three stories is the subject of what it means to be God's anointed. In the first and last encounters David vigorously proclaims that it is not permitted to "stretch out one's hand" against God's anointed. He states this conviction a number of times both to his own men and to Saul himself. The middle episode deals with the action of unlawful shedding of blood, not the blood *of* the anointed but *by* God's anointed, in this case David. David's future kingship is of concern for those who meet him in these chapters. Saul acknowledges for the first time his awareness of David's future kingship, overtly in chapter 24 (v. 21) and more obliquely in chapter 26 (v. 25). Abigail's words in the middle episode testify strongly to the conviction that David will one day be king (25:30) and that such a man should not be involved in shedding innocent blood (25:30).

These are vividly told stories to deepen our insight into the main characters in all their humanity. As Garsiel points out, the portraits of David and Saul are not simply that of positive and negative. Certainly, the middle episode depicts a hotheaded David willing to murder an entire household because of one man's insolence, while Saul in both encounters appears as a human being with the insight to rue the way he has acted toward his former protégé. Even though the king's remorse is not enough to bring about a true reconciliation, a more sympathetic Saul, and a less enigmatic David come to the fore in these chapters. Ironically, just at this point, the parting of ways at the end is final. They will not see one another again.

The Cave at Goat's Rocks (1 Sam 24:1-8)

"Anyone who has observed the extraordinary surefootedness of the mountain goats climbing the steep rock masses near En-gedi wonders whether Saul will be able to catch his prey . . . ." (Fokkelman 1986, 452)

David is hiding out in the area near the Dead Sea where there are plenty of caves for hiding, and Saul is hot on his tracks. As has happened before, it is easy enough for Saul to locate David but difficult to find him. He must have had spies on the lookout; there were always people willing to betray David, and the country is not large. Yet, so far, he has not managed to capture the fugitive. Once again, he comes close. The part of the tale in which the action takes place is brief. David and his men are hiding in a cave entered by Saul to answer a human need. This occurrence seems to provide an opportunity for David, as his men are all too eager to point out to him. Could there be a better occasion at which a man is so unwary? Surely this is a sign that God has put Saul in David's power. What could be clearer? David indeed approaches the defenseless king with his knife, but he cuts off an edge of his cloak instead of cutting down the man. The knife in David's hand may have misled his companions into thinking that he was indeed about to follow their advice, for he gives them no reply. Only afterward do they realize that he does not carry Saul's head but a piece of his cloak; only then does he make his pronouncement that an attack on God's anointed is out of the question.

> He said to his men, "The Holy One forbid
> that I did this to my lord,
> the anointed of the Holy One,
> to stretch out my hand against him,
> for he is the anointed of the Holy One." (1 Sam 24:7)

Even so, he has to restrain his men from going after Saul themselves. The very cutting away of a piece of Saul's cloak, the garment that in these texts symbolizes authority, is enough to give David heart palpitations (v. 6).

"I Know You Will Be King" (1 Sam 24:9-23)

". . . David's previous mock trial has made Saul publicly concede his knowledge of David's status as king-elect." (Edelman 1991, 200)

David is not content merely to retain the piece of Saul's cloak but follows the king and hails him. David's speech, the longest of the exchange, be (vv. 10-12), a declaration he follows with the request for God to judge between them (vv. 13-16). In the first half, David plaintively protests that Saul was in his power, and yet he refused to lay a hand on Saul's sacred person. He offers three negative phrases—"I will not stretch out my hand," "I did not kill you," "I did not sin against you" (vv. 11-12)—as his response to his men urging him to kill Saul. David appeals emphatically to the evidence that the king can see with his own eyes: "your eyes have seen," "see now, see," "know and see." Throughout this part of his speech, the word "hand" plays a central role. The piece of cloth is in David's hand, of course, and it is not something "bad or offensive." That is to say, it is not something with which to threaten an enemy; yet the cloak is all the same a powerful symbol of authority; cutting off the strip had caused David to be deeply disturbed. During the encounter with Saul, he wants it to be only the sign of his refusal to kill God's anointed. The same hand that holds the piece of cloth could have been the means to bring about Saul's death after God delivered Saul into David's hand, that is to say into his power. Even so, David would not engage in such an action against the anointed of the Holy God. It is an eloquent and intricate speech that begins by questioning the reliability of reports that malign David and his intentions and ends by pointing out the incongruity of Saul's pursuit of this obviously innocent and faithful servant of the king.

David addresses Saul twice in this opening salvo. First he calls out to him as "my lord, king" (v. 9), and he subsequently appeals to him as "my father" (v. 12). The first address puts him in the position of a loyal servant of the king, especially since he follows it with a prostration once the king has looked behind him. The second address, "my father," appeals to the personal relation that the two men have, in spite of all the hostility between them, and to the intimacy that once existed between them. This more personal and emotional appellation precedes exhibiting the piece of cloth as evidence of David's refusal to kill Saul, and so may have the intention of drawing attention away from the fact that David came too close to Saul's person and is now in possession of a powerful symbol of royal authority. The line of his argument then runs as follows: Why do you listen to bad reports about me? Here you were in my power just a moment ago and my men wanted me to kill you, but I refused and here is the evidence of that refusal. I could have killed you but instead "only" took a piece of your cloak. In addition, in the face of all that, you are the one who is hunting me down to kill me!

David is not done. In the second part of his speech, a mixture of appeal and reprimand, he allows that God may be the one to take vengeance on Saul, but if Saul has to be killed it will not be by David. Twice he asserts "my hand will not be against you," saying in so many words that not only has he refused to kill Saul in the recent past but he will continue to do so in the future (vv. 13-14). Two appeals to God as judge frame this part of David's address to the king (vv. 13 and 16). The repetition makes clear the emphasis on justice that David seeks (Fokkelman 1986, 465). It is after all to God, the highest judge, that David may safely commend his cause. Between these appeals and assurances, he cites half of a proverb and reminds the king of the extraordinary measures he is taking to do away with a single insignificant individual, comparing himself to a flea on a dog's carcass. The half of the proverb in v. 14 cites the part that evil people produce evil deeds and leaves unsaid the obvious counterpart, that good people produce good actions. Although David's speech is fairly long, he wastes not a word. Why belabor the self-evident truth that he, David, is one of the good ones? He is waving a part of the king's cloak in his face as proof, after all!

Now it is Saul's turn to speak (vv. 17-22). At first, he can only choke out a few words: "Is this your voice, my son David?" Clearly, this phrase, only four words in Hebrew, does not intend to elicit information but rather amounts to his saying, "Is it really you?" Saul was the pursuer with hostile intent, and now he finds himself pursued for a peaceful purpose by the one he sought. This is the same David he once loved, who brought him solace and healing in the midst of despair. To emphasize the fraught nature of Saul's state of mind, the narrator notes his weeping, an action that marks significant moments in the text of 1 Samuel. Hannah, the people of Jabesh, David, and Jonathan have all wept. Saul, who perhaps had more cause to weep than most, is said to weep only on this occasion. It marks the depth of the emotions that David has aroused. By calling on the bond between them through the address "my father," David has called forth Saul's humanity, a humanity out of which he now speaks.

Saul's subsequent words reveal how much he has taken David's speech to heart. First, he who once had declared open season on David, who has hunted him relentlessly, now allows that he was wrong. The phrase "you are more righteous than I" recalls the pronouncement of Judah on his daughter-in-law Tamar, whom he had condemned to death (Gen 38:26). To underscore the point, Saul compares their treatment of one another to his own disadvantage. He speaks his conviction that God indeed had delivered him into David's "hand," and that David's extraordinary act of grace compares to someone finding an enemy and sending him "nicely on his way" instead of killing him (vv. 18-20). Such an action deserves God's reward.

The king's final words give voice to both a certainty and a plea:

> "And now, look, I know
> that you will surely be king
> and the kingship of Israel will stand by your hand.
> And now swear to me by the Holy One,
> that you will not cut off my seed after me,
> nor destroy my name from my father's house."
> So David swore to Saul
> and Saul went to his house
> while David and his men went up to the stronghold. (1 Sam 24:21-23)

David asked Saul to "see" and "know." David has convinced Saul by what Saul "saw." Saul now moves to what he "knows" and lets his plea flow from his knowledge. "And now" precedes both phrases, lending urgency to his statements. First, like his son before him (cf. 20:15, 41; 23:17), Saul acknowledges that David will be king and that his kingship will be a lasting one (v. 21); then, again like Jonathan, he asks David not to exterminate his entire house. The acknowledgment of David's future kingship is enormously significant, for it means that for all practical purposes Saul admits that his own kingship is over. From now on, he will be a lame duck. If his descendants cannot be kings, then at least let them not die out altogether!

A heart-warming reconciliation! Yet, unlike the exchange between Jonathan and David, no covenant is made, and there are no embraces (cf. 20:41 and 23:17) to affirm the renewed bond. One gets the impression that each man keeps a safe distance from the other and only a fragile trust is established. Saul has had changes of heart before, and there is always a question as to whether his current state of mind will endure. At the end, each is back in the place whence he came.

A Death in Ramah and a Rich Man in Maon (1 Sam 25:1-13)

". . . moral stature is not a fixed 'given' but is something that a person must fight for repeatedly, struggling against his emotions and passions." (Garsiel 1985, 123)

The death notice of Samuel precedes the account of the events of chapter 25. One reason for this placement may be that the writers want to make clear that Samuel, the erstwhile leader, prophet, and kingmaker, no longer has a role to play. David must now go it alone, and Saul must find his inevitable end. The episode that follows introduces two new characters—Nabal, a rich man in Maon, and his wife, Abigail. The name of the man literally means "fool," probably a mocking referent rather than his real name. His wife will expound on it as the story unfolds (v. 25). In addition to their names, husband and wife are described in a contrasting way, Abigail as "sensible and beautiful" and Nabal as "a boor and ill-behaved." Finally, Nabal also gets his clan identification of "Calebite," a word that sounds uncommonly like the Hebrew word for dog.

The man, dog-like Nabal, is rich; the text literally identifies him as "very great," a man of substance with many possessions and status in the community. This type of man has become one on whose goodwill David depends, so David sends a request via a delegation of his lads for provisions out of the surplus Nabal must surely have. The words with which David instructs the delegates to approach Nabal are overtly peaceful; in fact, they repeat the word *shalom* three times (v. 6). Then the delegation points out that David and his men have not only never taken anything from Nabal's flocks but have also protected the shepherds and the flocks from harm while they were in the field. They voice their request only after the long introduction: "Give, please, what you have at hand . . ." (v. 9). David refers to Nabal in familial terms, calling him "my brother" and referring to himself as "his son." In spite of all the politeness, there is an implied threat here. The emphasis on David and his men not stealing but protecting highlights the possibility that things could have gone otherwise. This band is armed and can be dangerous!

Perhaps Nabal heard the threat all too clearly, for the appeals to his generosity send him into a rage. He not only refuses but does so rudely, calling David a "runaway slave" and casting doubt on his standing by referring to him as "the son of Jesse," an identification of David that is almost always negative in these texts. Since David is a nobody, why should he, Nabal, take anything from his possessions to give to one with no standing, a man from "I know not where" (v. 11)? Do they hold him for a fool? Four times he adds the word "my" to the goods he refuses to share, "my bread," "my water," "my meat," and "my shearers." It is all his, and were he inclined to share he would not do so with the likes of David! On receiving this reply, David in turn flies into a temper and orders his men to put on their armor, clearly intending a violent confrontation. Later we will hear more about his exact words at the time.

Abigail in Action (1 Sam 25:14-22)

"Power has less opportunity to turn a woman into a fool." (Goldingay 2000, 162)

Nabal's wife may not have known about the incident with David's men as she later will claim to David (v. 25), but one of the household servants informs her about the request and Nabal's refusal. The servant's report is elaborate and of some interest because of the frank tone with which he dismisses his master to the master's wife. The low esteem in which Abigail held her husband must have been well known in the household. The servant ends his report with a warning:

> And now, carefully consider what you should do,
> for it will go ill with our master and his whole house.
> And he is such a good-for-nothing,
> there is no reasoning with him. (1 Sam 25:17)

The fallout from Nabal's rude refusal will not just affect him but "his whole house," by the young man's reckoning. Then he adds a new epithet to the negative terms associated with his master; he calls him a *ben beliya'al*, a designation that we heard first from Hannah's mouth when she denied being a "worthless" woman (1 Sam 1:16), and for the second time in the description of Eli's sons as "worthless men"(1 Sam 2:12). Abigail herself will repeat this serious indictment in her address to David (v. 25).

Quickly, Abigail organizes a food column to send to David, while she will follow at her own pace. The provisions will be the first thing David will see, and she intends that this sight will stop him in his tracks. A mistress in charge of her household takes her servant's words seriously, and in agreement with his assessment of Nabal, she does not tell her husband about her errand. The text does not report any reflection on Abigail's part; nor does she reply to the servant with a verbal response. Rather, she goes into immediate action, packing up supplies in what would at least appear to be large quantities, even if not sufficient for 600 men, and rides off on her donkey.

Then, as the two, Abigail and David, ride toward each other, the narrator interrupts the story (v. 20) to reveal what David had said earlier when he gave the order for his men to gird on their swords. He voiced his anger at having guarded "this fellow's" possessions for nothing and swore he would not leave a single man alive in Nabal's household (vv. 21-22). The rough term he used for the word "male," literally calling them "wall-pissers," is no doubt an indication of the depth of his anger. The reference also calls to mind the implied comparison of Nabal to a dog (cf. Lozovyy 2009, 60)! The effect of the interruption, right when Abigail meets David, is to highlight the danger she is in by seeking out this enraged warlord. Surely, she too had heard the saying that "David had killed his tens of thousands." What would the life of one woman mean to such a man, especially the life of a woman belonging to a household such as Nabal's?

Abigail's Intercession (1 Sam 25:23-35)

"Abigail's discourse is a rhetorical tour de force *indeed." (Van Wolde 2002, 365)*

"A word fitly spoken is like apples of gold in a setting of silver." (Prov 25:11, NRSV)

Before Abigail says a word, she puts herself in the position of humble servitude, falling down before David and prostrating herself. (Note the similarity of her behavior to that of David vis-à-vis Saul in the previous chapter.) First, David must have already seen the provisions that had gone ahead of her, and now a reportedly beautiful woman faces him in a posture of entreaty. Then she opens her mouth and with her first words takes on all the blame: "On me, me alone, my lord, be the responsibility" (v. 24). This remarkable statement is clearly untrue, but it does what she intends, stopping David long enough to listen to the rest of her speech. Abigail has made a phenomenal diplomatic move, shouldering the blame for what was not at all her doing, disarming her opponent who must already have been mollified by the present she sent ahead. Next she asks for David's attention, identifying herself in an inferior position as an *amah,* a maidservant, and counsels him to pay no attention to "this good-for-nothing, this Nabal" (v. 25), for he is just like his name says, "a fool" who has "folly" as a companion. The words "fool" and "folly," particularly coupled with the designation *ben beliya'al,* which she, like the servant earlier, also uses, connote wickedness rather than simplicity or naivety (Lozovyy 2002, 52). She thus erases her husband as a subject worthy of consideration. She herself, as she now reveals, had been unaware of the visit by David's delegation—probably a true statement because she learned about it through one of her staff. Then she wishes on David's enemies the same fate that awaits Nabal/fool, anticipating Nabal's impending demise, and points to the gifts she has brought almost as an afterthought:

> And now, here is a blessing
> that your servant brought to my lord.
> Let it be given to the boys
> who follow the footsteps of my lord. (1 Sam 25:27)

The word "blessing" can also be translated "gift," but a literal translation may more readily bring to mind the story of Jacob and Esau in Genesis 33. There also two parties meet who were in a potentially hostile relationship; there also Jacob sends gifts ahead, bows to the ground before his brother, and calls his present a "blessing" (Gen 33:11).

In her opening words Abigail has referred to God, who has kept David from "committing a crime" by taking vengeance. This idea she now elaborates in the second half of her speech. She begins again by assuming culpability and makes an initial pronouncement about David's future that points to his impending kingship (v. 28), elucidating this idea further as she continues (v. 30). Both times, she adds to this forecast the reason David should stay his hand. Once in the position of ruler, he should not have to reproach himself for having taken the law into his own hands (Fokkelman 1986, 505). As she says,

> This will not be for you a stumbling block
> and a heartache for my lord:
> to have shed blood without cause
> to gain victory for himself.
> And when the Lord has done good to my lord,
> then remember your maid. (1 Sam 25:31)

Abigail provides a lesson in what makes a good ruler: one who is not out for personal vengeance, for that issue is up to the Holy God as David himself pointed out to Saul (24:13). Twice, she puts both David's and Saul's fates in God's hands. God will make a "lasting house" for David; God will protect him and set him up as a "prince over Israel"; God will deal with Saul (vv. 28-30). In everything she says, she emphasizes only David's interests with the exception of her last words, probably a discreet hint at her wish to become his wife. Thus she manages in one stroke to serve not only David's future well-being but also her own.

David needs no other persuasion. Perhaps her last words, showing her interest in his person as a potential husband, even tipped the scales. His first word to her is "Blessed" (v. 32). In fact, he uses the term three times, first blessing God, then Abigail's discretion, and finally Abigail herself. He sees clearly that she has saved him from incurring bloodguilt and sends her "in peace" to her house, this time indeed meaning peace toward Nabal's household. He cannot quite keep himself from revealing the destruction he had in mind, voicing the same threat he had uttered earlier, that all the wall-pissers in Nabal's household would have died—so help him God!—if she had not come to meet him. He speaks this time less in anger than in a show of muscle flexing before beautiful and well-spoken Abigail.

All's Well that Ends Well (1 Sam 25:36-44)

"Indeed, if she had been able to guess where all this would lead, she might have used her wiles to find some other destiny." (Goldingay 2000, 164)

On her homecoming, Abigail finds her husband drunk and so she waits to tell him her story until he has slept it off. This turns out to be unfortunate or an opportune moment, all according to one's perspective, for Nabal has what sounds like a stroke ("he became like a stone," v. 37) and dies after ten days, by the hand of God according to the narrative. Rather than waiting for Abigail until he has indeed become king, David, on hearing the news of Nabal's death, sends for her and she becomes his wife. The story ends with a note on David's other wives, Ahinoam, who became the mother of Amnon, and Michal. Here, the narrator also reveals that Saul had given Michal to another man, one Palti of Gallim. That is not the last we will hear of Palti or Michal, but it shows the lengths to which Saul was willing to go to sever the links between himself and David.

A remarkable encounter between two beautiful people, one that began fraught with liability and danger, has resulted in a positive outcome, a happy ending. Like Michal on an earlier occasion, Abigail is out to save David, this time not from the wrath of his enemy but from himself; unlike Michal, Abigail, with more independence and power, is also able to look out for her own interests. The story introduces her as sensible and beautiful, and she proves her sensibility by what she does and how she speaks. She saves David, she saves her household, and she saves herself. Only Nabal she does not save, but it is hard to feel sorry for him. In the end, God, who holds after all the "bundle of the living" (v. 29), takes care of Nabal. Yet one may wonder whether marriage to David turned out to be such a blissful event for Abigail. For what exactly had she exchanged the power and independence she once had as mistress of a large household? Once her usefulness is over, her importance in the story diminishes immediately through the mention of other wives of David (vv. 43-44), and for all practical purposes, she disappears from the narrative. She will appear only once more as the mother of David's son. "But then," as John Goldingay remarks, "the fact that she could not escape marrying first a fool and then a bandit perhaps itself reflects a woman's narrow range of options in this kind of society" (2000, 164). We may add that it reflects also the narrow range of options for the storyteller. For these are above all stories about men, their relationships, their exploits, and their road to glory.

For many interpreters, the parallels between Nabal and Saul are obvious, so that Abigail addresses not only the situation between Nabal and David but also between Saul and David (Van Wolde 2002, 355–75). In this reading, Abigail fulfills the role of prophet for David in Samuel's stead. For some scholars, the story has no historical merit but is purely a literary device, stuck between the parallel narratives of David sparing Saul's life, to highlight David's shortcomings and depict a complex hero (Biddle 2002, 617–38). Others see in it the foundation for David's eventual legitimization as king through a series of prudent marriages, including that to Abigail, who was a member of the Caleb clan. The capital for the Calebite patrimony was Hebron, where David will first rise to kingship (2 Sam 2:1-4; see Levenson 1978, 11–28). The truth may lie in a combination of perspectives. A historical incident of the sort described here, at the time that David spent his days as an outlaw in the Judean wilderness, is not impossible, and Abigail as David's wife is elsewhere referred to as the wife of "Nabal the Carmelite" (1 Sam 27:3, 2 Sam 2:2). All that remained for the creative narrator was to provide the story with detail that fit the context of risky encounters for David.

All three episodes in chapters 24–26 describe in some way the aversion of a violent conflict. Only the middle chapter features a woman as mediator. Abigail is not part of the male warrior culture and is unique in speaking out against the unnecessary shedding of blood. Such voices are rare in these narratives. She accomplishes her diplomatic mission first by soothing the agitated feelings of her opponent and thus mitigating the potential threat to her entire household. Furthermore, her initial words are of great importance because her assumption of responsibility for what happened, even if manifestly untrue, deprives David of the weapon of his righteous anger. Two forces are about to enter into a violent confrontation, and instead of more threats, muscle flexing, and weapon buildup, this woman falls from her donkey at her opponent's feet and states that it is all her fault. A formidable diplomatic model of peacemaking takes place, a model with no emulation in the context of her world and not one considered valuable in today's politics of negotiation between hostile parties. It is at least possible that the narrator breathed easier for a moment in the rarified air of Abigail's peacemaking efforts. The old world of military engagement and the clash of weapons, where a man's worth is proven not by his avoidance of violence but by his skill with spear and sword, is still present; it waits just around the corner.

A Secret Visit (1 Sam 26:1-12)

"The question at hand is how *this monarch will terminate." (Green 2003, 3)*

The next episode corresponds closely to the account of Saul and David at the cave in Engedi (ch. 24), a similarity that may suggest different versions of stories about such an encounter circulating at one time. While there are resemblances, there are also striking differences. Here, as in chapter 24, those out to betray David's whereabouts tell Saul where he is hiding (cf. 23:19 and 24:2), and Saul sets out with an overwhelming force to catch his enemy. As before, he puts himself in a somewhat defenseless state, this time sleep. On the other hand, in this account the role reversal between the hunter and the hunted is clearer. Where verbs with David as subject connote activity—he "sent," he arose," and "he went"—the one verb with Saul as subject is the repeated root *shakav*, "he lay down" (v. 12). In case one wonders why Saul or his soldiers feel relaxed enough to go to sleep during this expedition, the narrator offers the explanation that "a deep sleep of the Holy One had fallen upon them" (v. 12). Not only is Saul passive but his passivity is ascribed to God! In contrast to Saul, on this occasion, David takes on a far more active role than at Engedi, spying out the place where Saul lies encamped and acting more deliberately and with greater circumspection.

He also takes someone with him on his expedition, whether for protection or from the need for a witness is not clear. At his side goes Abishai, David's nephew, brother to Joab, both men eventually leaders in his army and sons of David's sister Zeruyah. They set out and come upon Saul's army with Saul and his general Abner fast asleep, sprawled on the ground, Saul's spear stuck in the ground beside him. Abishai offers to dispense with Saul once and for all:

> Abishai said to David, "God has delivered
> today your enemy into your hand.
> Now let me pin him with the spear to the ground
> with one stroke, no need to do it twice." (1 Sam 26:8)

As Saul had once tried to pin David to the wall with his spear, so now he is in danger of being pinned to the ground by David's commander. Abishai leaves nothing to the imagination with his offer, unlike the men at Engedi who had counseled David to do with Saul as was "good in his eyes" (1 Sam 24:5). David replies with words similar to the ones he used on that earlier occasion, twice referring to the taboo against killing "God's anointed," but this time he adds the phrase that the matter of Saul's death must be left up to God. Saul will either die a natural death or be killed in battle, a far more likely outcome of course. His death is, in any case, not in David's hands. He then asks Abishai to take the spear as well as the water bottle that is nearby, an action that takes from the king the symbols of both death and life. At the last moment, David apparently changes his mind and takes the spear and water container himself, perhaps not quite trusting that Abishai will be able to control himself and suspecting he might kill Saul after all (Alter 1999, 162).

A Wake-up Call (1 Sam 26:13-25)

"The alpha and omega of David's relationship to Saul is thus distancing from and undermining the ideology of weapons: you are not involved in my work, it is God's help I need." (Fokkelman 1986, 551)

Water bottle and spear in his possession, David removes himself to a safe distance and calls out, first to Abner whom he berates for not taking better care of his lord (vv. 13-16). Three times David repeats the phrase "Your lord," the third time adding that this lord is the anointed of God (v. 15). Unlike David—Saul's enemy, after all—Saul's own army and its commander have shown themselves careless in regard to the life of the king. Abner is not given a chance to reply before Saul also awakens. Unlike Abner, he recognizes the voice as David's. In response to Saul's query, identical to the one he uttered at Engedi, David again launches into a speech (vv. 18-20), defending his innocence, accusing others of slandering him, and lamenting a fate that has forced him far from his home and his God (v. 19). He ends his opening salvo with a plea for Saul to stop persecuting him, comparing himself, as he did in his address to Saul at Engedi, to two forms of life, this time the flea and the partridge. In effect, he points at the same time to his own insignificance and to the impossible task Saul has set for himself. The difficulty of finding a single flea or the elusive partridge in hill country should be obvious and needs no elaboration.

As earlier, Saul repents of his pursuit of David, declaring that he has done wrong and begging David to come back (v. 21). In addition, he promises not to repeat his wrongdoing, closing with a reaffirmation of his own sense of transgression. In response, David offers to return the spear, saying nothing of his own return to the king's household, and arranging for the handover of the weapon through an intermediary. He then reiterates his dedication to the notion that it is unlawful to lay one's hand on the anointed of God (v. 23), a declaration now heard not only by Saul and David's companion Abishai but also presumably by Abner and the entire army of Saul. David ends by commending his own life to God. Saul's final words to David are a blessing and a statement of the conviction that David will be successful in all that he will do (v. 25). Here, the entire conversation between Saul and David is public, so Saul refers in more covert terms than he did earlier to David's future kingship.

This is the last encounter between the two rivals. Although Saul speaks conciliatory words, at the conclusion each rival is back in his own place. David has kept his distance and will continue to do so. Not trusting that a repentant Saul will be able to stick to his posture of regret and conviction of personal wrongdoing, David will move further and further away from Saul's reach. Notably, David hands over Saul's spear but keeps his water jar. As others have observed, spear and jar symbolize the forces of death and life (Fokkelman 1986, 537). The spear in chapter 26 is the equivalent of the piece of Saul's mantle in chapter 24. The spear most likely also stands for the power of potency and manhood, a phallic symbol linked to a man's superiority in war, a logical connection in this warrior culture. Saul was very much the warrior king. By depriving him even temporarily of this representation of his potency in battle, David has shown the ultimate failure of Saul's kingship and in a way signals his final defeat by the Philistines. Although the spear goes back to Saul, its easy removal from a leader asleep at his job has been made clear. In addition, the sleep that overcame Saul originated with God, a sleep that can also indicate death. In contrast, the water, symbol of life, stays with David. Saul thus inches closer and closer to his demise.

Speaking of God

"The wild card in the deck, of the joker in the game, is God: what God wants, God will do." (Green 2003, 20)

Green points out that the role of God in these narratives, especially in 1 Samuel 24–26, is presented in what characters state about God, about what God wants, about whose side God is on, about God's protection. As she observes, it is all "talk about God and about how God is dealing with the two anointeds" (Green 2003, 21). She also puts the story in the historical context of those who were pondering the desirability of reinstituting kingship after the return from exile in the late sixth century. Nabal dies of his own stubbornness, his own wickedness, his own inability to deal with his people. That God finally killed Nabal is, according to her, a "red herring," making clear that the king and the kingship will die of their own deeds, "their own answerability" (Green 2003, 21). Kings, whether approved of or rejected by God, all turned out to be ambiguous heroes. At times they benefited the well-being of the community, as it was enjoined to follow God's *torah*, but many times they worked against the welfare of the community and resisted the demands laid on them to "do justice and righteousness," actions that the prophet Jeremiah compared to the knowledge of God (cf. Jer 22:15-17). A community may suffer more damage from a king who does not live according to the demands of *torah* than from not having a king at all. At this stage in the books of Samuel, judgment is still out on David, and only time will tell how it will develop for him, his house, and the community to which God appointed him as *nagid*/ leader.

The End of the Road (1 Sam 27:1–31:13)

"Saul is caught between his own turbulent personality and the antagonism of God toward human kingship." (Exum 1992, 41)

"Well over half the book of 1 Samuel finds Saul sitting among the ashes of his kingship, and the reader who looks upon him during this period is tempted to repeat the words of Job's wife: 'curse God and die.'" (Polzin 1989, 213)

Rather than moving the story along in a straightforward fashion, the next five chapters braid events together in a way that clearly compares the opposite courses of the main characters: Saul's star descends while David's star ascends. Neither ascent nor descent takes place rapidly, so detours along the way are unfolded with some detail, providing the narrative with needed texture, affording different perspectives on the protagonists, and adding ambiguity and interest.

First, the focus is on David, who succeeds in another try at allying himself with the Philistines and becomes the "servant" of the king of Gath, Achish. Granted the city of Ziklag by Achish, David goes out from there on a number of raids, letting his new master believe that he is fighting his own people, while in reality he strikes down Israel's enemies. Achish thinks one thing and David does another. A new light on David exposes the deceptive side of his character only glimpsed so far (see 1 Sam 21). This episode ends with the Philistines mustering for war against Israel, thus introducing a new note of anxiety into the story because it might potentially involve David in combat with his own people.

The narrative then leaps forward and tacks to King Saul, who, faced with the Philistine armies, becomes paralyzed with fear, applies for advice to the Holy One in vain, and resorts to calling up the spirit of dead Samuel with the help of a medium in a nearby town. Saul's encounters with the medium and the spirit of Samuel are told in fine detail, down to the last meal that Saul will be served in his life, the meal of the condemned man. The eerie cast and séance-like atmosphere combine with domestic detail and culinary preparations to create a poignant portrait of a king defeated before he has even begun to fight.

Meanwhile, Achish and David join the muster of the Philistine armies, an event that moves the story back some days, as the muster is recorded to have happened at Aphek, in the central west of the country, while the battle will eventually take place in the northeast. When the Philistine commanders notice "Hebrew" soldiers among the troops and Achish reveals that David is one of them, they will have none of it, a disapproval that forces Achish to send David and his contingent home to Ziklag. When they arrive there, it turns out that Amalekites have raided the town, and this event causes a severe crisis in David's career, as his own men turn against him for the first time. There follows an elaborate account of David's successful counter raid, involving a turncoat, worn-out fighters staying behind, and fair divisions of the spoils. This glorious victory on David's part against the Amalekites is thus juxtaposed with the final battle and defeat of Saul against the Philistines. Saul, driven into the mountains by the Philistine bowmen, dies by his own hand. Final notes to the narrative have the folks of Jabesh, once delivered by the hand of Saul at the beginning of his kingship, rescuing the mutilated corpse of their king and providing it with respectful treatment.

Here the book ends. Saul, the one "asked for," whose name echoes in the hope-filled story of Hannah that opens the books of Samuel, whose kingship was allowed by God as a means to take care of the Philistine threat (1 Sam 9:16), ends his life in defeat to this enemy. Together with him all Israel is defeated. It is not only kingship that lies in ashes; all Israel's hopes, invested in their choice to have a king who would fight their battles for them, appear to have come to an end on Mt. Gilboa. The situation recalls the words of Samuel to the people in chapter 12: "Swept away . . . swept away . . . swept away . . . !" (12:25).

Escape to Gath (1 Sam 27:1-7)

"It is all very well to trust in God, but this evidently does not exclude being shrewd." (Goldingay 2000, 165)

This short chapter opens a rare window into David's mind, revealing his thoughts for the first time since he appeared on the scene. His is not in a hopeful situation. In spite of Saul's conciliatory words at their final meeting, David appears to be convinced that he will never be safe from Saul. There is really only one place for him to go where he can be sure that Saul will not go after him: Philistine territory. Perhaps this time the Philistines will have heard of the breach between King Saul and one of his top commanders and accept David's presence. Once again, he chooses King Achish of Gath as a potential protector. It works; Achish accepts him and David settles in Gath with all his men and his household. Saul, informed as usual about David's hiding place, ceases to pursue his rival.

David wants to escape, as he emphatically states when he considers where to go to get away from Saul once and for all. So he "crossed over" to Achish (v. 2). The statement employs a verb that casts at least some doubt on David's ultimate intentions. Is his escape temporary, or does he contemplate siding with the Philistines permanently? What then would become of his ability to worship his God, an issue that concerned him during the last encounter with Saul? The sequel will show that he is of a divided mind, perhaps sometimes going with the flow, using Philistine protection as a shield against Saul for as long as possible, while at other times deluding his new masters and not doing their bidding. That he does not want his actions too closely scrutinized becomes clear from his request for a town to settle in with his entire retinue. Counting everyone, the size of his company makes his request for a place of his own eminently reasonable. In his appeal to Achish, David uses polite language, referring to himself as Achish's servant (v. 5). Achish grants him Ziklag, not too far away and not too close. There David settles down long enough that a sense of security and calm about his potentially treacherous presence pervades the mind of Achish.

A Servant to Achish Forever (1 Sam 27:8–28:2)

"What has David done for the king and what will he agree to do?" (Edelman 1991, 234)

David goes out about his usual business of warmongering, ostensibly against his own people but in reality against Israel's enemies, notably including the Amalekites. David's fighting against Amalek brings implicit comparisons with Saul to the surface. This enemy caused Saul all his troubles. They will cause trouble for David also, for Amalekites are wont to pop up again even when, according to report, they have been disposed of once and for all. For now, they are part of a defeated group, and David uses them as a ruse to deceive Achish into thinking he has turned on his own people.

For the second time in the story, the reader is made privy to David's thoughts. In killing everyone who could give away the actual victims of his raids, David hopes to mislead Achish (v. 11). Of course, one can never be sure in these cases that no one has survived to talk, so some anxiety may have been the result of these campaigns. In the short run, however, the ruse works. In counterpoint to the insight into David's mind, a glimpse is offered into the thoughts of Achish. So far, he is convinced that David's "crossing over" to Philistia, combined with his subsequent military actions, must be viewed as actual treachery against his own people, and that David will be his "servant forever" (v. 12). Contrary to some readings, Achish is not portrayed as a stupid man. Rather, these two, David and Achish, are well matched in duplicity. Their scheming is brought to the foreground in the concluding lines to the episode.

The Philistines have decided to go to war once again and get ready for another, perhaps a final, battle. Achish makes clear to David that this will put him in the position of fighting by Achish's side:

> Achish said to David:
> "You surely know that with me you will go out with the troops,
> you and your men."
> David said to Achish:
> "You yourself know well what your servant will do."
> Achish said to David:
> "Then I will appoint you my bodyguard for always."
> (1 Sam 28:1-2)

Each man uses the verb "to know." Achish even uses the double form to underline its significance, "you *surely* know." In case there was any doubt, this emphasis on David's knowledge includes the veiled threat that Achish expects David to go with him or else. David and all his fighting force are expected to follow Achish into battle. David in his turn throws the verb back at his lord with an emphasis on the pronoun, "*you* are the one who knows." At the same time, he uses deliberately ambiguous language wrapped in polite phrases. Achish tells David what to expect, and David responds with words to the effect of "you know me!" Nevertheless, Achish does not really know David or what he is up to, as has already become clear in this part of the story. Even though he has ostensibly trusted that David has gone out on raids as an enemy to his own people, he cannot be sure that the man will not turn on him in the middle of the battle. Therefore, he decides to keep him close by. As bodyguard, David will be fighting at the side of Achish, who will then also be able to keep an eye on his slippery ally. Earlier, Achish had expressed hope to himself that David would always remain in his employ. Now he cements the relationship by elevating him to bodyguard "forever." Once Saul had not let David go back to his father's house; now David is bound to the archenemy of Saul and his own people. It is worth noting that David does not swear an oath of loyalty, and nor does Achish demand it of him. It looks, however, as if this loyalty will be severely tested in the near future.

Seek Me a Woman (1 Sam 28:3-20)

"Nothing clothes Samuel and Saul alike in kingship better than the robes they wear throughout the book." (Goldingay 2000, 218)

The focus of the story shifts and also advances the action some days, as it is now the eve of the battle between Philistia and Israel. Significant events take place in the first five verses: Samuel's death is noted again, this time in connection with the expulsion of those who manipulate the spirits of the dead. An additional comment records the location of the opposing armies, with the Philistines encamping at Shunem in the northeast, while Saul and his armies gather at Gilboa, which makes the valley of Jezreel a likely place for the upcoming fight. For some reason the sight of the Philistine armies throws Saul into a debilitating fear, so he goes for advice to the Holy God who does not answer him through any of the usual ways of approaching the deity. The threefold reference to these efforts underscores the absence of a divine response to Saul's inquiry of God: dreams, in the ancient world often seen as divine revelations in need of interpretation; the Urim, a kind of holy rolling of the dice; and, finally, prophets, professional seers attached to centers of power. All these attempts, which required a good deal of effort and time, end in zero results, something that surely must have increased Saul's anxiety.

Why does the sight of the Philistine armies frighten Saul? He is a seasoned soldier who has been fighting all his life, so the mention of his fear at this point is a bit unexpected. Although the narration does not state it here, earlier it made clear that Saul knew of David's defection to Gath (27:4). Is he now afraid because he may meet his former protégé in battle, may be forced to kill him or face being killed by him? Alternatively, is he afraid because, knowing David's prowess, he is aware that this formidable fighter will lend the Philistine armies increased strength? Furthermore, what exactly does he ask of God? He will later say to Samuel that he did not know what to do. What are his choices, however? To turn tail and fight was surely not an option. Asking divine advice before war usually would be a way to find out about the outcome of the struggle. Is he asking whether to send secretly to David to regain his alliance and have him at his side? The text does not make it clear and so emphasizes the bewilderment of this soldier-king.

In his predicament, he resorts to a desperate gamble: "seek me a woman who is a necromancer, so that I may go to her" (v. 7). Once, when his spirits were distressed, he had asked his servants to "seek" him "a man" to relieve his torment, and David had come to soothe his agitated mind with his music. That day, which still held some hope, is long gone. Now Saul seeks a presence he himself had proscribed. Indeed, he must go to her in disguise, at night, to avoid detection by both the Philistines and the woman herself.

The trip from Gilboa to Endor (a journey of about 10 miles) would bring him close to the Philistine camp. It is thus a perilous journey Saul and his servants make to the medium at Endor. As Alter and others have noted, divesting himself of his clothes is symbolic, as 1 Samuel often uses the cloak to signify power. In a way, Saul divests himself here of kingship (Alter 1999, 173). He is already a condemned man, a "dead man walking" on his way to his doom. Once Saul is in the presence of the medium, the story slows the pace to record verbal exchanges of the main characters (vv. 8-14). The woman, who is never named, accuses her unknown visitor of setting a trap. Only when Saul gives his assurance that her efforts will not have repercussions does she ask whose spirit she is to raise. When Saul names Samuel, the narrative skips to her vision of Samuel without providing any description of her *modus operandi*. Either the narrator was nervous about describing details of a procedure so strictly forbidden according to the laws of ancient Israel (Lev 19:31; 20:6, 27; Deut 18:11), or other matters are too important for unnecessary detail to hold up the action. Because of the narrative technique, it now seems as if Samuel arises immediately on Saul's request: "He said, 'Bring me up Samuel.' The woman saw Samuel . . ." (vv. 11b-12a). Saul is coming close to the world of the dead. Yet it is not Saul but the woman who sees Samuel, a vision that causes her, ironically, to recognize Saul, who once again must reassure her that she has nothing to fear. Seemingly blind to what is occurring, Saul asks the medium what exactly she sees, and she identifies the apparition as "gods coming up from the ground" (v. 13). In need of more precise identification, Saul asks again, and finally she provides the identification necessary to convince Saul that he is indeed faced with his former mentor and nemesis: "An old man wearing a cloak" (v. 14). This description is sufficient for Saul to recognize Samuel and to bow down. This is the same cloak that he once held on to and that tore in his hand.

The woman now fades into the background, and the exchange that follows takes place directly between Samuel and Saul. It consists for the most part of a reprimanding speech by Samuel (vv. 15-19). Saul gets the floor only to explain why he is inconveniencing Samuel. In his explanation, he sums up his trouble succinctly: the Philistines are nearby and God is far off. So what else is he to do but to call on Samuel? At least he knows that he will hear the truth. It is of some interest that Saul declares that God has turned away from him. In fact, there has never been direct contact between the Almighty and his anointed, apart from the occasions when the spirit of God took hold of him, which was contact of a kind but not one initiated by Saul. Unlike David, who can count on divine counsel, Saul is not informed by divine support when he makes decisions. It could be said that God turned away from Saul a long time ago. Only now does Saul himself give voice to this particular trouble in his life.

In Brueggemann's words, "Death has not mellowed Samuel" (Brueggemann 1990, 194). His speech is filled with reproach and the sure announcement of doom, not only of Saul but also of Saul's sons and of all Israel, not some time in the faraway future but "tomorrow." God has turned from Saul all right, indeed has become his enemy, has torn the kingship from Saul's hand and given it to David, Saul's "neighbor." For the last time in these chapters, David's impending kingship is announced, this time with the full authority of the dead prophet. A rhetorical question precedes the diatribe: "Why ask me?" (v. 16). To hammer everything down, Samuel uses the name of the Holy One seven times. It is a sharp and bitter speech, leaving no room for compassion and ending with a death sentence. It is not surprising that on hearing it Saul falls down. He, who once stood tall among his people, noticeable because of his size, now lies without strength full length on the ground.

Saul and the Mistress of Ghosts (1 Sam 28:21-25)

". . . it also needed this woman to pick Saul off the floor afterwards." (Goldingay 2000, 180)

Enter once again the medium, the "ghost-mistress" as Saul called her earlier in the story (v. 7). During the events of the night she faced a demand for powers she was not supposed to exercise, a demand that caused her to question her visitor who dared put her in jeopardy. Once she executes her task, she recognizes not the one she has called from the world of the dead but the one who is still alive before her: King Saul. Again, she questions the powerful man in her presence and accuses him of deception. Once assured on the point of her vulnerability, she fulfills her task in describing who has appeared before them, a being Saul is unable to see. In the aftermath of the exchange between the living and the dead, she sees before her one whose power has drained out of him, and she attempts to minister to him.

First, she speaks in a rather peremptory tone, emphasizing her positive response to his request and requiring the same from him toward her. The surprise comes in what she wants of him. One might expect her to ask for a reward, at least for continued protection in her difficult marginal situation. Rather than protection, the reward she seeks is for the king to have a bite to eat. She recognizes the exhaustion of the man, who though a king is also a vulnerable human being, and so she tends to his vulnerability. After a first refusal, Saul consents.

> The woman had a fattened calf in the house
> and she hastily slaughtered it,
> took meal, kneaded it, and baked flatbread.
> She brought it to Saul and his servants and they ate.
> Then they arose and went on that night. (1 Sam 28:24-25)

This is a strange, somewhat anticlimactic end to a story that began in the realm of the forbidden and awe-inspiring. The necromancer turned cook receives more attention for her work as chef than her act of conjuring. The "gods" that came up from the ground have gone back to where they came from, and it all ends with everyone eating veal together. A woman with great powers turned out to be the first one aware of the human needs of the man before her in whose hands lay the power over her life. It had all begun for Saul with a meal in the company of his mentor, Samuel. On the eve of his death, it ends with a meal together with the one who brokered Samuel's presence for the last time. We leave them there, Saul, his two companions, and the woman who bestowed on him this kindness, in a lull before the great disaster that will happen.

David Rejected by the Philistines (1 Sam 29:1-11)

"Is there a sting in the tail?" (Fokkelman 1986, 570)

From the dark of night and the spookiness of the visit to Endor, the story switches back to the Philistines and David's presence among them in their preparations for the fight against Israel. The time line has moved back to the war preparations, with the Philistines still at Aphek, some days march south of Shunem. There, the parade of troops marches by the commanders. All is well until they notice a foreign element among the last contingent, perhaps noticeable because of dress. "What," they say, "are these Hebrews?" In using the term reserved for Israelites in a subservient position, they are in fact asking what this riffraff is doing here. This observation stops the action, which from here on devolves into conversation.

First, Achish, in his defense of the presence of Israelites, lets slip that David is the one who has brought them on board. His reassurances that David is really a reliable fellow, who has served him faithfully for a long time, fall on deaf ears. The enraged commanders order Achish to "send the man back" (v. 4). The Philistine army commanders assume that David will happily return to Saul with appropriate Philistine trophies, most likely more foreskins! In their castigation of Achish, they repeat once again the victory song that once celebrated the young hero at Saul's side, a song that was the first occasion for Saul to become suspicious of David. This refrain has now become proverbial for David's prowess, but not on behalf of Philistines! Throughout their speech, the commanders refer to David in derogatory terms, as "the man" or "this one," clearly indicating their distrust.

Achish presents David with the bad news, which may of course have been good news to David. This turn of events will let him off the hook in an honorable way. He makes a protest, but it is clearly pro forma, and Achish in response, while reaffirming his own trust in David, also repeats the demand of the Philistine officers. His last words to David are a repeated "rise early," a phrase echoed by the words "David rose early." They then go in reverse directions, David south to Ziklag, far from the site of the battle, and the Philistines north to face their foe Israel.

The short chapter is humorous and provides some relief from the depths of despair faced by Saul in the previous episode. The Philistine commanders, the Pentagon of their day, clearly have great power and practically order Achish to get rid of David as fast as he can. Achish may have been shrewd, but in their opinion he has not taken the full measure of "this Hebrew." Achish's words to David drip with honey, filled as they are with praise for this apparent traitor, calling him "good" and like an "angel of God." "But you know how it is. I must bow to the voice of the generals, and they want you gone." David, in his role of faithful vassal, protests his dismissal, asking what he has done wrong that he should not be allowed to stay at Achish's side. His protest sounds hollow, but he may also be fishing for whether Achish has found out anything about his activities back in Ziklag, when he left Israelites unscathed during his raids. Has someone been talking? When Achish responds to him with the highest praise, David must have heard him in great relief.

The Trouble with Amalek (1 Sam 30:1-25)

"David is a man who lives by the infinitive absolutes of God's speech." (Brueggemann 1990, 202)

It is a bitter homecoming to Ziklag. Going on a march in the opposite direction from the battle, a two- to three-day march as the text notes, David may have forced the pace somewhat so that the men would have arrived tired and hungry, ready for some rest and recreation (Fokkelman 1986, 581). Instead of refreshment, they find a burned-out town and their families gone into captivity. The Amalekites have miraculously resurrected themselves once again and gone on the rampage, no doubt in revenge for David's earlier military actions against them. David and his men do not know the identity of the raiders, although they may have suspected it. They also do not know that their family members are still alive, of course, so the lamenting is loud and bitter. Hungry and exhausted, David's men turn on him in their anguish and are actually ready to kill him. David faces not just his own losses—his two wives, Ahinoam and Abigail, are gone and for all he knows dead—but for the first time a rebellion among his followers. David's actions may have begun to seem inexplicable to them. First, they were supposed to go over to their archenemy the Philistines, which might have put them in the position to have to fight their own people. Then, those "foreskins" had the temerity to reject them and send them packing on a long march home. It was all doable as long as there was plenty of spoil to be had, but now look what happened! This insane idea of joining up with the Philistines has come down to a huge disaster!

It is no mean crisis that faces David. Like Saul, according to his report to Samuel at Endor, David is in "sore distress" (v. 6). Yet for David the source of the distress is abundantly clear, and unlike Saul, he finds strength in God (v. 6). The phrase "David took strength in the Holy One his God" precedes the consultation that takes place by means of the priest Abiathar (vv. 7-8) and proleptically refers to the consultation. Putting it at the end of the lines that begin with the mention of his distress, however, emphasizes the contrast between the two anointed ones: no answer for the one, easy access for the other. The oracle David receives is interesting for the extra information it provides. When David receives a positive answer to the question of whether he should go in pursuit to overtake the foe, the response comes that he must do so and will be successful and will "certainly" rescue, with the emphatic repetition of the verb. This promise makes clear that there will be something or someone to rescue and therefore inspires great hope. In one of the most serious crises David faced during his time on the run from Saul, he, in contrast to Saul who only hears prophecies of doom, receives a view of a positive outcome.

He can thus set out, in spite of exhaustion, having found new strength. He must have inspired his men with hope for them once again to follow him. That they are tired is made clear by the advance mention of a contingent that can go no further and stays behind about ten miles south at Wadi Besor (v. 10), so that David must continue with only two-thirds of his force. Exhaustion and lack of food run like a red line through these episodes for Saul and for David and his men. The part of the narrative that has David in the center shows also a nearness to death, although the outcome is positive, unlike the story of Saul. The presence of death is next embodied by a starving fugitive found in the field, left behind to die by his Amalekite master (vv. 11-15). Once fed, he provides crucial information about the identity of the raiders and the place where they may be. The raiders have been slowed down not just by their captives but also by the booty and their premature celebration of their conquest, degenerates that they are! For David and his men, tired though they may be, lashed on by their anger and thirst for vengeance, these are easy prey (vv. 16-17). Thus, all ends well for David and his followers, for everything that the Amalekites took is returned and more. We note that plunder from the Amalekites caused Saul to be rejected as king. As Brueggemann observes, "The Amalekites are resented for taking spoil; Saul is rejected for taking spoil; David is saluted and championed for doing the same! David is subjected to none of the restrictions, held accountable to none of the old norms" (Brueggemann 1990, 203). It is true that no edict about total dedication had been laid down in this case, and yet the contrast is remarkable:

> David took all the flock and the cattle.
> They drove before them that livestock
> and they said, "This is the plunder of David." (1 Sam 30:20)

Another incident unfolds on the return of the victorious group to the ones who had been too tired to come along on the pursuit at Wadi Besor. Some malcontents, "every wicked and worthless character," grumble that they refuse to share the booty with these weaklings. Just give them their families back and send them away. David will not hear of it and makes it a rule that everyone, fighters and stragglers, will share equally. There is an echo here of the fairness of Saul, who, when faced with grumblers on their return from the fight with the Ammonites, would not allow anyone to be killed who had originally been against him (11:12-13). That fair victor is soon to meet his end, however, while David's fairness is to become "a rule in Israel until today" (v. 25). The entire episode ends with the record of a grand distribution of the plunder among those in Judah, thus creating goodwill among his future constituents (vv. 26-27). David, the rising star who will soon take center stage, has overcome a situation of "sore distress."

Saul Falls on Gilboa (1 Sam 31:1-6)

"You could say that Saul lived an undistinguished early life, then had his one moment of glory, and then fell into a morass from which he never found the exit, unless you could say he found it in his last 24 hours." (Goldingay 2000, 182)

In contrast to the detailed report about David, the account of Saul meeting his fate is told in quick strokes. The actual fight with the Philistines, most likely on the same day as David's raid against Amalek, took place in the Jezreel valley, where the Philistines would have the advantage with their chariots. Saul and his army retreat into the mountains, where Philistine archers pursue them. Hence it is on Mount Gilboa that Saul faces his end. With his three sons, including Jonathan, already dead, his enemy sets upon him. Badly wounded, he determines at the last to take control at least of the manner of his death, and asks his weapon bearer to do the task for him. When his man out of fear refuses to do the task, not wanting to lay hands on God's anointed, Saul throws himself on his sword. His weapon bearer follows him in death and the story of Saul ends:

> So died Saul with his three sons,
> and his weapon bearer,
> and all his men on that day together. (1 Sam 31:6)

The ground upon which he fell after hearing Samuel's foretelling has received his last fall. The once bright star of Saul has descended and come to rest on this mountain. A hush falls over the story, and it will be up to his erstwhile enemy to lift his voice in lament over the demise of the valiant soldier king who in spite of all adversity stuck to the task he had initially taken up with reluctance to the end.

A Deliverer King (1 Sam 31:7-13)

"The first book of Samuel ends in a cemetery with a tamarisk tree in Jabesh." (Brueggemann 1990, 209)

With the Israelites in a rout, the Philistines do what victorious armies did in those days; they mutilate the corpses of the slain king and his sons. As once the head of the gigantic champion had been cut off by David, they cut off

Saul's head, sending his weapons around to bring the good news, the "gospel" of the victory of their people and their gods to everyone (Brueggemann 1990, 209). Beth Shan, where they impale the mutilated body of Saul, is about ten miles east of Gilboa, west of the Jordan. A bit further to the southeast and across the river is the town of Jabesh Gilead, where the inhabitants still remember their rescue by the fledgling king Saul when they were under Ammonite attack (1 Sam 11). These folk do not remember him as a failed king or as the one who disobeyed God's commandments; to them he is their deliverer. They pay their respects, therefore, to his body and the bodies of his sons by going on a secret rescue mission. They burn the bodies, too badly mutilated for a decent burial, but they bury the bones in Jabesh under the tamarisk tree and hold a mourning ritual in Saul's memory. It is not such a bad resting place for the remains of Saul, and those of Jabesh are not the worst ones to honor Saul.

David, who might have been able to turn the tide, has been absent from the battle. As Polzin points out, he is in the position of the ones who "have stayed behind with the baggage," and his own rule will come down on his head with both advantages and disadvantages. "The king who hid himself among the baggage when called upon to rule (10:22) is replaced by one who stays by the baggage (30:24) as he waits for a chance to rule" (Polzin 1989, 223). For Polzin, Saul's fate, foreshadowed by Abimelech's fate in Judges (Jdg 9:54), illustrates the fate of Israel in the Deuteronomist's perspective: "kingship despite all its glories, constituted for Israel communal suicide." When the king falls, all Israel falls, because from now on their fates are intertwined. There may still be hope for Israel in exile, but it will no longer reside in having a king to rule over them.

We may also read the narrative in a more ambiguous way. The narrator does not criticize Saul's act of suicide, though generally considered an abhorrent deed in ancient Israel, and many commentators view it as a kind of final display of heroism on Saul's part. The failure of the first king to meet the demands put on him by those whose mindset on the whole issue was divided from the beginning does not decide the fate of kingship. God and Samuel were not happy with the people's request and, not surprisingly, the first attempt at the new adventure ends in failure. Nevertheless, there is yet a new star on the horizon, another anointed one who may fulfill the role more adequately. The future is not closed and the sun has not yet set on this young kingdom.

Then too, by letting Jabesh Gilead have the final act in the drama, the narrative shows that different views of kingship, even Saul's kingship, may exist simultaneously. For those of Jabesh Gilead, Saul would always be the one who rescued them from extreme danger, their redeemer-king. Perhaps, in the wake of failure, a different vision of kingship was forming itself in embryo. Like the vision of the land, for which the actual ground under the feet of the Israelites was only the concrete picture of the utopian vision created by the promise, actual flesh-and-blood kinship only faintly resembled the ideal. Against the negative picture of the future painted by Samuel in 1 Samuel 8, against the brute facts of the reality of the kings that will be in power, a positive picture arose. It was the vision of a deliverer king, one who would embody justice and righteousness, who would defend the cause of the poor and the needy, who would uphold the rights of the stranger, the orphan, and the widow. Great expectations were thus shaped against the concrete background of failed monarchs, or unjust and greedy ones—expectations that would stay alive through the exile and beyond.

Part 3

The Story of David

(2 Samuel 1–24)

Introduction

Second Samuel divides easily into three parts. The first eight chapters give an account of the early years of David's reign after Saul's death on Mount Gilboa. Half of these chapters concern themselves with the period when there is a Saulide pretender to the throne besides David (1:1–4:12), while the second half reviews the early years of David's kingship over the entire nation (5:1–8:18). The first half includes David's lament over the fall of King Saul and his son Jonathan (1:17-22), a poem that functions as counterpoint to the praise-song of Hannah at the opening of 1 Samuel. In language and tenor very different from Hannah's prayer, David laments the demise of Saul and Jonathan in their capacity of warriors and the fall of their weapons as symbols of their valor and strength. Whereas Hannah assigned all power, whether in armed struggle or social context, to the Holy One of Israel, David allocates the strength of weapons of war to the men who wield them. Stories of military and political manipulation follow this testimony to David's artistic talent. The road to kingship is strewn with violent and murderous encounters, and funerals are the order of the day. David is able to distance himself from direct involvement in the fighting on both a national and a personal level. The final murder removes Saul's son Ishboshet and, with all obstacles out of the way, David can ascend to the throne of Israel.

The chapters concerning his early kingship (5:1–8:18) involve the capture of Jerusalem, henceforth the nation's capital and the place of David's residence, the settling of the Ark in this city, David's thwarted attempt to build a temple to house the Ark, and military campaigns of aggression enriching the royal treasury. The prophet Nathan appears for the first time in this section, as God's representative advising David on his course of action in constructing a sanctuary. Communication between David and the Deity always proceeds smoothly, mostly through David consulting God on a course of action. In this way, David finally removes the Philistine threat in two decisive battles, both of which involve divine assistance (5:17-25). God interferes negatively only in the matter of temple construction by means of Nathan, who includes a mild reproof in his speech to David (7:5-8). Nathan's speech also contains promises of an enduring Davidic house. David responds to this communication with a long prayer, expressing his gratitude and devotion and asking God to bless his house. A chapter on military campaigns, aimed at expanding David's kingdom and securing the borders, follows (8:1-18). This last account leaves the impression that David practiced unwarranted cruelty and violence in the conquest of neighboring peoples.

The second main part (9:1–20:24) deals first with David's kindness to one of Jonathan's descendants and, subsequently, with a war against Ammon that ensues when a diplomatic mission of David misfires (9:1–10:19). At that juncture, the narratives turn to present a close-up tale of events at David's court during the long years of his reign (11:1–20:24). This story depicts in great detail nefarious doings on the part of David and two of his sons. David rapes the wife of one of his soldiers, a soldier whose murder he arranges surreptitiously (11:1–12:25). One of his sons, Amnon, rapes his half-sister, Tamar, a deed that provokes his own death in turn by the hand of another of David's sons, Absalom (13:1–14:33). God's displeasure with David's actions becomes evident through the words of the prophet Nathan, who makes a second appearance in the text, this time as critic of royal behavior and announcer of divine chastisement to descend on David and his house (12:1-12).

Four chapters (15:1–18:32) tell of the rebellion of Absalom, who has managed to win a great number of people over to his side and who presents a serious threat to David's reign. David is forced to flee Jerusalem and crosses to the other side of the Jordan, where eventually his own and Absalom's troops fight a battle in the region of Mahanaim (18:1-18). Absalom suffers a total defeat and is himself killed by Joab and his soldiers (18:15). The death of his son throws David into a tailspin of grief, from which he arises only on the passionate urging of Joab (19:1-9). Divisions among the tribes become apparent during David's return to Jerusalem and soon another rebellion breaks out, quashed before it can take on full force by General Joab (19:42–20:22). A list of David's cabinet concludes the detailed story of relationships and dysfunction at David's court for the time being. It will receive a conclusion in the first two chapters of 1 Kings.

Finally, chapters 21 through 24 present a closely constructed series of texts that recount two tales of disaster brought on by God and resolved by God (21:1-9 and 24:1-25) and two lists of heroes and their valiant deeds during David's reign (21:15-21 and 23:8-35). In the center of this last part of 2 Samuel, we find two poems (22:1-51 and 23:1-7), the first in praise of the power of God who supports the military engagements of the anointed king; the second in celebration of the God who supports the house of David and David as a righteous ruler.

Second Samuel portrays God in different ways. In the first part David consults God in his endeavors and in turn receives God's support. In the large middle part God chastises David for his failures, but is mostly in the background, although we see the divine hand in the disasters that befall David and his family. The final chapters depict a God who acts in seemingly arbitrary ways, whose judgments are inscrutable and who punishes where no shortcoming is present. This portrayal leaves the impression that in the end the power of the king is subject to God's unfathomable will and that the Davidic house is subject to the reign of God.

Character description is especially vivid in the largest part of the book—the account of David's court and the relationships between the ruler and his family on the one hand, and the royal siblings, David, and his retainers on the other hand. Women come to the foreground infrequently; on two occasions they intervene to thwart the course set by the monarch (14:1-20; 20:11-22). More often, women function as pawns or outright victims in the game of male politics.

The Road to Kingship (2 Sam 1:1–4:12)

"Is David perhaps like Charles de Gaulle, patiently waiting, knowing that sooner or later the nation must turn to him because it has no alternative?" (Brueggemann 1990, 210)

Saul is dead, but the matter of kingship is not resolved, and David's path to kingship is far from smooth. Violent deaths follow Saul's, and many episodes in this set of chapters end in funerals, laments, and curses. While still in Ziklag, David receives a report about Saul's demise on the battlefield that causes him to react with both violence and mourning. David has the unfortunate and deceitful messenger executed, and launches into an eloquent dirge for Saul and Jonathan (ch. 1). Subsequently, David becomes king in Hebron, but the rest of the country has a son of Saul, Ishboshet, as king in Mahanaim across the Jordan, at the instigation of Saul's erstwhile general, his cousin Abner (2:1-11). Abner together with his counterpart Joab, David's cousin, play central parts in the sequel involving two kings in the land. First, a battle between the two sides comes out in favor of Joab but ends with both parties withdrawing from the field (2:12-32). A crucial incident during the struggle occurs when Asahel, Joab's brother, dies at Abner's hand. The episode ends with a count of the dead and the funeral of Asahel. Back in Mahanaim a disagreement breaks out between the puppet king Ishboshet and Abner over the possession of one of Saul's concubines, Rizpah, a dispute so enraging to Abner that he decides to switch sides and begins to make overtures to David (3:1-11). David and Abner start negotiations, involving the retrieval of princess Michal and ending in a pact, with Abner promising to bring all of Israel over to David's side (3:12-21). Joab, incensed at the notion of Abner's support, still fuming over the death of his brother, or truly believing that Abner is up to no good—or a mixture of all three notions—lures Abner, who had already left Hebron, back to the city and murders his potential rival in secret (3:22-30). The episode ends with Abner's funeral and David lamenting Abner's death while calling down a curse on Joab and his house (3:31-39). The bloodbath is not yet done, for in the next chapter, two of Ishboshet's commanders sneak up on him while he is taking his siesta and murder him. They triumphantly carry the head of the unfortunate victim to David, who, rather than rewarding them, has them executed (4:1-12). With the head of Ishboshet buried next to his faithless general Abner, the road is finally clear for David to become king over all the people (5:1-5).

During all this "sordid sorry mess" (Brueggemann 1990, 235), David is absent from much of the action. He is not, for example, out in the field fighting the battle at Gibeon; he makes overtures to different groups and individuals but does so through messengers; he is on the receiving end of much of the action, reacting to events rather than setting them in motion. On the other hand, he is once again privy to divine counsel (2:1) and is depicted as the head of a thriving fertile family (3:2-5), a house that is becoming stronger, while clearly the house of Saul is dwindling (3:1). He makes certain to absolve himself from gratuitous violence, while declaring judgment on the perpetrators. The narrator strives to keep the king as free from bloodguilt as possible. The text describes David as king, speakers address him as king, and, for the first time, the narratives call him "King David" (3:31), even before the entire people have come over to his side. Here then David is becoming a king in the center of much political maneuvering, of power factions, and of those who try to take advantage of the moment to benefit from his rise in power.

Against the violent background of male antagonists, women stand in the background: the wives of David appear as his entourage and mothers of his children (2:2-3; 3:2-5); Zeruiah, David's sister and the mother of Joab, Abishai, and Ashael, receives mention three times (2:13, 18; 3:39), but we hear nothing further of her; Rizpah and Michal occur as objects of male possession and male power; finally, two women without names in chapter 4 further the collapse of the house of Saul. The women receive no voice; they do not rejoice or lament; their presence either enhances male presence and power or enables their demise. Women eventually occupy space of their own in the story, and when they do, it will be as contributors to David's decline as a person and a king.

News Comes to Ziklag (2 Sam 1:1-16)

"Eager for a fat reward, he thinks that the war-lord of Ziklag, who was regarded as a collaborator by the Israel of Saul, will be happy at the king's demise . . . ." (Fokkelman 1986, 642)

David is back in Ziklag after his defeat of the raiding Amalekites, when a messenger arrives with obviously bad news, judging by his torn clothing and the dirt on his head. Once he has learned that the man comes from the battlefield, David inquires about the outcome with the same words blind Eli once used to ask the harbinger of news in Shiloh: "What's the word?" (1:4). Like that earlier messenger, the escapee first reports on the defeat of the Israelite army and ends with the deaths of the most important people among them: "also Saul and Jonathan his son are dead." On David's request for more information, a detailed story unfolds, one constructed of half-truths and lies. Because the reader already knows how Saul's death took place, this version of events raises doubt. In addition, the messenger clearly seeks to win favor with David, someone he knows to be Saul's antagonist and therefore believes would be glad at the news of the king's death. It is a clever tale in which he reveals himself as an Amalekite who, as a foreigner, would presumably be exempt from the taboo of finishing off a king already in his death throes. As proof that Saul is truly dead, the messenger holds out Saul's regalia: his diadem and bracelet.

Convinced that the messenger has spoken the truth about the death of the king if not the manner of it, David and his entourage go immediately into deep mourning:

> Then David took hold his clothes and tore them
> and so did all the men with him.
> They wailed and wept,
> and fasted until evening,
> on account of Saul
> and on account of Jonathan his son,
> and on account of the people of the Holy One,

and the House of Israel
for they fell by the sword. (2 Sam 1:11-12)

David is not done with the messenger; he asks him to explain himself further. When it turns out that he is a son of a stranger, a *ger*, he is held as accountable as any Israelite would have been who should not have stretched out his hand against God's anointed. David, after all, had twice refused to do so himself. *Gerim,* who were strongly protected by multiple regulations eventually codified in the Torah, were those from outside who had come to live with the tribes permanently and who therefore were responsible to live by the same codes as insiders (cf. Num 9:15; 15:14-16, 29), certainly insofar as it pertained to ritual matters. Thus, the messenger is executed and posthumously receives David's curse of bloodguilt, having condemned himself by his own words (v. 16). The account does not make clear whether David believes the Amalekite's report because his confidence in the truth at this point is not of great significance. What is clear is that Saul has died, that mourning needs to take place, and that the one who claimed responsibility must die, so that David will not appear to rejoice in the demise of the one who stood in the way of his road to the throne. He himself, in the face of that reality and in the presence of Saul's animosity and persecution, had not dared to lay a hand on God's "anointed." How dare this alien, this stranger, dependent on the goodwill of his host country, take it upon himself to do so!

Lament over Saul and Jonathan (2 Sam 1:17-27)

"There is a moratorium on power for the full honoring of grief." (Brueggemann 1990, 214)

David had a long and complicated history with Saul. He had strong attachments, was unable to cut his ties to the unstable king for a long time, and in the end had refused to harm him when he was twice within his grasp. With Jonathan he shared a relationship on its face less complicated, which was instigated in the first instance by Jonathan's love for him. Bound by covenant ties and family relations, the two were able to maintain friendship and love. Yet Jonathan remained Saul's son, and throughout he stayed loyal to his father, fought at his side, and died at his side, torn in this complicated tangle of relationships.

David composes his dirge over the fallen heroes in a poem of great economy and beauty. Five strophes weave themselves around a refrain lamenting the death of the heroes: "How have the mighty fallen!" (vv. 19, 25, 27). The refrain has variations, the first two referring to the hills where the dead lie slain, and finally to the instruments of war that now lie abandoned:

> The glory, O Israel,
> on your heights lies slain;
> how the mighty have fallen! (2 Sam 1:19)
>
> How the mighty have fallen
> in the midst of the battle;
> Jonathan on your heights lies slain! (2 Sam 1:25)
>
> How the mighty have fallen,
> have perished the devices of war. (2 Sam 1:27)

These lines surround a series of addresses to people and nature. First, the poet admonishes an unspecified group not to announce the tidings of the defeat as "good news" in Philistia, where the women will sing the victory songs welcoming their warriors home (v. 20). Then he addresses the hills themselves, forbidding them to show signs of flourishing in view of the despoliation of Saul's shield (v. 21). Mention of the shield leads to a stanza about the weapons of the two fallen heroes—the bow for Jonathan, the sword for Saul—and a paean of praise for the two united in battle (vv. 22-23). While the first address proscribes the daughters of the Philistines from rejoicing, a third commands the women of Israel to weep for the royal leader who provided them with clothing. The second refrain begins with the fall of the two warriors then focuses on Jonathan alone. Drawing Jonathan to the center occasions an outburst of grief over the death of this friend, addressed to him personally:

> Distress is upon me over you, my brother;
> Jonathan, you were very dear to me,
> wondrous was your love to me
> more than the love of women. (2 Sam 1:26)

In comparison with the song of Hannah in 1 Samuel 2:1-10, there is a striking absence of any mention of God in David's lament. In her poem a man is not a hero by strength (v. 9), and "the bow of the mighty is broken in pieces" (v. 4), for God reverses the fate of the weak and the strong. In David's dirge about the dead warrior/hero, the bow and sword make a man mighty indeed and their fall is indicative of the hero's fall. The roots *gavar* (to prevail) and *nafal* (to fall) recur throughout the poem, indicating strength and the terrible defeat when strength fails. Hannah's poem ascribes all power to God. David's poem ascribes power to the sword and bow and to those who carry them, the "mighty men/heroes" of a warrior culture. While its tone is that of a lament, it is also a celebration of men of war and war machinery. There is no mention of Saul as Israel's first anointed king; in fact, the word "unanointed" occurs in reference to Saul's shield (v. 21).

Two Kings in the Land (2 Sam 2:1-11)

"Ishboshet has much territory / but little time—David has little territory / but a lot of time." (Fokkelman 1990, 34)

At this point it is a matter of some urgency for David to get out of Ziklag and his Philistine alliance, so, on the advice of the deity, advice that as usual he has no trouble receiving, he moves east with family and followers. Within a few sentences, he has settled in Hebron, where "the men of Judah" come to anoint him as king (v. 4). The royal title occurs in connection with David in this first section in three key places, twice linked to the verb "anointed" (vv. 4, 7, 11), a word that now clings to David rather than the house of Saul. Immediately, David opens negotiations with the folks in Jabesh Gilead, praising them for their loyalty to Saul and promising them unspecified benefits from his side (v. 6). Twice he refers to Saul as "your master," while, seemingly as an afterthought, he mentions that the Judahites have already anointed him as king (v. 7). What his address amounts to is that the Jabeshites were kind to their former master, who is now dead, so if they know what is good for them they will recognize David as their new master, for he has just been made king.

Meanwhile, the house of Saul has not quite disappeared, for one hears next that Abner, Saul's cousin and his general, moved across the Jordan with one of Saul's sons named Ishboshet and "made him" king (v. 9). This section (vv. 8-11) resounds with words for king and ruling as king, occurring four times in the span of three verses. Three of them attach to Ishboshet, and one at the end to David. There are now two kings in the land, yet only one of them is "anointed"; the other has been "made" king by strong man, general Abner. It will become clear where the power lies in that arrangement.

Will the Sword Devour Forever? (2 Sam 2:12-32)

"The pursuit of kings within the house of David ultimately will be an exercise in self-annihilation on both a personal and national level." (Polzin 1993, 34)

Alas, the devices of war have not perished, and bloodshed marks the beginning of David's reign. First, the armies of Joab and Abner meet, with David notably absent from the battlefield, to witness a joust or gladiatorial contest between twenty-four combatants, all of whom die simultaneously (vv. 14-16). It is hard to imagine how this could have happened or that this was the intent of the "play" (v. 14) suggested by Abner, but such is the upshot of the picture created by the narrator. The result is a battle and the pursuit of Abner by Asahel, whose presence is noted, together with Joab and Abishai his brothers, as the offspring of David's sister Zeruiah (vv. 18-23). A close-up highlights a curious exchange between Ishboshet's strong man and the fleet-of-foot Asahel in pursuit. The scene portrays Abner as hesitant to kill a brother of Joab, an act he fears will set Joab against him. Abner shows throughout the unit a grudging respect or concern for his counterpart on David's side. It does not become clear whether Joab responds in kind. In any case, Asahel does not take Abner's advice to pick someone else as victim, and Abner thus kills him in a particularly gruesome way with the butt of a spear.

The last scene (vv. 24-31) portrays the armies of the generals at a standstill with Abner addressing Joab, pointing out the futility of continuing this fight any further. In view of the count of victims on each side reported later (v. 31), Abner was clearly unable to gain the upper hand, which may have colored his perspective. Joab agrees to the cessation of armed struggle, remarking that Abner should have spoken up sooner (v. 27), and the troops go their separate ways. Each general holds the other responsible. In his address to Joab, Abner indicates that this fighting could go on for a long time, with enormous bitterness as a consequence, and asks why Joab continues to let brothers kill each other. Joab in turn puts the responsibility on Abner, implying that there would not even have been a fight if Abner had spoken up earlier. With this response he may also imply that his brother Asahel would still have been alive in that case. The narrator provides the uneven count of victims on each side, 19 of David's men and 360 of Ishboshet's, before noting the burial of Asahel in Bethlehem (v. 34). It will not be the last funeral in these early days of David's kingship.

The divided kingdom has occasioned a civil war in which neither of the generals, it seems, is eager to engage. Abner suggests the contest of the twenty-four (v. 14), a combat that would supposedly have decided the winning party but that instead unleashes a battle. The narrator calls the contest "play," but it is surely an odd kind of play that results in twenty-four dead bodies. The rest of the chapter deals with the oppositional movements of pursuit and standing/stopping, denoted by the Hebrew verbs *radaf,* pursue, and *'amad,* stand. Asahel runs after Abner, and Abner stops him forever. Next, the spectacle of Asahel's dead body stops the troops in their tracks. Then Abner's men stand/stop behind him on a hill, he calls for a cessation of the fight, which causes Joab's men to stand/stop their pursuit:

> Then Joab blew the ram's horn,
> and all the people stood
> and no longer pursued Israel,
> and did not continue to fight. (2 Sam 2:28)

Polzin reads the emphatic use of the verbs combined with the preposition "after" (Hebrew *ahare'*), as indicative of the question mark cast on kingship by the Deuteronomist. Could or should the people at this point have "stopped" their fatal pursuit of kingship, their going "after" kings who in the end would not help them? Could they have halted the sword that devours forever once the inevitable bloodshed of kin by kin was staring them in the face? How many funerals will it take for everyone to come to his or her senses? (Polzin 1993, 33–34)

A Transfer of Allegiance (2 Sam 3:1-21)

". . . you take me to task over a woman today?" (2 Samuel 3:8)

Chapter 3 opens with notes on the long struggle between the house of David and the house of Saul, on David's increasing strength and the weakness of Saul's house, with no mention of the name of Ishboshet. To offset the difference between the two even more, David's family and abundant offspring receive detailed remarks. His potency and flourishing are clear, while Saul's son is not worth mentioning by name. The one in Ishboshet's house who does deserve notice is Abner, whose strength is cited also.

The scene switches to the household of Ishboshet, who questions Abner about having sexual relations with one of Saul's concubines named Rizpah. This reproach cloaked in question form sends Abner into a fury. He gives his master a tongue-lashing and announces without further deliberation that he is switching sides; not only that, but he also swears to deliver all of Israel to David. Ishboshet is so afraid of his "strong" man that he does not utter a word. Obviously, Abner rules this house rather than Saul's son, the "made" king. Perhaps Abner has had enough of being a puppet master and is looking for the first opportunity to abandon Ishboshet. The previous episode made clear that he has at least respect for Joab, while his words on that occasion evidence that he saw little benefit in endless bloodshed between folk who profess the natural allegiance of kinship. The narrator does not reveal whether Ishboshet's accusation against Abner is true, but Abner's vigorous protest leads one to suspect that Ishboshet had the correct information. To possess someone else's concubine indicates a claim to power and in this case may point to the true state of affairs, not only in the household but in the realm still ruled by Saul's descendant. Women are little but pawns in the struggle for superiority waged by powerful men.

Abner opens negotiations with David, who is eager to enter into the partnership under one condition: his wife Michal must be returned to him. Saul had married Michal to another man (1 Sam 25:43), and now David wants her back in his household. He sends a message to that effect to Ishboshet, who engages Abner to execute the task. Ishboshet's almost automatic accession to David's demands affords another glimpse of his weakness. The subsequent pathetic scene depicts Michal's removal from her household to be returned to David, with her husband following her in tears only to be shooed away like a dog by Abner, who has no sympathy for weakness. Abner is far too busy with other more important matters, such as convincing the tribes who are loyal to Saul's house that David is really their man (vv. 18-19). In so doing, Abner attempts to tap into a current of discontent that may have existed among certain groups, as well as into a desire for a king who would finally get rid of those annoying Philistines. In any case, one hears nothing of any resistance to his efforts to win people over to David.

David, meanwhile, hosts a banquet for Abner during which Abner promises to deliver "all Israel" to David, calling him "my master the king" (v. 21): "I will get up and go and gather," he announces, and no one doubts that he can indeed deliver the goods. He has, after all, delivered Michal back to her rightful husband, even though not a word is said here about her reunion with David or whether she received any welcome at all from the man she once saved from her own father's vengeful nature. Abner has much business to conduct, and David sends him off "in peace" (v. 21).

A Murder in Hebron (2 Sam 3:22-39)

"The narrator is at great pains in this matter, because he knows that bloodguilt has now come to dwell very close to the person of David." (Brueggemann 1990, 229)

It soon becomes clear that one person in David's entourage is not content with the way things are going and with Abner's gaining the confidence of the king. On hearing about all the "peace" (vv. 21-22) that now exists between David and Abner, general Joab flies into a rage and aggressively questions David about Abner's presence. He bluntly accuses Abner of being a spy at David's court (vv. 22-23), lures Abner back to Hebron while David remains ignorant, and kills him with the help of his brother Abishai, as revealed later (v. 30). The precise motivation for the deed is not entirely clear, although the narrator recounts that it was because Abner killed Asahel. No doubt, Joab also felt Abner to be a potential rival, and, finally, Joab's mistrust of Ishboshet's erstwhile supporter may not have been entirely unwarranted. We notice that throughout this episode David appears fairly passive, one who finds out crucial matters belatedly, subtly hinting perhaps of a David who may be "losing his grip on developments" (Fokkelman 1990, 101).

On the other hand, it is important to keep David in ignorance, lest the bloodguilt that results from the killing of Abner should cling to David. It is crucial that everyone knows that David had nothing to do with the murder, so he makes sure that the mourning over the fallen general and the funeral are very public:

> And all the people took notice
> and it was good in their eyes,
> as all that the king did
> was good in the eyes of all the people.
> All the people and all Israel knew on that day
> that it was not from the king
> the killing of Abner, the son of Ner. (2 Sam 3:36-37)

All the running around, the "coming and going" of the chapter, ends with a mournful procession behind a bier and with another funeral, where David and "all the people" weep. David composes another lament in which he virtually accuses Joab and Abishai of being "scoundrels" (v. 34). He calls Abner a commander and a great man (v. 38), calls down a curse on Joab and his house, and declares his cousins, the sons of his sister Zeruiah, to be "too hard" for him, softie that he is (v. 39).

Abner remains a somewhat enigmatic figure, since his thoughts, and therefore his motives, never become clear. Questions frequently accompany his appearance in the story: "Will the sword devour forever?" "Do you not know the bitterness that will be after?" (2:26). "Whose is the land?" (3:12). Polzin understands him as an artificial construction of the Deuteronomist, never becoming a "full-fledged character in the story" and functioning as an "artificial vehicle for the foreboding purposes of the Deuteronomist" (Polzin 1993, 39). The questions so often found in Abner's mouth may lend some support to this viewpoint, pointing as they do to issues of lasting concern for the nation and its eventual demise.

Whatever the truth about the motives of the writers, it could be that Abner never comes into his own as a character because his person is attached to the falling star of the house of Saul. He established Saul's son as king because he served this house as both a soldier and a relative. At first, he may not have counted on the strength of David and his deft political maneuvering. Once he has considered the landscape and reviewed both his master's weakness and David's growing following, he uses the first opportunity to change allegiance. He sounds like a soldier's soldier who is not interested in internal fighting but rather in taking care of the real threat to the fledgling nation, the Philistine armies. Abner must have been a part of the battle at Mt. Gilboa, even though his presence there is not reported, and he sees little value in a fight of kin against kin that ultimately will weaken the Israelite troops (2:26). Thus, in aiming to convince the rest of Israel to accept David as king, part of his argument is that David will be capable of delivering the people from "the hand of the Philistines" (v. 18). Abner does not come across as a manipulator but as a man most at home on the battlefield, and as such he would, of course, have been of great use to David. David's weeping behind Abner's bier may not have been entirely feigned.

A Murder in Mahanaim (2 Sam 4:1-12)

". . . his fate is sealed, and already he is a dead man." (Exum 1992, 107)

The mayhem and bloodshed are not yet over. Two brothers murder the next one to succumb, Ishboshet, on his bed at siesta time. Because of the way the story introduces the two, following the note on Ishboshet's fear at hearing of Abner's death, the narrator may lay down a false trail for the possibility of a positive outcome for this hapless son of Saul. In addition, the narrative veers away from the court of Ishboshet to report on the rescue of a son of Jonathan, Mephiboshet, who was lamed during flight at the news of the deaths of Saul and Jonathan.

The story takes a sharp turn when the two "naturalized Benjaminites" (Alter 1999, 217) under false pretenses penetrate Ishboshet's sleeping quarters and behead him. They triumphantly bring the head of the fallen scion of the house of Saul to David, making the same mistake as the Amalekite escapee in thinking that he will rejoice in the death of the rival king from Mahanaim. They call Saul David's enemy and address David as "my lord, the king" (v. 8). David responds to them as only David can with sharp and eloquent words, telling them exactly what he thinks of those who think to bring him "good news" (vv. 10-11) about a death. He has them executed and Ishboshet's head buried next to Abner. Again, David has managed to distance himself from the misfortune that overcomes the house of Saul.

As Alter has observed, "mayhem and dismemberment" mark the end of these episodes, which also spell the beginning of David's kingship over all Israel (Alter 1999, 219). In addition, much of what has taken place has been between "brothers." This is true either in a literal sense, as in the case of Joab and Asahel and the subsequent embittered relations between Abner and Joab, a circumstance Abner already foresaw (2:22), and in a wider sense as in David's reference to Jonathan (1:26). We may think also of Abner's remark to Joab that there will be no end of kin pursuing kin if the state of affairs continues (2:26, 27). The murderers of Ishboshet are literally brothers, but they are also tribal "brothers" of their victim. The bloodbath that has ensued in the early stages of David's kingship can in no way be viewed as a positive beginning, and it will not be the last time that family members rise up against each other in the narratives that relate the period of early kingship. From the Deuteronomists' perspective, this ruinous beginning may well mirror the eventual collapse of the kingdoms (Polzin 1993, 47–49).

A Presence of Women

"Since in patriarchal texts women are frequently made to speak and act against their own interests, an important question faces us: what patriarchal function do these narratives serve?" (Exum, 1991, 178)

Women have no active role in these chapters, but many episodes mention them, and their place and function in the narratives are of interest in view of the role that women will play in the eventual decline of David's moral stature. In addition, the absence of women in an active capacity as agents in the plot contrasts with the strong figure of Hannah in the opening chapters of 1 Samuel. David has aroused love in masses of people and individuals, including women, but there has been no mention of reciprocity on his part; so far, his strongest emotional bond has been with Jonathan. It is worth considering how women are portrayed in the early stages of his reign.

In his lament over Saul and Jonathan, David mentions women twice with the group name "daughters of . . . ." First, he depicts the Philistine women as the singers who might welcome the triumphant warriors home (1:20), as we encountered the Israelite women upon the return of Saul and David from the battlefield (1 Sam 18:6-7). Rejoicing and exulting on the part of Philistine women is a thing to be prevented. Further, the poet admonishes the women of Israel to lament over their king, who dressed them in fine garments and lavished ornaments on them (1:24). These descriptions allow the "daughters of the foreskins" the role of participants in triumph as they sing and dance in celebration, even if the intent of the poet is to prevent them from doing so. The poet commands the "daughters of Israel" to lament, but we never meet them in the following stories participating in lamentation. They are present here as passive receivers of finery, the only benefit the "sweet singer of Israel" can think of as having come to them from

Saul. Women appear in David's lament as a group to be silenced and as interested only in fine clothes.

Next, individual women appear at David's side, as wives and the mothers of his sons (2:2; 3:2-5), with Ahinoam and Abigail, as usual, mentioned together with their tribal origin. Abigail always appears as the "wife of Nabal the Carmelite," an association that highlights her ties to Hebron, probably of some advantage to David as he initially settles there. In addition, the story mentions David's sister Zeruiah a few times as the mother of David's commanders, Joab, Abishai, and the unfortunate Asahel (2:18 and 39). One may ponder the significance of the silence regarding Zeruiah as the body of Asahel is brought home and is buried there. Was she alive? Was she there to weep over the dead body of her gazelle-like son? She had given birth to "hard sons" according to her brother, and perhaps this reflects on the mother by implication. Only men weep and lament in these stories.

Chapter 3 mentions four other wives besides Ahinoam and Abigail as mothers of David's sons (vv. 2-5), pointing to an increasing harem and offspring as signs of his growing power. Two women play a role in the episode that follows the list of David's wives and sons. The first is Rizpah, one of Saul's concubines, who becomes a cause of contention between Abner and Ishboshet. We know nothing of her at this point, not even whether Ishboshet's accusations were true. Abner's furious retort dismissively refers to her as "a woman," when he asks incredulously, ". . . you take me to task over a woman today?" (3:8). By implication, this is the least important thing that Ishboshet could reproach him with and is therefore all the more infuriating. Yet the possession of a man's concubine indicated a power grab, as Abner must have known. Rizpah is a tool in this part of the narratives to further or thwart the ambitions of powerful men. She never speaks, is only spoken of, and has no agency or power of her own. Her association with Saul makes her a lightning rod for the disagreement between Ishboshet and Abner and indirectly causes Abner's defection.

The second woman whose presence is noteworthy is Michal, the daughter of Saul, whom he had given to be married to another man (1 Sam 25:43). David wants her back in his household and makes her return the condition of Abner's joining his side, a test of the sincerity of Abner's intentions. Abner retrieves her on Ishboshet's orders:

> And Ishboshet sent
> and took her from her husband,
> from Paltiel, the son of Laish.
> And her husband went with her,

going along weeping behind her,
as far as Bachurim.
Abner said to him,
"Go home!" And he turned back. (2 Sam 3:15-16)

Not a word addresses Michal's reaction to the forcible removal from her husband; nor is there any comment on her reunion with the husband she once "loved." David had Michal to thank for his original escape from Saul, but he made no attempt at reuniting with her when he still had the opportunity to do so (1 Sam 20), and nor did he seek refuge for her as his wife when he begged a safe place for other family members in Moab (1 Sam 22:4). Michal's function in the present episode seems to be merely one of adding to David's stature as the future king of Israel; like Rizpah she serves only to enhance male power. She is "reduced to nothing more than a pawn in the game of politics on a grand scale" (Fokkelman 1990, 91). Michal's place at David's side is, of course, filled with ambiguity and possible tension. David refers to her first as "Saul's daughter" (3:13) and second as "my wife, whom I betrothed to myself" (3:14). As Saul's daughter and David's wife, she is the potential birth-giver to offspring that will continue Saul's as well as David's house.

In the episode of Ishobshet's murder, two other women appear, both in some way falling short in their responsibilities. First, a nurse appears, who fled in the aftermath of the defeat at Gilboa with one of Jonathan's sons, Mephibosheth, an incident mentioned almost as an aside in the lead-up to the killing of Ishboshet. "In her haste to flee," the narrator reports, "he fell and was lame" (4:4). A change of subject in the sentence avoids a direct mention of the nurse's failure—i.e., that she dropped the child—but the inference is clear enough. Finally, at the time the two killers enter their master's quarters, a female guardian at the door may have been derelict in her duty: "And look, the woman who kept the gate, had been gleaning wheat and nodded and fell asleep" (4:6 in the reading of the Septuagint). Two women, even if they do not engage in outright criminal behavior, certainly participate in the demise of the house of Saul, one leaving the sole descendant lame, symbolic for a crippled house, the other unable to warn her master of his impending doom, futile though it might have been.

Totaling the tally, absent from scenes of grief, women are present in the prelude to David's reign as spectators and receivers of finery, as contributors to David's rise and potency, as enhancers of the political power of the men to whom they are attached, and as unable to execute the duties they have been assigned. They represent quite a contrast to the "swift eagles" and the "strong lions," symbols of male prowess, lauded in David's lament and portrayed as main actors in the narratives. At the same time, David, as the epitome of strong leadership, is also the one who weeps and laments the many deaths that occur and who claims "weakness" (3:39). The "daughters of Israel" dressed in the "finery" bequeathed to them by Saul shine by their absence in any active role. These are the stories of warriors and heroes, fighting and falling in the struggle for the upper hand. Yet the main hero, David, will come to grief over the presence of women in his life, and it will be through his association with one of them that it will finally be impossible for him to avoid the bloodguilt from which so far he has been able to distance himself.

David Reigns in Jerusalem (2 Sam 5:1–8:18)

"The shepherd and his flock belong together and are destined for each other." (Fokkelman 1990, 141)

With the last obstacle on David's road to kingship removed, the moment is right to record foundational events of his rule. "All Israel," formerly terrified, come to claim kinship and allegiance with David, and so his kingship over the entire people begins (5:1-5). He makes it a first item of business to establish a capital, choosing Jerusalem, a city to which none of the tribes has allegiance, where he settles and thrives as the founder of a dynasty (5:6-16). In a final episode he takes care of the Philistine threat in a double defeat, two battles in which God plays a decisive role (5:17-25). In chapter 6, the Ark of the Covenant reenters the story and comes to Jerusalem, here consistently called "the city of David." While jubilation and festivity accompany the entry of the Ark, two sour notes darken the mood of the episode: a death occurs during its initial transport (6:1-9), and when, on a second try, David succeeds in housing the Ark in Jerusalem (6:13-19), he receives a sharp rebuke from Michal, Saul's daughter and David's wife who was brought back to him earlier (6:20-23). Chapter 7 consists almost entirely of speech, in contrast to the two preceding chapters, and concerns building a temple. David expresses a desire to build, but he is halted by God through the agency of the prophet Nathan (7:1-17), who appears here for the first time. David responds to the divine refusal with a long prayer (7:18-29). Finally, an overview of Davidic campaigns is provided in which David expands the kingdom and, from the tribute paid by subdued nations, enriches the coffers that will eventually be used by Solomon to build the temple in Jerusalem (8:1-18; cf. 1 Kgs 7:51).

Robert Polzin titles his discussion of chapters 5–7 "Houses" and points out how the material revolves around the issue of "house," both in its narrow literal sense and its larger meaning of family and dynasty (Polzin 1993, 54). This insight helps to lend cohesion to what might otherwise seem disparate data. A house is a central resting place. Once he is king over the entire people, David, for so long perforce on the move, finds a place for himself and for his administration in a city that requires conquest, another show of his military prowess, and one that will not be a cause of contention among his subjects. David can only establish a secure place when enemies no longer present a threat, so the defeat of the Philistines is of primary importance in achieving his objectives. Subsequently, since politics and religion closely intertwine in the Davidic realm, David needs to find a place where the presence of God is above all visible. The Ark of the Covenant, long kept out of sight though perhaps not out of mind, is the most logical object associated with the notion of God's presence, and its placement in Jerusalem will accomplish the purpose of solidifying David's political and religious power. The next logical step is a building to house the Ark, and that is where all the housing comes to a stop, for this appears to be against God's will. Chapter 7 offers a reflection that includes some of the tension and ambiguity when it comes to houses, both for human and divine rulers. Once David has all the houses he needs, a stable place of his own and a center of operations, he engages in disturbing the houses of others in a series of military campaigns. These destructive efforts will also enrich the royal treasury and eventually make the manufacture of a house of God possible.

As is frequently the case in the narratives of Samuel, the chapters alternate between fast and slow tempos. Everything at the beginning takes place at a fast clip; no time is wasted on superfluous detail, and some passages take a large leap forward in reporting on house construction and the great increase of David's family, which with a sizeable harem must have taken some time (5:9-16). The transport of the Ark to Jerusalem slows the tempo significantly, and in the next chapter everything comes to a halt with the lengthy report of speech. In contrast, the battles of chapter 8, described briefly, take place over a number of years and may well represent a long period of David's reign (Fokkelman 1990, 256). After the bloody battles with his neighbors, much is in place to begin the telling of David's decline to which the contents of 2 Samuel will devote such detailed attention.

A Place for a King (2 Sam 5:1-16)

"David is something quite new." (Brueggemann 1990, 239)

The removal of obstacles on David's road to the throne of all Israel means, for a good part of the people, that they are now leaderless. With Abner and his puppet king Ishboshet gone and no other pretenders from Saul's house in sight, the tribes visit David to claim him as their king. First, they claim kinship with their king-to-be, a statement we should take in its broadest sense as pointing out that the people and David belong together. After this claim, they bring to the fore David's gifts of leadership even when Saul was still king, and cite God's promises for David's future as "shepherd" (v. 2). The shepherd metaphor, conventional for that time and place, connotes the particular care a king should exercise over his people in leading, nurturing, guarding, and protecting them. In David's case, God called him as a shepherd boy to become the shepherd of God's people. The speech is interesting for its indirectness: "we belong together, you were always a leader even under Saul, and God promised you would be our shepherd/leader, so . . ." (vv. 1-2). Without spelling out their request, the tribal representatives in the next breath come to "the king" in Hebron, where David, now called "King David," makes a covenant, after which they anoint him as king (v. 3). This noteworthy sequence of events constitutes the only time in the Bible that a king makes a covenant with his people before taking up his official kingship. The text does not provide any detail on the type of covenant David makes; we may assume that it involved a pledge on David's part to provide continued leadership and on the people's part not only to acknowledge him as king at this moment but to remain loyal to David and his house. Concluding sentences provide an anticipatory review of the total years that David reigned, headed by the information that David was thirty years old at the time he became king (vv. 4-5)—not a young man for those days, with the largest part of his reign still ahead of him. Names abound in this unit: David, Israel, Judah, Hebron, and Jerusalem, all of which surround the title "king" (eight times). This is the king, these are the people, and these the places of importance. Hebron signals backward, while Jerusalem points forward.

The description of the siege and capture of Jerusalem is particularly sparse, even for a narrative that ordinarily wastes few words on the details of military encounters. There is no mention of the number of combatants, the length of the siege, or how David accomplishes his feat. It opens with a taunting saying by the inhabitants of the city that David will never enter it, with the report of the capture immediately following, so that we find two sharply contradictory phrases in close proximity: "David will not enter here / And David captured" (vv. 6-7). The choice of Jerusalem as a neutral site was no doubt an astute one; even the fact that it had to be captured could be turned to an advantage in showcasing David's talents as a military tactician and leader. The inhabitants of the city were Jebusites, part of the original inhabitants of Canaan, a notation that attests to the survival of indigenous groups long after the struggles of the tribes' settling the land. Without devoting a line to its method, the account reports David's capture of the stronghold laconically as though it took no effort in spite of the inhabitants' words of defiance. The short report devotes the most space to two statements that are not readily comprehensible regarding the blind and the lame (vv. 6 and 8). The absence of detail together with the impenetrable nature of the verbal expressions lends a somewhat mysterious nature to the enterprise. David comes, sees, and conquers.

The drive of the unit is toward David's settling down there and making it his city, "the city of David" (v. 9). David "resided," "built," and "continued to grow great." All David's success takes place because of the support of the Holy One who is with him and who established him as "king over Israel." So great is David's fame already that outside help comes from the king of Tyre in the form of the necessary materials and labor to build "a house for David" (v. 11). The report of the resounding success of the new king culminates in a list of more sons and daughters, born to David after he acquired more "concubines and wives" (v. 13). We note that he took these "from Jerusalem," meaning they were Jebusites.

Defeat of the Philistines (2 Sam 5:17-25)

"The Holy One has broken through my enemies before me . . . ." (v. 20)

Now that David has a place, he can take care of the second and perhaps most important issue: defeating the Philistines. No doubt they are up to date on what has transpired and may be as eager to take care of this threat to their dominance as David is to overpower them. In any case, they take the initiative and march up to face their foe close to Jerusalem, some distance to the southwest of the city. The struggle that ensues recounts a double defeat for the Philistines, both times with direct aid and intervention of God. David, as he was wont to do, asks divine counsel before he sets out. When the go-ahead is given, the text simply records that "David struck them down," providing no count of victims or any other battle detail, but David's declaration that God broke through the enemies like a "water breach" may indicate there was some type of flash flood (v. 20). The place therefore bears the name Baal-Perazim, the "master of breaches." Precise instructions from God to mount an attack from behind trees precede the second defeat:

> When you hear the sound of marching
> in the tops of the willow trees, then act boldly.
> For then the Holy One has gone out before you
> to strike down the Philistine camp. (2 Sam 5:24)

"The sound of marching" may be a reference to "mysterious unseen agents" of God, or it may simply be the sound willows make when the wind blows through them that would provide "a cover for the movement of the troops as they advance stealthily" (Alter 1999, 224). In any case, the direct agency of God is at work here. This time David achieves a more complete victory than previously and deals the Philistine threat a serious blow. The emphasis in the brief account is on God's support of David, a theme that runs through these first chapters in 2 Samuel. Now, in Robert Alter's words, David has "completed the consolidation of his rule over all the land, and his real troubles are about to begin" (Alter 1999, 224).

A Place for the Ark (2 Sam 6:1-19)

"The covenant chest is a piece of hot theological and ethical property." (Goldingay 2000, 210)

"There is . . . an unpredictable danger, a risk, in seizing the Ark." (Polzin 1993, 64)

As Goldingay argues, Jerusalem, a city lying outside the tribal areas, needs a connection to God, and the Ark of the Covenant will serve that purpose nicely. Again, the story plunges into the action without introduction. It begins with David gathering 30,000 men to retrieve the Ark from where it has been residing since the Philistines brought it back to Beth Shemesh (1 Sam 7:1). That return had a close link to the defeat at Ebenezer at which 30,000 of the tribes had fallen to Philistine victory (1 Sam 4:10). Thus, the number of men David takes with him to retrieve the Ark echoes the number of slain soldiers in that earlier battle, when the Ark was lost.

In the first attempt to bring the Ark into Jerusalem (vv. 3-9), the means of conveyance recalls the way the Philistines returned the Ark to Israelite territory (1 Sam 6:7-13); a new cart will carry the holy object. This time, priests are in charge of the correct course instead of cows, while David and his entourage play musical instruments. One of the priests, Uzzah, is unfortunate enough to touch the Ark, perhaps because the cattle slipped, and God strikes him down. As earlier the awesome and destructive power of the Ark became evident against both Philistines and Israelites (1 Sam 5–6), the numinous quality of the container is once again evident. It may not be useful to ponder in what respect Uzzah fell short. He simply came too close and thus died. In turn, his death unleashes the anger of David, who halts the entire parade in its tracks and diverts the Ark to another house, that of Obed Edom, a Gittite Philistine.

David's first reaction is not fear, although there is a reference to fear of God secondarily (v. 9). The narrator notes that he "became enraged, because

God broke out against Uzzah" (v. 8). "Breaking out" on God's part is all fine and good when it affects David's enemies, but this kind of turning on one of God's own servants is another matter. This may also have been a first for David, who was unaccustomed to being on the receiving side of God's wrath. For the first time, God's presence is not entirely benevolent and supportive toward David and his company. In any case, he needs time to reflect on this matter, for it is now unclear how to achieve the purpose of bringing the Ark to Jerusalem. Obed Edom, most likely well aware of the circumstances, must accept the presence of this fearsome object whether he likes it or not.

Once again, the unpredictable nature of the Ark appears when God "bless[es] Obed Edom and his entire house" (vv. 11, 12). This expression is rare in the material edited by the Deuteronomists and all the more remarkable because it concerns a Philistine. This situation, lasting three months, is enough to convince the king that it is now safe to continue with the earlier plans, and so they proceed, albeit with extreme caution, making appropriate sacrifice after the first six steps (v. 13). David acts here in a priestly function, bringing the sacrifice and wearing a "linen ephod," the priestly garment. In addition, there is loud jubilation, the sound of the shofar, and dancing and leaping on David's part, all to indicate the "gladness" with which the Ark is brought into the city. Once there, the Ark is placed in an especially constructed tent, and David once again takes on his function as priest by bringing sacrifice and sharing largesse with the people.

The Rebuke of Michal (2 Sam 6:20-23)

"How eloquent is the goaded ego!" (Fokkelman 1990, 203)

"She cannot avoid her tragic fate as a member of Saul's house; she can only protest it, and that she does forcefully in 2 Samuel 6." (Exum 1992, 85)

In this episode, David's weeping and lamenting of the earlier chapters are a part of the past, with gladness, dancing, and leaping taking their place. David's behavior does not impress everyone favorably, however. To put the reader on guard, the narrator inserted a note on Michal's observing her husband's behavior from a window and despising him "in her heart" (v. 16). The note is a warning that a disturbance will arrive together with the happy homecoming, as indeed happens when Michal goes out to meet her husband:

> David returned to bless his house
> and Michal, the daughter of Saul,
> came out to meet David and she said,

"How glorious the king of Israel today,
who exposed himself today in the eyes of his servants' maids,
as exposed as the exposure of a worthless person." (2 Sam 6:20)

Here, as earlier in v. 16, Michal is named "the daughter of Saul," perhaps partly to emphasize the fact that through these two the perpetuation of the house of Saul may be possible, and partly to highlight that her loyalties may be divided and still lean toward the royal house rejected by God. Alternatively, it could be that the naming indicates a divide between her person and her husband, the king.

Michal's sarcasm and David's searing anger mark the exchange between wife and husband. This is the only time that the two exchange words, a meager harvest for a union that began, at least on Michal's side, with love. She reproaches her husband for exposing himself to everyone, high and low, as if he were himself part of the riffraff, alluding to what may indeed have been the case if the ephod consisted of only a short skirt. Michal, one of the few who was not with the throng to welcome the Ark home, has come out of her house to protest against David's display of joy that in her eyes was not befitting a king. She uses the words "king of Israel" and "honor" to point out how far David's behavior was from that of a true king. She uses the root "to expose" three times, thus combining the word for honor/glory (Hebrew *kavod*) with the word that also can mean "to go into exile" (Hebrew *galah*), a combination that was found also in the mouth of the dying wife of Pinhas when she commented on the capture of the Ark by the Philistines (1 Sam 4:21-22). Words that combine a reference to the Ark with one that contains echoes of exile sound an ominous note in these stories.

Michal's words clearly goad David into a stinging reply tantamount to "I will play as I like, for after all I play before God, the one who chose me, David, over your father. What is more, I do not care how low I will get and will get as low as I want and still find honor in the eyes of the maids!" Michal must have touched a nerve for him to reply in this way; perhaps he was not as sure of his origins as a shepherd boy or of his prowess as a husband, at least toward Michal, as he would like to have been. These cruel and dismissive words are the only words we hear from David toward his wife, who helped him escape from her father's anger, who lied on his behalf, whom he ignored while on the run from Saul, and whom he neglected to welcome home when she was torn from her loving husband as a prize possession. It is not a pretty picture.

One note on Michal's fate closes her appearances in the narratives: "Michal, the daughter of Saul, had no child until the day of her death"

(v. 23). Whether the intent is to point to a divine punishment because she upbraided David or to a cessation of sexual relations between the two characters is left to the imagination. Childlessness was largely viewed as due to divine interference, so her lack of children must have at least been interpreted in this way. Offspring produced by Michal and David would of course perpetuate the house of Saul as well as that of David, but this road is barred by the words of the Almighty. The account is all about "houses," after all, and the house of Saul must end. Therefore, a chapter that reports on the joyous return of the symbol of God's presence to the new capital, the city of David, begins and ends on a somber note. Uzzah's death casts an aura of gloom over the beginning of the endeavor, and the announced death of Michal without offspring closes the account. Like the wife of Pinhas, whose words she echoed, and the house of Eli rejected by God from priesthood, Michal is a woman who resides under the shadow of death and of a dying house. Already then, in this tale of David's rise to royalty, somber threads are woven into the fabric.

A Place for God (2 Sam 7:1-17)

"Did I ever ask for a house?" (Goldingay 2000, 221)

Once settled in his city, with the Ark ensconced in a tent, David decides that this is not a suitable place for housing the most important religious relic of Israel. He observes as much to the prophet, Nathan, who tells him to go ahead with whatever plans he may have. The phrasing is significant, for David never states outright that he intends to build a temple. Rather, he compares the two ways of residing, literally "sitting," he in a house of cedar and the Ark in tent fabric, implying that this does not feel right and that he wants to upgrade the quarters of the Ark. David's intentions and God's reply, which comes unasked to Nathan, address notions of sitting or staying, always stated with the Hebrew verb *yashav*. The episode opens with a double reference to David *sitting* in his house (vv. 1 and 2), and God's word to David begins with the rhetorical question, "Is it you who will build me a house for my seat (literally *sitting*)?" (v. 5).

God's long speech points out essential truths about God's presence and about who is in charge of establishing leadership and houses, and it contains a strong promise for the future. The first half (vv. 5-11) emphasizes the nature of God's presence and who derives benefit from it. Staying/sitting in a house is not the way God has ever been present, and a house is not something God demanded as guide and shepherd of the people (vv. 6-7). God has now appointed David to be the shepherd of God's people so that they may have a secure place (v. 10). Both God's presence and David's presence are shown to be in service of the well-being of God's people. It is not David, however, who is responsible for establishing houses—not even his own—but God (v. 11).

The section thus closes with an assurance that forms the link to the second half of the speech (vv. 12-16), which promises the establishment of a lasting house through David's son, who will also be the one to build a house for God. Or, rather than for God, the house will be for "God's Name" (v. 13). David's current "sitting" will eventually turn to "lying down" at his death, after all, and what matters is that the kingship founded in him endure. The bond between the two, God and David's offspring, will be like that of father and son, familial and unbreakable, even though it may involve punishment. Thus, the words Nathan conveys to David conclude,

> Your house will be solid
> and your kingship before you for the ages,
> your throne will be established and endure. (2 Sam 7:16)

The perspective and style of the unit differ from the preceding material. It is more theological in outlook and more hortatory in style, pointing strongly to Deuteronomistic editing. Yet it fits well in the span of the narratives, providing a needed reflective pause on Davidic kingship, on God's role in appointing kings, on palace and temple, on the people who were eventually supposed to benefit from both and who certainly have been uprooted from their place when the editors assembled this material. God's "forever" is not always to be relied on, as we learned at the beginning of 1 Samuel from the threat to Eli's house, also a house to which God had promised endurance (1 Sam 2:30). Human behavior and human irresponsibility also weigh in the balance and are able to unsettle even the most secure promises of God. But then again, in the end, neither palace nor temple guaranteed the ongoing life of the community and God's presence with them, and God would once again go about with the people as in the beginning (cf. v. 7).

We note that in the opening of the chapter, David does not ask for God's advice, as he usually did in the past, nor does Nathan consult with God on the plans envisioned by the king. God's intervention takes place as a corrective to the prophet's insights, but it does so without reprimand. This is the first appearance of the prophet Nathan on the scene, at David's side, where he will emerge twice more in the stories, always concerned in some way with the establishing of the dynasty (2 Sam 12 and 1 Kgs 1:22). Although Nathan initially utters approval of David's implied plans, God corrects him and he brings the correction to David (v. 17). The prophet functions as God's mouthpiece to the royal administration, speaking truth to power, a feature already discernible in Samuel, who still combined in his person the functions of prophet, priest, and political leader. From now on, the role of the prophet will be distinct and not bleed over into that of priest or administrative leadership.

Torah for the People (2 Sam 7:18-29)

"David is a hard bargainer both on earth and before heaven." (Brueggemann 1990, 261)

Nathan's message causes David to "sit in God's presence" (v. 18), an unusual posture for prayer that once again underlines the difference between the human and the divine being. He then speaks his astonishment before God and his awe at God's greatness. Three questions link the first part of his speech together (vv. 19-24): Who am I and what is my house? Who is great like God? Who is like God's people? The questions lead to a reflection on God's greatness and goodness that echoes with the praise of God in Hannah's song when she sang the incomparable greatness of God and declared that God is the God of the great reversals, who "raises the poor from the dust . . . to seat them with nobles" (1 Sam 2:8). David was taken from the modest position of shepherd of a flock to become the leader of God's people. God had brought him this far; yet this was still not enough, and now God has made him a promise that exceeds all expectations: a lasting house to rule over God's people.

The question about God's people, a people that "God went to redeem for himself" (v. 23, twice), also leads to a reflection on God. Redemption as a social mandate in ancient Israel's laws existed so that those who had the means could take care of those without resources. The ones in need of redemption were not the strong and the powerful, people of substance; they were the ones in need of help, the small and insignificant, as was the case for Israel. God did not fall in love with them on account of their size and power but because they were "littler than all nations" (Deut 7:7). God's nature becomes clear through God's preferences for a forgotten youngest/smallest child in a large family of tall sons, for the unruly crowd of an enslaved and dominated people.

A line at the beginning of this reflection puzzles many interpreters. While the words are not difficult, their intention is obscure: "and this is instruction for a human being, my Lord, Holy God" (v. 19c). What is this torah/instruction? And who is the "human being"? Without becoming lost in possible interpretations, one could read the line as an interjection that posits the entire reflection on God, God's dealings with the individual, David, and with God's people, Israel, as instruction for human beings. This is who we are: honoring what is high and mighty. This is who God is: lifting the poor from the dust and listening to the cry of the destitute. This God does not regard appearance but both sees in the heart and looks with the eyes of the heart (cf. 1 Sam 16:7).

David is not quite done. Being David and still not completely secure in his chosen-ness, he asks for confirmation and blessing (vv. 25-29). The plaintive "and now" (vv. 25, 28, 29) precedes each petition. The last lines of the speech contain the root "to bless" three times, and the final words of David's petition are that his house may be blessed for the ages by God's blessing. Like his ancestor Jacob before him, he refuses to let go until a blessing has been given (Gen 32:26), but unlike the case of Jacob, the narrator leaves the request hanging in the air without furnishing a reply from God. It is indeed a question of whether David's house was blessed or whether this ruling house turned into a blessing for the people. Polzin views David's request for blessing as a misunderstanding on his part, because the degree to which David's house would be blessed and be a blessing would depend on his behavior and that of his descendants (Polzin 1993, 86–87).

The Ghastliness of War (2 Sam 8:1-18)

"The treatment of prisoners provides a means of establishing total control over enemies, of melting their hearts in terror of the fearless and guiltless way with which the tyrant takes life." (Niditch 1993, 130)

"Who was this man before and who is he afterwards?" (Goldingay 2000, 195)

Chapter 8 recounts a series of battles fought by King David, probably over an extended period. We should therefore view it as a summary of the wars fought during David's reign. David defeats the Philistines to the extent that they do not rise up again in the narrative to threaten Israel, and then he turns his attention east and north. First, he tackles Moab, meting out particularly cruel treatment to the vanquished survivors, and then takes on the large Aramean kingdom in Mesopotamia. Although not mentioned as a site of battle, Edomites and Ammonites also fall victim to the armies of David. All become subservient to David, and he takes home a great deal of loot, most of it forcibly taken and some voluntarily donated as tribute by peoples, before this aggressive and expansionist-minded king can set out on the warpath against them. All booty goes to Jerusalem to be consecrated to the God of Israel, thus establishing a sizeable storehouse of material for use by David's successor in his building program:

These also King David consecrated to the Holy One,
with the silver and gold that he consecrated,
from all the nations that he subdued.
From Aram and Moab,
from the Ammonites and the Philistines
and from Amalek;
and from the booty of Hadadezer,
the son of Rechob, king of Zobah. (2 Sam 8:11-12)

Thus far, we have encountered many battles and scenes of war in these texts. Most of the stories of Samuel, Saul, and David take place in a context of military strife, where participation in a warrior culture forms character. Saul becomes emboldened to embrace his kingship by taking on the task of military leadership, only to be rejected from his position as the result of imperfectly executed military engagements. David rises to prominence not primarily as a talented poet-musician but as the champion fighter of Israel. "Saul struck down his thousands, David his tens of thousands," the women sang to their victorious heroes (1 Sam 18:7). David's most eloquent words are devoted to Saul and Jonathan as champion fighters (2 Sam 1:17-27). According to the testimony of the first chapters of 2 Samuel, bloodshed marked the initial period of David's reign. In that sense, then, there is nothing remarkable about the events recorded in chapter 8: David fought, God was with him, and he was victorious. On the other hand, the military engagements occurring here are different enough that a fundamental shift seems to take place, one that may well anticipate the shift in subject matter for the largest part of the remaining chapters of this book.

For the first time, battles are not fought on a defensive or semi-defensive basis, or because of provocation on the part of an enemy. At this turn, David, as a king who is also a military leader, wages battles of aggression and expansion. The arbitrary violence and cruelty apparent in his treatment of the defeated Moabites—a group that earlier had sheltered him and his family! (cf. 1 Sam 22:3-4)—and of the horses of the army of Hadadezer (8:2-3) have the ability to stop us cold and inquire what exactly is going on here. The text pushes us up so sharply against the ghastliness of war that we must pause to consider more closely the phenomenon in its entirety as it occurs in the Hebrew Bible, in particular in the books of Samuel.

In her book *War in the Hebrew Bible: A Study of the Ethics of Violence*, Susan Niditch explores in detail the various ideologies of war in the Bible. War may take place if the cause is considered just, and a ban (Hebrew *herem*) may be imposed that considers the booty, including human life, to be God's portion. As Niditch points out, this type of warfare actually values human life highly as it becomes a sacrifice to God and does not demonize the other. A second and more common understanding of war that includes the ban views it as deriving from God's justice; war under the ban is then a way to gain God's favor through rooting out abomination. We encountered the *herem* in 1 Samuel 15, where in Niditch's view a tension is present "between the ban as sacrifice and the ban as a rooting out of what is unclean and sinful" (Niditch 1993, 61). Amalek suffers punishment for past mistreatment of Israel, testimony to the ban as God's justice. On the other hand, Saul keeps the best of the cattle and spares the king's life, by which he misinterprets the sacrificial character of the ban. Both the ban as sacrifice and the ban as God's justice make killing in war acceptable, the one by reducing guilt that might accompany killing and the other through a desire to eradicate evil.

At times, war in any text, and certainly also in Samuel, may occur as a defense against an aggressive enemy. Most of the Philistine-Israel encounters happen in this context. David's military exploits against enemy groups during his service to Achish (1 Sam 27) may be viewed in light of his need for establishing credentials with his new lord, as well as creating goodwill among those of his own people who saw these groups as threats. War may take on a liberating character, as the fight of David against the Amalekites who have captured family members of himself and his troops (1 Sam 30). War may also be initiated by God, in which case the human group becomes spectator to God's violence (Goldingay 2000, 184–201; cf. 1 Sam 7:10). Finally, war occurs in the bardic tradition as serious sport with codes of combat and kinship. We found such traditions in David's lament over Saul and Jonathan and in the encounters between the sons of Zeruiah and general Abner (2 Sam 2:12-28). According to Niditch, war in the bardic tradition "reveals a courtly, even a chivalric view of war that has more in common with a work such as the *Iliad* than with the banning texts" (Niditch 1993, 105).

War as we encounter it in the present chapter may fall under the heading of "war in the context of an ideology of expediency" (Niditch 1993, 130). Perhaps one may view the extermination policies of David under Achish in this light also, but there at least one could explain his actions as arising from despair about having to find a safe haven with the archenemy as a last resort. In some way, chapter 8 does not fit with what has taken place in the context of war to this point, and it should come as no surprise that it stops one cold and causes questions regarding the issue of armed struggle, as it permeates much of the biblical text, especially the historical books of the Bible. The bloody execution of a helpless defeated enemy described in 1 Samuel 15:33

may horrify and repel, but at least one can discern a theological vision that may have informed it, even if one disagrees with such a perspective. What vision motivated David when he measured off helpless victims arbitrarily to leave some to die and some to live (8:2)? Does this not recall death-camp selections under the Nazi regime? Not surprisingly, in the television play *God on Trial*, the men in one of the death camps on the eve of their execution cite David's violent treatment of war victims. It forms part of the argument in the trial, illustrating the exercise of vicarious violence by a revered Israelite leader of the past, violence that ostensibly enjoyed God's support. In turn, the men feel that they are now delivered to senseless and brutal treatment, abandoned without divine intervention.

What about the character of David? Is he operating here only out of an expansionist desire, perhaps also as a preventative against possible aggression on the part of neighboring peoples? Is he working with the overweening conviction that God will be on his side no matter what? It appears that he has indeed stepped onto fundamentally different ground, from which he emerges a different person. A last question raised by this chapter is why we find it here, or rather why it is not attached to chapters 21–24. These last chapters in 2 Samuel fit the tone and content of 2 Samuel 8 by providing a review of David's career as warrior-king, opening a window on the cast of characters that made up his armies and on incidents that took place during his reign. That is, however, not where the story goes. Rather, it veers off in a different direction that takes a close-up view of David and his behavior in intimate settings. The issue of how chapters 9–20 fit with the rest of the material has interested many students of the Bible; these chapters, together with 1 Kings 1–2, may have made an original unit, sometimes called the Court History of David.

Wherever the origin of this material may lie, as it stands, it interrupts the narrative of David's royal exploits on the larger political and religious scene. In addition, it leaves a rather negative picture of the once almost spotless shining figure of the young warrior who stepped on to the scene to play healing music for his lord, and in the same breath almost brazenly to defy the most impressive bully the Philistines had to offer. After chapter 8 we meet a David who commits adultery and murder, who ignores the rape of one of his daughters by one of his sons, and who is weak in his personhood and in his fatherhood. Finally, this weakness bleeds over into the political realm when we view him cravenly fleeing throne and city, leaving the very position to which Samuel anointed him and for which he struggled so long and hard. Could it be no coincidence that this picture follows almost immediately on the military forays of David in chapter 8? Does he perhaps emerge from this scene more blood soaked and with a beclouded moral vision that will shape other disastrous choices he will make? If so, then what follows fits eminently with the tenor of the events portrayed here and should come as no surprise. After meting out death in the way David did to the Moabites, what is the death of one more soldier, even if one technically under his own command? After the cries of hamstrung horses, what are the cries from a desecrated woman, even if she is one of his children?

A King in His Own House (2 Sam 9:1–12:31)

"David has grown used to killing people, used to deceiving people, and used to treating women as things." (Goldingay 2000, 243)

The story line that broke off at the end of chapter 6 picks up in these chapters, which we can divide into two parts. Chapters 9 and 10 portray a David intent on showing "loyalty" (Hebrew *hesed*), in both cases to a son on account of a perceived debt to the father, one on a personal level and one on the larger political scene. The first instance, the retrieval of Jonathan's son, succeeds and ends with Mephibosheth living at the court and eating "at the king's table" (9:13). The second instance, paying homage to the heir to the throne of Ammon, backfires spectacularly and lands David and his generals in a devastating war against Ammon, with victory achieved only at the end of part 2 of this sequence (12:2-31). The second part of the unit, chapters 11 and 12, depict David in the grip of adultery and murder, with personal bereavement and the threat of more grief to come in its aftermath. As a sequel to the bloodbaths of chapter 8, it becomes especially clear in the David-Bathsheba-Uriah episode how David's moral vision is beclouded to the extent that it jeopardizes his status as God's anointed king. Here is indeed a king who takes and takes (cf. 1 Sam 8:11-17) without regard for the consequences to those who fall victim to his caprice. The events at David's court that follow (chs. 13–19) show a weakened king incapable of dealing with his errant offspring and irresolute in the face of national crisis.

If we view the accounts of chapter 8 as a survey of campaigns during David's entire reign, then we may assume the episodes of chapters 9–20 to have taken place in the context of those campaigns. Chapter 10 and the end of chapter 12 make clear that what takes place in the intervening chapters happened during the war with Aram and Ammon. It is important to view the tragic events of the violence David perpetrates against Bathsheba and Uriah in the context of a war.

The Kindness of the King (2 Sam 9:1-13)

"King David came into Jerusalem whirling and dancing before the Lord; the surviving Saulide limps into Jerusalem, crippled in both legs." (Alter 1999, 243 n. 13)

In contrast to the previous descriptive chapter, the tale told here is full of dialogue from the moment of its opening with the words "David said." What comes out of David's mouth constitutes a request and a promise. The request, presumably to his servants, is to find out whether there are any surviving Saulides. When someone closely allied to Saul's house turns up, a servant named Ziba, David articulates more clearly that he is looking for a male survivor: "Is there not still a man left from the house of Saul?" (v. 3; cf. v. 1). The first four verses, marked by questions, first as to the existence of a descendant of Saul and next as to his whereabouts, concern themselves with the search for the survivor. The storyteller wedges David's promise between the questions, both times framed as his intention to "show loyalty" (Hebrew *hesed*), once "on account of Jonathan" (v. 1) and once with reference to the Deity (v. 3) in an expression that serves to underscore the weight of his allegiance. On encountering Jonathan's son, David will once again state his intentions in this fashion (v. 7), returning to the promise he had made to Jonathan (1 Sam 20:14; see also 1 Sam 24:22-23).

The remaining son of Jonathan, Mephiboshet, made a brief appearance in an earlier chapter as the victim of an accident during the flight after the defeat of Saul and Jonathan on Gilboa (2 Sam 4:4). This accident left him crippled in both feet, a fact that Ziba mentions as the first piece of information before he reveals his location to the north in the Transjordan, a place not far from Jabesh Gilead, known for its loyalty to Saul. Mephiboshet's host Machir will turn up later in the story as a supporter and ally of David (17:27). Mephiboshet may not have been so sure of his welcome, for he makes full prostration, a difficult and painful act for someone in his condition, and evidently shows some fear because David's first words to him are "Do not be afraid" (Fokkelman 1981, 29). David assures Jonathan's son of his intentions to take care of him and provide for him in perpetuity: "you will eat food at my table for always" (v. 7).

Subsequently, King David orders Ziba to work the land that was originally Saul's, now belonging to his grandson, and to bring the yield to the court for Mephiboshet's provisions. Presumably, this directive was of some benefit to Ziba also, and all parties seem satisfied with the solution. The phrase for eating "at the king's table" attracts attention by its emphatic fourfold recurrence (vv. 7, 10, 11, and 13), sounding especially redundant at the end when we hear again that "Mephiboshet . . . always ate at the king's table"

(v. 13). Finally, the account notes once more that the one who so benefits from the king's largesse is "crippled in both feet" (v. 13).

So what is this story about? Is David indeed overflowing with loving-kindness, and are his actions here above reproach, as some would have it (Fokkelman 1981, 25–30)? It is of special interest that a story, fitting perfectly as a sequel to the death of Ishboshet (ch. 6), found its place just here, following on the heels of the account of David's conquests. Polzin, who believes that the portrayal of David here is implicitly negative, points out the frequency of words related to service (Hebrew *avad*) occurring in this chapter. Paired with words for serving are those that refer to king and master, the latter gaining density and velocity in vv. 9-13. While chapter 8 emphasized the servitude of the nations, this episode draws attention to the servitude of individuals to David by the repetition of certain words and phrases, including the verb "to bow down" (vv. 6 and 8), a verb that takes on heightened significance in reference to kings (Polzin 1993, 96–99). Certainly, it strikes one as somewhat odd that David would only now, after the death of at least one main rival to the throne, think of his once sworn loyalty to Jonathan. It could be that a later episode describing the gruesome killing of seven remaining Saulides (21:7-10) took place before the events of chapter 9. There may be an intention of kindness or loyalty on David's part, but it is clearly rather late in the day to consider his pledge to Jonathan. Furthermore, a crippled survivor does not pose much of a threat and is hardly in any position to mount a challenge to David's reign. Certainly, this kindness costs David nothing; even the sustenance for his guest, who in a way endures enforced hospitality, comes from the guest's own lands and does no damage to the royal coffers.

Polzin argues that the phrase "eating at the king's table" refers back to the prophecy of 1 Samuel 2 against Eli's house, and by implication against the house of all the kings that were to result from the demand made of Samuel by the people. In the end, only a subservient king will eat at the table of the Babylonian overlord (2 Kgs 25:27), a situation the narrator alludes to in 2 Samuel 9 by references to "survivor," to servitude, and to eating "at the king's table." According to Polzin, the Deuteronomistic historian shapes the telling of the history to signal a prelude to the final debacle that was eventually to befall Israelite kingship. In this way, the status of Mephiboshet ultimately reflects back on the Davidic house and its fate (Polzin 1993, 103). Whatever may have been the purpose of the writers in inserting this story just here, a note of ambiguity creeps in about David's behavior toward those around him.

Disturbance on the Eastern Front (2 Sam 10:1-19)

". . . the war and the affair at the court are interwoven and attuned to each other." (Fokkelman 1981, 41)

Chapter 10 recounts another military campaign that has its conclusion at the end of chapter 12 (12:26-31). The lead-up to the story is another of David's attempts to prove loyalty, *hesed*, this time in the arena of international politics as he sends gifts to the Ammonite king, Hanun, in consolation over the death of his father Nachash. There had apparently been a show of goodwill from Nachash's side toward David (v. 2), although we hear nothing of this in the biblical text. Whatever the grounds were for David's gesture, it backfires in a spectacular way when Hanun sends the ambassadors on their way in a state of humiliation, with hair and clothes cut off to expose nakedness both above and below (v. 4).

For David, the treatment of his messengers is a cause to engage in immediate war with Ammon, and he sends Joab with a war party to fight the Ammonites, who in the meantime have found reinforcements by hiring foreign troops, Arameans and their vassals. Verses 8-14 recount the battle scene with Aram and Ammon in more detail than is usually the case with stories of military engagements in Samuel. Perhaps, as Alter suggests, this attention to detail has the purpose of highlighting the talents of Joab as an able commander (Alter 2001, 246). With words of encouragement, Joab divides his forces between himself and his brother Abishai, the latter taking on the Ammonites while Joab draws up against the Arameans. Because Joab succeeds in his efforts, the Ammonites withdraw, and for the time being the fight with Ammon stops. Joab returns to Jerusalem, and this time David engages a counter attempt initiated by Aram and their king, Hadadezer, to regain the upper hand. A fight ensues at Helam, across the Jordan to the northeast, and David defeats the Arameans so conclusively that they are loath to come again to the aid of the Ammonites who are still lurking in their city pending a decisive battle. It looks then as though all has turned out well for King David, although there is more fighting to come, as the initial verse of the next chapter makes clear.

Most likely, we should view the narrative of these campaigns as providing details of the summary of wars given in chapter 8, where both Aram and Ammon ended in a defeated and subservient position to David. War and all its violent context is in any case the context in which the next episode takes place.

David at Rest (2 Sam 11:1-13)

"This is not a thing men do in Israel, but David is Israel." (Schwartz 1991, 20)

"We have to conclude that David does not actually like women very much, and certainly has no fun with them." (Clines 2009, 226)

By all previous accounts, David is a "man of war." David Clines reports that David's total body count is "something like 140,000 men" (Clines 2009, 216–17). David's masculinity was located for a great part in his capacity to be a battle hero, the very characterization of which made Saul begin to see him as a potential rival (1 Sam 18:6-8). It is the more surprising then that David sends Joab for the next fight while staying at home. Emphatically, David "sends" Joab, while he "sat" in Jerusalem. The opening line places the scene in the spring of the year when "messengers" or "kings" go out to battle. If one omits a Hebrew consonant from the word translated "messengers," the result is the word "kings," and many translations opt for it. In that case, David, by staying home, acts in a way that is uncharacteristic for what kings usually do. Some scholars opt for the reading "messengers" because the word emphasizes the constant going back and forth of messengers and the crucial role they play in this part of the story (Polzin 1993, 115). We note also that in the previous chapter the very "sending" of messengers set off hostile encounters. Perhaps we should read both possibilities in the line, each resounding with its own echoes of contrast and centrality.

Kings at leisure pose a risk to the women in their environment, and so it proves for Bathsheba, whose beauty catches David's eye. When he "sends" to inquire about her, the reply details her family circumstances as both a daughter and a wife, in other words belonging to at least two other men. In a few lines the story recounts that David concludes his sexual activity with Bathsheba as if it were the most ordinary thing to have intercourse with someone else's wife:

> David sent to inquire about the woman
> and they said, "Is this not Bathsheba,
> the daughter of Eliam,
> wife of Uriah the Hittite?"
> So David sent messengers and he took her,
> and he entered her and lay with her,
> and she was ritually clean of her impurity
> then she returned to her house. (2 Sam 11:3-4)

The heretofore sedentary king suddenly engages in a great deal of activity: "he sent (twice), he took, he entered and lay with her" (reading "he entered" with the Septuagint variant as the more logical reading with David the agent). The only action accorded to Bathsheba is that she "returned" to her house. David has apparently no intention of keeping her with him in the harem, which would force her into a divorce from her husband, who is, as it will appear, absent from home (unlike his king!) and at the battlefront.

Rape I (2 Sam 11:1-5)

". . . alas, the story of David and Bathsheba has been mostly read as a love story . . . ." (Scholz 2010, 100)

"Since her consent does not matter, his action equals rape." (Scholz 2010, 100)

The violation of women will become a central part of the unfolding events at David's court, and we pause here a moment to consider more closely the scene many view as David's adulterous affair with Bathsheba, one in which Bathsheba certainly had a role to play. As the story progresses with a king in bed instead of on the battlefield, first for a siesta and then for a sexual encounter, the narrator describes the episode with the greatest economy of words. Instead of fighting, David is "sending" and "lying down," key verbs delineating the actions of the king in this chapter and the next. For a king at rest, David launches rather a good deal of activity. First, he "arose," "walked," and "saw" (v. 2), then he "sent to inquire" and subsequently "sent messengers," "took her," "entered her," and "lay with her." With very few exceptions (vv. 3, 4) David is the subject of the action.

Until v. 5, the narration states of Bathsheba only that she was beautiful, that she just had her menstrual period, and that she returned home. A woman who was subject to the king, who could hardly deny him her body, does not receive a voice in the story until the last lines; thus, she is denied participation as a subject. Certainly, all the signs point to rape. In her discussion of Bathsehba, Cheryl Exum points out that the absence of a role ascribed to Bathsheba amounts to a violation of her "by means of the story." "By portraying her in an ambiguous light, the narrator leaves her vulnerable, not simply to assault by David, but also to misappropriation by those who come after him to spy on the bathing beauty and offer their versions of, or commentary on, the story" (Exum 1996, 23). While this is one way to perceive the narrative, it is also possible to view the silence of Bathsheba and her absence as a subject as pointing an accusing finger at David. At this juncture, the unraveling of his character, made clear in the unnecessary bloodshed and violence on the battlefield in chapter 9, bears its unsavory fruit. His compromised moral vision will unfold more in the next episodes, but here we begin to see the fault lines that run through the king who was a king after God's heart. When he learns that Bathsheba is one man's daughter and another man's wife, he does not hesitate for a moment. She did not belong to him, but he took her anyway, as he took lands and booty from any peoples that came under his rapacious eye.

We note that, with one exception, the text refers to Bathsheba as "the woman" (vv. 2, 3, and 5). The one exception inserts her name with a question mark: "Is this not Bathsheba?" (v. 3). Subsequently, references to her will be as "the wife of Uriah" (11:26; 12:9, 15), until she becomes Bathsheba once again after a resolution of sorts is accomplished (12:24). In the current episode, she might as well not have had a name as far as David is concerned. She serves only in the role as "the woman" to slake his lust. The dreaded "taking" on the part of the king, announced earlier by the prophet Samuel (1 Sam 8:11-16), has come to pass, superseding even that vision, for this king has taken the wife of another, something that was not part of Samuel's dire predictions. Although with a harem at home, and at least one other woman noted for her beauty in his household, he *takes* the one who does not belong to him without consideration, or question, or apparently any opposition from anyone in his environment. The revelation that Bathsheba is ritually clean anticipates her eventual announcement that she is pregnant, but first she goes back to her house. With everyone back in place, there is no reason to suspect anything untoward! That is, however, only the beginning, for she finds out that she is pregnant and at the same time finds her voice:

> Then the woman was pregnant,
> and she sent and told David and she said,
> "I am pregnant!" (2 Sam 11:5)

Her words, only two in Hebrew, *harah anokhi,* occur elsewhere in the Hebrew Bible in the mouth of David's matriarchal ancestor, Tamar, when she faces Judah, her father-in-law by whom she is pregnant, with the evidence of his role in her presumed immoral behavior for which he has condemned her to die (Gen 38:25; *anokhi harah*). Bathsheba, like Tamar, has outsider status as the daughter and wife of a Hittite. Unlike Tamar, Bathsheba does not possess damning evidence, but for the careful listener, her statement, "I am pregnant," echoes the other woman who made the same declaration on the brink of death. Both women suffer violation, one by her father-in-law, one by her king; both send their message as a pointing finger: you are the man!

David is not there yet; he is not ready to face the fact that he has set his feet firmly on the path of wrongdoing and is still unable to look his errors in the face. Rather, he continues to hang on to his sense of being right. He is after all the king and can do as he pleases, certainly with regard to the women in his life.

Murder (2 Sam 11:6-27)

The cruelty, the atrocities, and killing, again and again the main features of the theater of war, have here 'found their way inside' and taken over David's court." (Fokkelman 1986, 94)

We can divide this unit in four subsections: (A) vv. 6-13—David's manipulations in trying to make Bathsheba's husband, Uriah, sleep with his wife in order to hide his own crime and ultimately make Uriah believe he is the father of Bathsheba's child; (B) vv. 14-17—David's orchestration of Uriah's death via his agent, general Joab; (C) vv. 18-15—Joab's instructions to the messenger who will bring the news to David as well as the actual verbal exchange between the messenger and David; and (D) vv. 26-27—a coda to the account, with the notation of Bathsheba becoming a part of David's harem and giving birth to their child. While the narrative could have ended there, the last lines of v. 27 open in a new direction with the note that God has taken serious exception to David's actions. The verb "send" remains key throughout, with the first two sections beginning with a sending by David's hand and the third with Joab's sending, while the coda contains another sending on David's part.

David's Manipulations (vv. 6-13). Verse 6 contains the verb "send" three times, ending with the *sending* of Uriah to David by Joab. Much of the unit consists of speech between the two protagonists, David and Uriah. The location is the palace, the "house of the king," while Uriah's house remains out of bounds by his own intention. The word "house" occurs eight times in the span of seven verses, alternating between the "house of the king," the center of power, and the "house" of Uriah, the soldier, the house that poses a threat to the house of the king. The magnitude of the threat the soldier's house poses to David's house will only gradually become clear. David tries to make Uriah "go down to his house" to lie with his wife, but each time Uriah instead "lies down" with the staff at the palace gate, thwarting the intent of "his master" (vv. 8, 9, 10, 13).

David's opening words to Uriah as he faces the man he has betrayed are all about well-being:

> Uriah came to him
> and David asked if it went well with Joab,
> went well with the people,
> and went well with the war. (2 Sam 11:7)

Each time he inquires, he uses the word *shalom*, inserting a note of heavy irony for he certainly does not have *shalom* in mind for the man before him. Without further niceties, he orders Uriah to go home and "wash his feet," creating a note of ambiguity as the biblical text may use the word "feet" to refer to genitalia. Uriah, however, does not go home, but "lies down" instead at the palace gate, a use of a verb that can indicate sexual intercourse in contrast with the soldier's custom of refraining from sexual relations.

When David hears of this, he questions Uriah (v. 10) and receives a reply that makes clear Uriah has no intention to take his ease with his wife "while neither Ark, nor the troops, enjoy proper shelter" (Alter 1999, 252). These are the only words Uriah speaks, and they cast him as a paragon of virtue. On the other hand, he may have heard of David's shenanigans with his wife and is simply not going to oblige the king. His thoughts or knowledge are not recorded. He was in the company of palace folk, who would almost certainly have known of the matter, as servants often do, and they may well have informed him. On the other hand, his words may reflect a sincere determination to share in his comrades' deprivations, even while away from the battlefield. In any case, he speaks passionately and takes an oath on refusing the king's order (v. 11). Despite the strong language, David makes two more attempts, going so far as to inebriate Uriah, but all is in vain, and it ends with Uriah not going down to his house (v. 13).

David's Orchestrations (vv. 14-17). Once again, David "sends," this time a letter by the hand of Uriah instructing Joab to bring about the soldier's death by placing him alone in a vulnerable spot. David thus makes Uriah the conveyor of his own execution, and Joab his henchman—particularly sordid notes in a tale filled with examples of David's cruel and manipulative behavior. The brief story of Uriah's death exhibits great economy; before we know it, David achieves his goal. Among other deaths in the siege of Rabbah, there "died also Uriah the Hittite" (v. 17).

The manner in which Joab follows David's instructions is not entirely clear. David instructs Joab to put Uriah in the front and then to withdraw from him so that he will be killed. Joab, on the other hand, puts Uriah in a place "where he knew there were warriors" (v. 16). It could be, as Alter and others surmise, that Joab did not agree with his master's plan, which would make the ploy all too obvious, and therefore arranged to have others die together with Uriah (Alter 1999, 254). It could also be, however, that Joab simply did not comply. Who, after all, was to tell David of this failure to carry out orders of which only he and David knew? He could simply pretend to have done as his king asked and, should Uriah survive, assert that the plot had not worked. As it happens, arranged or not, Uriah does die together with other soldiers.

Joab's Report (vv. 18-25). Now it is Joab's turn to send, and he does so by means of a messenger who brings David news of the battle and the death of Uriah. Joab's speech to the messenger is elaborate and hypothetical. It consists of words Joab anticipates the king to speak in anger, but his anger never comes to pass (v. 20). The hypothetical speech Joab imputes to David makes reference to the story of Abimelech (Judg 9:52-54) and his death by the hand of a woman, leaving a strong impression that Joab disapproves of David's sexual encounter with the wife of one of his solders, which to his mind can only lead to disaster.

As it is, there is no report of David's asking the question Joab expected. It could be that he did ask, since the messenger's speech begins in the manner of a response: "because the men were strong against us" (v. 23). The messenger dutifully reports the death of Uriah, the Hittite—"your servant Uriah, the Hittite, is dead" (v. 24)—repeating the root "to die" for the third time in this unit. There is an anticipatory note here of the events of the next chapter where deadly catastrophe will envelop another innocent. At this point, David lets the messenger go back to Joab with a platitude about war causing many deaths and encouragement not to let it bother him. In Alter's words, he counsels the messenger to tell Joab that "every bullet has its billet" (v. 25). David's words that "the matter should not be evil" in Joab's eyes anticipate the note at the end of the chapter that the matter is evil in someone's eyes indeed (v. 27).

Coda (vv. 26-27). In a few strokes, the narrative speeds up the story through the period of mourning on Bathsheba's part, her becoming a member of David's harem, and the birth of their son. All has come to a good end with David's "house," it seems. David's machinations have worked, and he has done the right thing by Bathsheba. Had it not been for the last words, this could have been the wrap-up of the events. Another "sending" is about to begin, however, for the matter that should not seem "evil" to Joab, or to David, or perhaps to the reader, does not sit well with God at all:

> And evil was the matter that David had done
> in the eyes of the Holy One. (2 Sam 11:27)

There is one who does not always agree with David's intentions (see ch. 7), one served by those ready to speak truth to power.

The Verdict (2 Sam 12:1-15)

"Far from making us reevaluate our beliefs, external opposition—especially opposition that we perceive as threatening or insulting—tends to make us dig our heels in even more." (Schulz 2010, 151)

In her discussion of our love of being right and our distaste for being wrong, Kathryn Schulz reviews the difficulty in swaying people from erroneous beliefs and actions, with the example of the Swiss Canton of Appenzell, where women did not gain the voting franchise until 1990. In that case, under a great deal of outside pressure, the Appenzellers stood firm in their wrongheadedness for a long time. Outside pressure made them, in fact, even more adamant, and moved them to a "more extreme position" (Schulz 2010, 151). If one looks at the previous sequence of events from this vantage point, it becomes clear that David had several opportunities to see the error of his ways and to do something about it instead of bending all his energies to making his problems go away. First, he receives information that Bathsheba has a husband, a man who is one of his own soldiers. This information should have been sufficient to turn him from his immediate desire. In stark contrast, the text records that David "sent . . . and took her" (11:3). Next, Bathsheba sends him a message about her pregnancy, which could have given him pause for thought; he might then have sought to remedy the situation in a way that would preserve Bathsheba's honor and save Uriah's life, even if at some cost to his own reputation. He could have used this revelation to confess his wrongdoing and to set himself once again in the sanctuary to seek God's counsel in prayer. Rather, Bathsheba's announcement drives him into another wrongheaded action, the attempt to manipulate Uriah into a position where he would eventually appear to be the father of the child to be born. At this point, Uriah defies him, showing him that even a Hittite can be a more faithful believer than an Israelite king. Another opening then appears for David not to continue on his destructive path. Faced as he is with Uriah's implacable opposition to his plan, he might have come to his senses and seen the error of his ways. But, as happened with the Appenzellers of Switzerland, Uriah's opposition drives him further into his erroneous way of thinking and acting. He may well have felt Uriah's words to be insulting. This soldier, not even an Israelite, points out to him that everyone else is out in the field fighting, so he should not take his ease at home. Is Uriah implying that he, the king, should be out on the battlefield, too? Hence, the disastrous decision to have Uriah killed follows with David digging in his heels and letting one bad decision create another. Finally, Joab's hypothetical speech regarding the threat to a political leader's life from a woman's hand, which the messenger may have conveyed although the text does not repeat it, could have served as a warning and afforded the occasion for David's eyes to open to the extent of the crimes he had committed. Rather than having this effect, Joab's words solidified his sense that he had made the right decisions; Uriah is dead, after all, so now life can go on as if there had been no rape, no Uriah. Joab's words, too, may have felt insulting to David. Who, after all, was Abimelech compared to the anointed King David? To convince someone that they are wrong, especially in serious matters, takes a special and artful type of argument, and by now David has missed several opportunities to become aware of what he has done.

The unit opens with God "sending" Nathan, who, rather than announcing judgment on God's behalf, begins by telling a story, ostensibly placing a case before the king that demands his judgment. "There was a man" is a traditional way of beginning a tale (1 Sam 1:1, for example). The sparse language paints a vivid picture of the two main characters with the pet lamb between them. The two men are opposites, one rich and one poor; one has everything, the other nothing. Well, he had something—a ewe lamb that was like his own child ("It was to him like a daughter," v. 3). Regardless of the position of the lamb in the household, regardless of the affection she received from her owners, she ends up in the pot of the rich character, who makes a meal of her for a wayfarer. David does not even have to be asked, and bursts out with his verdict before Nathan requests it. He pronounces the death sentence on the rich man with a penalty of fourfold restitution for the lamb. The sternness of David's tone and the disproportionate nature of his sentence make clear how efficiently Nathan has told his story.

Now David is caught in the net of fabrication that Nathan has woven for him. Once he declares the reason for his sentence, that "he did this thing and had no pity," the words rebound and David sits self-accused. "This thing" (Hebrew *davar*) was the thing that David counseled Joab not to feel bad about, the thing that was indeed bad in God's eyes, the rape of Bathsheba followed by the murder of her husband. David did "this thing" and "had no pity." Once Nathan has the king exactly where he wants him, he can turn David's accusing finger around to point to himself.

Nathan's story turned out to be a parable, and, as all parables do, it demands a judgment. As with all parables also, the listener's judgment may in the end fall on her or his own head. Parables are mirrors for listeners to look into and recognize themselves and their shortcomings. It takes a moment before David gets there, but with Nathan's help he does, for after Nathan utters his "you are the man!" there is no doubt that David recognizes himself as the rich man who took the one cherished being in the household of his poor neighbor. If we consider the parable again, the identity of the rich man may be obvious, but the identity of the lamb is less clear. The lamb is slaughtered, but in the real world Uriah was murdered and Bathsheba lived. Yet the mention of the lamb as daughter, *bat* in Hebrew, is a clear reference to Bathsheba. The lamb, denoted by a word that occurs only in three other places, two of which refer to it in the context of sacrifice (Lev 13:10; Num 6:14), is also female. A lamb has no voice, of course; it cannot protest its fate or have agency of its own. The parable clearly points to David's dealings with Bathsheba as that of a rich man who takes a defenseless, voiceless being for his own gratification and pleasure. The violation of Bathsheba is as much an assault on her being as the murder of Uriah is:

> and he thought it a pity to take from his flock and cattle,
> to prepare a meal for the one who came to him.
> He took the ewe lamb of the poor man
> and prepared it for the man who came to him. (2 Sam 12:4)

The word here used for pity can also be translated "to spare," a word that reverberates with meaning in the Saul and David story. Saul once "spared" the life of the Amalekite king and was severely punished for it (1 Sam 15:9, 15); Saul once praised David because David "spared" his life (1 Sam 23:21). When David pronounces judgment on the man, he gives the word another twist on the grounds that "he had no pity." Precisely then Nathan utters the statement "You are the man" (v. 7a), because it was David of course who had no pity, neither for Bathsheba or Uriah nor for Joab, whom he forced into collusion with his nefarious plan.

Once David prayed before God, enumerating all the great things God had done on his behalf (2 Sam 7:18-22). In the judgment speech that follows the accusation, God flings back in David's face all the things God has done for him: anointing David, rescuing David from the hand of Saul, giving David the house of his master, the wives of his master, and the house of Israel and Judah. In return for all this *giving* on God's part, David started to *take*, unlawfully, the wife of Uriah and Uriah's life. So God sets up a new process of giving and taking: taking the wives of David and giving them to "his neighbor" (v. 11), who will lie with David's wives in broad daylight, in contrast to the secretive way in which David behaved. These harsh, punitive words drive home the truth that in all this, David "despised" the God who had treated him so generously. The verb "despise," which occurs here twice (vv. 9 and 10) in relation to God, recalls the prophetic speech to Eli in 1 Samuel that informs Eli's house of its doom on account of having *despised* God (1 Sam 2:30).

David confesses his sin but is not able thereby to avert the immediate consequence, the death of the child born to Bathsheba, a death that follows the gratuitous murder of Uriah. The narrator unflinchingly makes God the cause of the illness and death of the child, creating one of the most unpalatable events in this difficult history, the death of a being who was no less innocent than the ewe lamb in the poor man's lap—a newborn child—at the hand of God. Another victim falls in the chain of events set in motion by David's wrongdoing, and it will not be the last one.

Death of a Child (2 Sam 12:16-25)

"In place of David the seeker and wielder of power, we now see a vulnerable David, and this is how he will chiefly appear through the last half of the story." (Alter 1999, 262)

Whereas the first part of the chapter consists almost entirely of speech, the text now turns to narrative. In a sparse yet vividly descriptive report, it tells of the illness and death of the child, presenting in detail David's reactions both to the sickness of the baby and to his death. First, David does what he should have been doing all along when faced with the consequences of his wrongdoing: he prays (v. 16). He also fasts, an action more appropriate for mourning a death than trying to forestall one. His servants obviously think his reaction inappropriate and extravagant, perhaps a sign of their master not being in his right mind. In vain, they try to raise him. Then the child dies, and one can almost see them whispering in a corner, too afraid of their master's reactions to tell him of the death of the boy. David has become a true king wielding great power and sometimes unpredictable in his reactions.

> And on the seventh day the child died.
> And David's servants were afraid
> to tell him that the child was dead;
> for they said, "Look, while the child was alive,
> we spoke to him and he did not heed our voice.
> How can we say to him, "The boy is dead!"
> He will do something evil."
> David saw his servants whispering to each other,
> and David understood the child was dead;
> so David said to his servants,
> "Is the boy dead?"
> They said, "Dead!" (2 Sam 12:18-19)

Six times the verb "die" occurs in this passage, three times before and three times following the line, "He will do something evil." Death thus encircles the mention of *evil*, the evil that the servants fear David will do, in an ironic note, for of course David has already done the evil that caused the death of innocents of which this boy is the most striking example. The end of the section shows extreme economy with David uttering two words in Hebrew and the servants replying with one.

As soon as David hears the news, he resumes ordinary activities, rising, cleaning, and dressing himself, worshiping God in the sanctuary, and finally eating. This activity clearly baffles his servants, who question him about the absence of signs of mourning, fasting, and praying now that the time for it has come (v. 21). David answers them with a clear and unvarnished sample of his state of mind. He prayed because during the child's illness he continued to believe in the possibility of God relenting—"I thought, 'Who knows, the Holy One may repent'" (v. 22)—resulting in the healing of the child. Fasting and praying were appropriate for that moment. Now that the child is dead, that time is over. David's fast was anticipatory but also an attempt to avert the disaster and, as such, it resembles the fast of Esther before she goes to implore the king to ward off the ruin that is threatening to overcome her people (Esth 4:16). He cannot bring the child back to life. Instead, he, David, will eventually end up just like his now dead son: "I am going to him, and he will not come back to me." David thus faces his own mortality through the death of a child and speaks of it in a bleakly realistic tone, stripped of all deception and blandishments. For the moment, the deceitful, violent, manipulative David has disappeared. Yet the sequel will show a weakened character who has lost the clear-eyed decision-making skills that once served him so well.

Subsequently, comfort follows death, as David resumes sexual relations with Bathsheba, who now appears in the text as "his wife" (v. 24). The tempo of the narrative speeds up. She gives birth once again to a son who receives a second name, as God's beloved, in a message related by the prophet Nathan (v. 25). Solomon, here set on the stage, will eventually benefit from Nathan's support of his claim to the throne (1 Kgs 1:11-40) when Nathan's intervention on Solomon's behalf will prove crucial, a reason perhaps for inserting the note on this double naming (Alter 1999, 263). His mother gives him a name that connotes well-being, *shalom,* while the God-given name points to the favor he will find with God. Hopeful notes for the future thus round off a story of violation, deception, and murder.

The Sack of Rabbah (2 Sam 12:26-31)

"The reports of war form the framework in which 11:26-31 is enacted . . . ." (Fokkelman 1986, 94)

Continuing with positive reports, the chapter ends with a short account of the final victory over Ammon, with whom war began in chapter 10. According to Fokkelman, the coda about victory over Ammon at the end of the narrative that tells of David, Bathsheba, and Uriah is a flashback, intentionally inserted here to create a note of optimism at the conclusion and above all to construct a frame of war and violence around the central story, which is essentially a "war episode" (Fokkelman 1986, 94). In addition, the brief review depicts Joab in a favorable light as having done the heavy lifting, but wanting to leave the glory of the moment to his king (v. 27). David goes to battle and conquers, gathering more booty to his already accumulating hoard and, rather than slaughtering Ammon's population, putting them to forced labor (v. 31). Instead of the "sitting" king who engaged in all manner of mischief (11:1), we now have the king "returning" to Jerusalem, crowned with the laurels of victory, as a proper war leader should.

Certainly, the end brings into view a David we thought we knew: competent, victorious, and not overly cruel toward defeated populations. Yet, in a sense, one may also view the framework of war as ironically contrastive. The public David is still a competent military leader, while the private David has shown an altogether different picture of a man whose machinations, though successful, belonged to a category of evil that God did not countenance. It remains to be seen how much of the private David will bleed over into the public arena, as it inevitably must in the case of political leaders.

A King and His Sons (2 Sam 13:1–14:33)

"This is a man's story, a story about kings and would-be kings." (Goldingay 2000, 257)

Like Eli and Samuel before him, David has sons who do not show loyalty to their father, and as in Eli and Samuel's case, his sons' rebellious ways are intricately interwoven with the larger political scene. Oddly, it was the unworthy Saul whose sons remained at his side, in spite of his irascible and capricious nature. David's sons fight not only against their parent but also among one another. Their rivalries, with both their father and each other, will prove a serious threat to the stability of the young kingdom. The two chapters before us form a prelude in two major parts to the larger story of Absalom's rebellion against his father. The first part, chapter 13, unfolds the tale of Absalom's brother Amnon and his rape of Tamar, who was Absalom's sister, with its aftermath, the murder of Amnon by Absalom. In the second part, chapter 14, a wise woman comes to convince King David to bring Absalom, who lives in self-imposed exile, back to Jerusalem. In truth, David's general Joab has sent the woman to him. At the end of chapter 14, the turmoil seems to have died down, with David and Absalom reconciled, but the peace is only superficial and will not last long.

Each part of this introduction to the story of Absalom's treachery exhibits a weakened king who is in turn hesitant to dispense justice when it concerns his wayward sons, just as Eli and Samuel had been, too harsh in his treatment, or too forgiving in the face of heinous crimes. David becomes the unwitting participant in his own daughter's violation by her brother and in the aftermath is helpless to stop the carnage brought about by Absalom. Just as once David came on the scene as a beautiful young pretender to the throne (1 Sam 16:12), so the would-be king Absalom appears as a beautiful specimen (14:25-26). Counselors will play a significant role in each of the two chapters and in the sequel, although their counsel may be ambiguous, while, from now on, God is almost entirely absent and does not intervene in the debacle about to take place.

The location of the story narrows from the concluding section of chapter 12 with its return of the king to Jerusalem to focus on the royal residence with its separate "houses" for David's offspring. The Hebrew word for house, *bayit*, occurs first in v. 7 and thereafter in key places (vv. 7, 8, 20). Tamar moves from her own residence to Ammon's to end up in the house of her brother Absalom. The subtext here is that the *house* of David in a larger sense is becoming less and less stable. The evil that God threatened to bring against the king from his own house (12:11) has begun to play itself out. Of course, within an even larger framework, the fate of the "house" of the nation comes into view also, a fate that in the perspective of the story's writers ended in a ruin for which perhaps Tamar, the "desolate woman" of v. 20, functions as the metaphor. The significance of "house" arises once again at the end of chapter 14, with King David and his violent son Absalom each residing in their separate houses until a reconciliation of sorts comes about. This seeming appeasement of alienation between the two houses is only temporary. Soon the house of David will be shaken to its foundations.

Rape II (2 Sam 13:1-22)

"Sustain me with raisin cakes,
refresh me with apples,
for I am sick with love." (Song 2:5)

"You have ravished my heart, my sister, my bride,
you have ravished my heart, with one glance of your eyes." (Song 4:9)

This section of chapter 13 stands out among the narratives of the books of Samuel, material that in general exhibits outstanding skill in storytelling, for its vivid detail and the attention it pays to the inner lives of the characters who participate in the events. As Bar-Efrat has observed, one clearly delineated scene follows another with a slow building of tension (Bar-Efrat 1989, 276). When tension partially resolves itself at the end of the episode, the text introduces renewed tension by mentioning the hatred Absalom feels for his brother Amnon, a hatred that must eventually find an outlet. The story begins with love, but for quite a while the reader/listener is unsure of the nature of this love. Only when the love finds its outlet in a hateful deed does one become aware of the precise quality of Amnon's feelings for Tamar, the sister of Absalom. Love's path ends in hate for both brothers, as Amnon hates Tamar after his violation of her (v. 15), and Absalom hates his brother for what he has done to his (Absalom's) sister (v. 22).

Words for siblings occur more often in this section than anywhere else in the texts of Samuel. Tamar comes on the scene as Absalom's sister rather than David's daughter (v. 1), and so Amnon identifies her when he speaks to his friend Jonadab (v. 4). Jonadab calls her Amnon's sister (vv. 5, 6), and Amnon appears as her brother (vv. 7, 8, 10, 12, 20). Amnon addresses Tamar once as "my sister" before he forces himself on her. In the end, the narrator returns to calling her the sister of Absalom (vv. 20, 22). If love turning to hate is the motivational fuel that moves the story forward, Amnon's hate for the sister he violated precipitates Absalom's hate for his brother. Tamar is caught between these two as the victim of male power. While she does not go silently to her doom, she ends up silenced by her powerful brother who, at the same time, acts as her protector and provides her with shelter: "Tamar stayed desolate in the house of Absalom her brother" (v. 20).

Throughout the episode, the terminology reminds the reader both of relations between lovers and of violence among "brothers" that swirls around an initial deed of sexual violation. In the Song of Songs, the declaration "I am sick with love" occurs twice (2:5 and 5:8), the first time with an appeal for food to provide comfort (see above). The term for the nourishment that Tamar is asked to provide derives from a rare root in Hebrew, *barah,* occurring only in the 2 Samuel material as a word for food intended to revive one stricken by grief or mourning. The same verb occurred in the previous chapter in connection with David's intense grief over the illness of his child (12:17). A link to the Song is also visible in the baking of "heart-shaped cakes" as well as in Amnon's appeal to Tamar as "my sister" (v. 11; cf. Song

4:9 and Fokkelman 1981, 105–106). Finally, multiple references to "lying down" and the substantive "couch," which in Hebrew directly derives from the root for lying down, evoke images of lovemaking. In contrast to the connotations of love, the threat of violence, never far from the action in this chapter, echoes other tales of rape and destruction (cf. Gen 34; 39; Judg 19). The mantle of love actually thinly camouflages the hatred that simmers just beneath the surface and that comes to full boil at certain points.

Spatially, the action moves from residence to room to inner chamber (v. 10), thus casting a net over Tamar that becomes more and more restrictive and confining. As a victim of incestuous rape, in the end she has lost her social standing, to say nothing of her peace of mind, even though only her brother Absalom and a few intimates of Amnon know of what took place. The Hebrew word "desolate" refers elsewhere to places that have been ravaged by an enemy and made uninhabitable (Lam 1:4; Isa 54:3; Jer 12:11). Tamar has become a site of loneliness and desolation, like a city made uninhabitable by the rampaging power of the enemy.

The scene opens with Amnon ill on account of his love for Tamar, the beautiful sister of Absalom, whose name takes first place among the four names that come to the fore in the opening, signaling the figure who will be central to the story for a good deal of what follows (v. 1). In addition, both Absalom and Amnon receive the specific designation of David's sons. Instead of introducing Tamar with the expected label of David's daughter, the narrative identifies her as Absalom's sister, thus as one caught between the two brothers from the beginning. Sick with love for Tamar, it seems impossible to Amnon "to do something to her," "for she was a virgin," an issue that apparently weighed heavier than the incestuous implications. When the latter subject arises in the narrative, it is according to Tamar's words a solvable problem (v. 13).

Seeing his friend and cousin Amnon sick with love, Jonadab counsels him to make a plan to get Tamar to visit him and revive his body and spirit. In each reference to the plan, first by Jonadab (v. 5), then by Amnon (v. 6), and finally by David, the word "nourishment" occurs with its association of restoring a person to health and healing. The narrator leaves the purpose of Tamar's visit and provision of nourishment, as planned by Jonadab, unclear, and it is not certain that he had in mind what eventually takes place. Jonadab may have been a true friend to Amnon, wanting to see Amnon's spirits revive through watching the movements of his beautiful sister as she prepares food. On the other hand, it may have been Jonadab's intention all along to aid Amnon in his attempt at greater intimacy than watching. When asking his father to send for Tamar, Amnon introduces the refinement of the "heart-shaped cakes," where Jonadab's counsel mentioned the more general word "food," Hebrew *lehem.*

Heart-shaped cakes Amnon wants and these he gets, as Tamar prepares them in his presence. In v. 8, the action slows almost to a standstill as we watch Tamar taking dough, kneading, shaping it into hearts, and baking it "before his eyes." Tension rises with every verb of which she is the subject. Next, Tamar offers her brother the cakes she has prepared, but instead of eating, Amnon orders his retinue out of the room, clearing the stage, and invites his sister into yet another, more private space, the "inner chamber," promising that there he will eat from her hand. The inner chamber is the closeted private space where there will be no observers. It is the space of lovemaking in the Song of Songs (1:4 and 3:4), where the king and the female lover in turn "bring" the beloved. Now Tamar is ordered to "bring" the nourishing, reviving food into the most private space the prince, her brother, can think of—his bedroom.

Once confined with her in the most private space, his true purpose becomes clear as he grabs her and invites her to yet greater intimacy: "Come, lie with me, my sister" (v. 11). The invitation echoes the words of Potiphar's wife to Joseph (Gen 39:7, 12), while the address "my sister" uses the language of love (Song 4:9). Amnon's true intentions toward his sister are now clear, and for the first time Tamar speaks. Thus far, she has been a silent and compliant participant in the proceedings, doing exactly what her father and brother tell her to do. Tamar, however, will be not be a silent participant in the ravaging of her person that will leave her a desolate woman:

> She said to him,
> "No, my brother, do not abuse me,
> for such is not done in Israel.
> Do not commit this disgrace!
> As for me, where would I carry my shame?
> As for you, you will be one disgraced in Israel.
> Now speak please to the king
> for he will not withhold me from you." (2 Sam 13:12-13)

With great presence of mind, she utters a refusal, describes the consequences of what her violation will do to her, and offers a solution. Her first word is "no" followed by "do not," recalling, as several scholars point out, the plea of the Ephraimite in Gibeah to the rapist mob: "Do not, my brothers, do not commit this disgrace" (Judg 19:23). In all, Tamar utters the negative four times. The deed would amount to abuse of her person, and it is a thing "not done" in Israel. She calls it "a disgrace" that would bring shame on her and disgrace on her brother. Other places with the word "disgrace" refer to sexual crimes (Gen 34:7; Deut 22:21; Judg 20:6, 10). After all, Tamar observes, if Amnon has honorable intentions toward her, he only has to speak to the king, who will certainly be accommodating in this affair.

Amnon's response to her pleas is to force sex on her (v. 14). Time speeds up, and the report of the wicked deed requires only one verse that omits particulars, for the story hastens to tell of a second crime he commits against his sister. Having had his way with her, his love turns to hate, and his hate is greater than the love he once thought to have. With harsh words, he orders her to leave. When she protests, almost in a stutter of despair and indignation ("Do not . . . This wrong is greater than the other that you did to me, sending me away!" v. 16), he calls a servant to throw her out. In his orders to the servant, he refers to Tamar with the pronoun *zot*, "this one," treating her as "something loathsome, as someone without identity" (Bar-Efrat 1989, 256). To add yet more to his despicable treatment of his sister, he orders the door closed behind her, as though he expects her to return and importune him. The last sounds we hear from Tamar are her loud cries of protest and despair (v. 19).

Between Amnon's order to his attendant and the action of leading her out, the narrator notes that Tamar's clothing is "an ornamented tunic," such as the ones worn by the virgin daughters of the king. While the mention of specific garments is rather rare in the biblical material, it is even more striking here because the word for Tamar's robe is the same as the word for the one Joseph wore before he underwent the abusive treatment of his brothers (Gen 37:3, 31-33) and does not occur outside these two narratives. Joseph's robe was also torn and bloodied, serving as silent witness to kin strife, just as the robe torn by Tamar testifies to the disgrace her brother meted out to her. She, who went in to her brother's house ready to provide reviving nourishment, is now outside in a posture of loud and public mourning. The verb for her crying out carries implications of protest and legal action.

Absalom finds her in this state. He counsels her to be quiet and end her public commotion, for Amnon is after all her brother and she should not "take this thing to heart." Absalom's words, although perhaps motivated by kind intentions, have the effect of silencing Tamar for good. No longer one of the "virgin daughters of the king" or in a position to enter into marriage with anyone, she "stayed desolate in the house of Absalom, her brother." Neither brother behaves toward Tamar in a way that recognizes and honors her personhood. One rapes and humiliates her, and the other silences her so that it becomes impossible to take her plight to the king, the one expected to dispense equity and justice.

Amnon, who early in the story may have elicited some sympathy for his plight, has lost all right to feelings of respect and loyalty. He was the firstborn son of David, born to David and Ahinoam from Jezreel (2 Sam 3:2-3), and has acted in a disgraceful way. Like David in his dealings with Bathsheba and Uriah, he had a number of opportunities to change course and refrain from violating his sister. He could have done so when Jonadab first proposed his plan, or when the king visited him, or when Tamar prepared the cakes in his presence. He could certainly have done so when she uttered her protest and pled with him to take a different approach. Finally, the door is still ajar to a possibility at least of easing the suffering of Tamar by marrying her after the rape, an obligation spelled out in the Torah (Deut 22:28-29). Neither time does he listen to her: "he did not want to heed her (voice)" (vv. 14, 16). Like his father, he persists in his wrongdoing, piling humiliation on his act of violence until it is too late to reverse course.

The last two verses of the story bring into view the reactions of both the king and the brother Absalom to what has transpired. David "heard all these things" and became very angry, but does not do anything to call his son to account (v. 21). He who made it his priority to dispense "justice and equity to all his people" (8:15) is not able to act justly within his family circle. About Absalom, the narrator explicitly states that he kept silent vis-à-vis Amnon, and ends with the observation that Absalom hated Amnon "because he had violated Tamar, his sister" (v. 22). This ending clearly introduces new tension into the story, alerting the reader/listener that there is more to come. For the moment, the situation may seem quiet, although grievous, but it will probably not stay that way for long.

Death of a Son (2 Sam 13:23-39)

"In Israel there is no place for Amnon." (Schwartz 1991, 208)

The mayhem and destruction in the aftermath of David's wrongdoing toward Bathsheba and Uriah are only just beginning. We can divide the second unit of chapter 13 into three parts: Absalom's preparations to murder Amnon (vv. 23-27); the murder itself and the reaction to it by David and the court (vv. 28-33); and Absalom's flight to his grandfather's court (vv. 34-39). Whereas the space of the preceding encounters confined itself to royal residences, narrowing down to an inner chamber, the events that follow take place in a larger arena, opening out from Jerusalem to the countryside and ending in another country altogether. Yet the wider, fresher air of the story portrays not freedom and liberation from evil plans but rather forms the backdrop for the ever-widening violence that spreads out over royal family and kingdom. The lead phrase in each of the subsections, "all the sons of the king," indicates the danger threatening the Davidic house (vv. 23, 27, 29, 30, 32, 33).

We may imagine Absalom nursing hate for his brother Amnon on account of his sister Tamar and at the same time contemplating the possibility of getting rid altogether of the one first in the line of succession, while he, Absalom, is only the third. An occasion presents itself after two years during a sheep shearing, commonly a time of celebration and feasting and of showing hospitality to invited guests. Two years have elapsed, a time signifier that shows Absalom knows to bide his time. Enough time has gone by for King David, who may have had his suspicions about Absalom's feelings, at least to have set aside the thought that Absalom might be up to no good where it concerns his brother Amnon. Even so, Absalom first invites the king himself to the celebration, clearly overreaching so that his eventual request will not sound so outrageous. When, predictably, David refuses, the appeal to have Amnon attend the festivities appears as a kind of compromise. He is, after all, the crown prince, and therefore an appropriate stand-in for the king. In this way, Absalom cleverly maneuvers his father into cooperating with the eventual demise of one of his sons. The king, probably aware of the estrangement between his sons, may imagine that Absalom is looking for an occasion to reconcile with Amnon. That he is not entirely easy in his mind regarding Absalom's intentions becomes evident from the fact that he sends all his sons with Amnon: "and he sent with him Amnon and all the sons of the king" (v. 27).

The preparations for the murder of Amnon show Absalom in a new light. In the aftermath of Tamar's rape, he revealed himself as a protective brother who in his efforts to protect his sister deprived her at the same time of voicing the crime committed against her. In addition, while, like his father, he kept silent, he hated his brother for what he had done, a comment that raises expectations for the future of these two, because hatred of this nature needs to find an outlet. As Absalom prepares for the sheep shearing, he initially invites "all the king's sons" (v. 23), then singles out his father, who is unlikely to take time off for such an occasion, and finally focuses on Amnon, a seemingly unnecessary move because he would be one of "all the sons." The mention of "all the sons" at the end of the unit underlines the danger that looms for the house of David in the person of Absalom, a theme that will continue in the sequel. Absalom shows himself to be both clever and manipulative in his dealings with his father, who is beginning to appear all too indulgent toward his sons.

The narrative wastes no time on placing the characters in the correct location, but moves directly to the plan and execution of the murder, which Absalom arranges through the agency of his servants (v. 28). The tale of the murder itself takes up little space, revealing no detail, simply stating that the "lads of Absalom did to Amnon as Absalom commanded" (v. 29). The somewhat bland verb "to do" (Hebrew *asah*) paints only the most general picture, but harkens back to the "*doing*" of the thing that was "not *done* in Israel," as Tamar put it. Later she reproaches her brother for piling on her a greater wrong than the "other you *did* to me" (vv. 12, 16). The doer of all these misdeeds now is done to, and the hand that metes out justice is not that of his indulgent father but that of his far more violent and dangerous brother. The murder causes "all the king's sons" to panic, and they flee the scene of feasting that has now become a place of bloodshed.

A switch in focus turns the attention to David and his courtiers, who react to the erroneous news that Absalom has murdered "all the king's sons." Whereas the murder received little attention, the narrative dwells at relative length on the reactions of king and court. The report that all the sons of David are dead causes a scene of general mourning, with the king the first to tear his clothes and his servants following his example. The mourning that in the earlier episode caused Tamar to tear her tunic now has spread to the entire court, even though the report is false. As such, it also anticipates David's subsequent reactions to his traitorous son's behavior (15:30) and to the death of the same (19:1-5). Once again, Jonadab enters the scene. He who earlier had counseled Amnon now tries to convince David that this report about "all the lads, the king's sons" must be false and points out that it concerns only Amnon, whose death had been in Absalom's mind since the violation of his sister. Twice he states "Amnon only is dead," his entire address to the king ending with the word "dead" (vv. 32-33).

The final section brings Absalom in view once again and begins with the news of his flight, clearly in a different direction than his brothers, whose return to Jerusalem we see through the eyes of a guard. Jonadab again reassures the king, and the father and his sons are reunited, all of them weeping. The word "look" (Hebrew *hinneh*) three times draws attention to the arrival of royal sons: first from the perspective of the guard who says, "Look, a great many people" (v. 34); then from the point of view of Jonadab who declares, "Look, the king's sons have come" (v. 35); and finally through the eyes of the narrator who announces the safe arrival of the sons with the same phrase, "look, the king's sons came" (v. 36). All this safe arriving causes no rejoicing, however, but only more tears.

The section ends with a precise indication of the location of Absalom's flight. He seeks refuge with his grandfather Talmai in Geshur, in the northeast, a place where he could apparently count on safety. David, meanwhile, mourns his son every day (v. 37), although it is unclear which son he mourns, Amnon or Absalom. In reality, three sons have now been taken from him, two by death and one by self-imposed exile. This part of the tale, one that began with the word "love," ends in death, as the narrative once again mentions that Amnon is dead (v. 39). This will not be the last death, and the cycle of violence is far from over.

A Wise Woman and Her Son (2 Sam 14:1-20)

"Convoluted or awkward language combines with narrative opacity to make interpretation difficult." (Polzin 1993, 139)

The ending of chapter 13 is opaque in regard to David's feelings toward Absalom, as it mentions either David's continued pining for Absalom or an abatement of hostility on his part (13:39). Equally, the opening lines of chapter 14 do not reveal whether David's mind was fixated *on* Absalom or *against* him (Fokkelman 1981, 131–33, and Polzin 1993, 139). The Hebrew preposition *al* can be explained either way and, in fact, occurs ambiguously three times in this part of the story (vv. 1, 8, 13). Could it be that the ambiguous wording points to the ambiguous feelings of David himself? He must have been angry over Amnon's treatment of Tamar, yet he did nothing; he grieved over the death of his firstborn and must have felt great anger toward Absalom, yet, as becomes clear from the sequel, he loved this son extravagantly. David is divided, torn between anger and love, now leaning more in the one, then in the other direction. This incapacity to steer a clear course in terms of Absalom will cost him dearly. As much as the previous scenes are filled with movement, the subsequent chapter consists almost entirely of conversation, reporting an exchange between the king and a "wise woman," except for the very end, when Absalom once again enters the picture.

It appears that, for whatever reason, Joab does not consider it good for David to have Absalom so far away. Perhaps Joab would also rather have Absalom close by, under his eye, rather than at a distance where he could be plotting who knows what. He corrals a woman known for sound counsel (like Jonadab earlier, she is called "wise," v. 2) and instructs her both as to her appearance and her words, although there is no report on the latter and we must assume that Joab left her a good deal of freedom. She must appear in mourning, however, to draw the immediate attention of the king who will recognize the gravity of her situation from her appearance alone. The woman does as Joab has instructed, and her first words are a plea for help (v. 4). From there on, a conversation between the two takes place. As terse as Nathan's story to make the king see the error of his ways once was (12:1-4), so elaborate and convoluted is the woman's discourse. Her story has many twists and turns before she gets to the point, and there is no sudden reversal of judgment on David's side, as happened on that earlier occasion, but rather a gradual discovery of who orchestrated the encounter and for what purpose.

The Tekoite's speech has three parts: first, she lays out her "case" before David, a case in which one of her sons has killed another with the result that family members are demanding the death of the killer, who turns out to be her only remaining son, the "ember" who would carry on his father's name (vv. 5b-7). To this presentation, the king replies that he himself will give "orders concerning" her (v. 8), using the ambiguous preposition *al.* Clearly, the wise woman is not satisfied with this vague reply and resumes her discourse, making sure that she has the solemn promise of the king that her surviving son will not be harmed (vv. 9-11). She opens her second plea with words proclaiming the king's innocence that echo those of Abigail when she met rebel David in the hills around Carmel (1 Sam 25:24): "On me, my lord, be the responsibility" (v. 9). When the king has assured her that "not a hair of your son's head will fall to the ground" (v. 11), taking an oath on it, she would have gone home in the knowledge that her "case" had found the resolution she sought, had her situation been actually true. Of course, she has not yet revealed the real object of her request, so she goes on speaking (vv. 13-17). In her third and last appeal she addresses the king in the second person, opening with a question about the king's devising (for or against?) the people, which introduces the verb "banish." In contrast to her earlier emphasis on the king's "innocence," she now introduces the thought that the king might be "guilty" in not having recalled "his banished one." Her speech becomes increasingly convoluted, but a few elements stand out. The king has *devised* a plan that may not be in line with the *devising* of God in respect to the "banished one," and he may thus be guilty. As she winds up, references to herself as "maid/servant" come thick and fast, and she ends by comparing the king to a "messenger of God" (v. 17), surely an affirmation that comes across as ironic to the reader/listener who has observed the David of the last episodes.

Most likely, the term "banished one" serves as a revelation for the king, and he now requests whether he may ask the woman something. The man who has been called a messenger of God is shrewd enough to detect which of his servants may be behind this female envoy. She confesses that indeed Joab told her what to say. She ends with a last ironic flourish, both calling the king "wise" and comparing his wisdom to that of a "messenger of God, knowing all that is on earth" (v. 20). That is the last we hear of the wise Tekoite, whose discourse brings to light crucial parts of the affairs of the court up to this point: murder and revenge, guilt and innocence, the schemes of the human heart that go contrary to God's devising, and the huge flaws that have opened up in David's behavior and run directly counter to the flamboyant praise the wise woman heaps upon him.

A Son Returns (2 Sam 14:21-33)

"David continues to see him as a child to the very end." (Fokkelman 1981, 145)

Both Joab and David have "done this thing" (vv. 19, 21), Joab by maneuvering the king into the position of having to recall Absalom, and David by taking an oath, seemingly on behalf of the Tekoite but in truth on behalf of his son. Without further consultation with himself or others, the king orders Joab to bring Absalom back. Tellingly, he refers to his son as "the lad, Absalom," clearly conveying the indulgence he feels toward his wayward offspring. When this same son has turned in full-fledged rebellion against his father, he will once again refer to him in those terms, commanding his soldiers to "go gentle for me on the lad, on Absalom" (18:5, 12). At the same time, he makes what is probably a mistake by emphatically forbidding his son the royal presence: "my face he shall not see!" (v. 24). That phrase, issued once from the king's mouth and repeated affirmatively at the end of the short section, raises renewed tension where all could have been satisfactorily resolved. Joab's machinations have succeeded; prince Absalom is back in Jerusalem. What good, however, is this outcome with father and son separated, each living in their individual houses? As Absalom will observe, he might just as well have stayed in Geshur (v. 32).

An interlude temporarily delays a solution to the tension raised by the emphatic notation of Absalom's presence in Jerusalem with a forced separation from his father (vv. 25-27). It draws attention to the person of Absalom first by describing his extraordinary beauty: "from the sole of his foot to the crown of his head there was in him no blemish" (v. 25). While the beauty of both his father and his sister received mention (1 Sam 16:12; 2 Sam 13:1), the notation here is exceptionally elaborate. The implication is that his appearance made him attractive. Clearly, Absalom's own preoccupation with his looks underlies the subsequent description of his hair, which he had to shave off each year because of its weight. Shaving is one thing, but weighing one's hair may indicate a self-absorption that is not altogether healthy. In addition, of course, the hair provides a proleptic reference to the manner of his death. Alter suggests that there may also be an implied comparison with

Samson at work here, another strong man whose hair became his undoing (Alter 1999, 208). The interlude closes with a reference to Absalom's offspring, an observation that contradicts a later reference to his lack of children (18:18). Here, sons are born to him as well as a daughter, and, contrary to the usual custom of Hebrew narrative, only the daughter receives a name while the sons remain nameless. The name of the daughter is Tamar, like his sister; and like her aunt, she is beautiful (v. 27). The sons may or may not have been; their existence is of no account, for the story once again draws attention to Tamar, the violated sister of Absalom, incestuously raped by her brother, an act that gave rise to the spreading pool of violence that is far from over (Fokkelman 1981, 150). A twofold mention of beauty thus frames the interlude, neither one of them intended to allay tension, even while they postpone the solution of the immediate problem. One mention refers to the future and the larger problem presented by Absalom that is looming on the horizon, and the other refers back to the incident that propelled Absalom's most recent actions forward.

In the concluding unit (vv. 28-33), Absalom is in charge of all the action and controls most of the dialogue. Clearly, the present situation of life in Jerusalem without seeing his father is untenable for him, and Joab, his earlier spokesperson, is unwilling to push matters further. The opening lines once again emphasize the distance between father and son, this time adding a time span of two years: "and the face of the king he did not see" (v. 28). Eventually, Absalom engages in intensive "sending," calling on Joab to help. When Joab refuses twice, Absalom forces him into a confrontation by destroying Joab's property. During the interchange with Joab, which takes place in person, he manages to convince the general to intercede with the king once more, and a reconciliation of sorts comes about.

The picture of Absalom at the end of chapter 14 is now more sharply drawn: a beautiful, vain, and proud prince who does not refrain from violence to obtain his objectives. His words to Joab get at the truth of his predicament and yet leave a taste of duplicity at the same time (v. 32). It is true that self-imposed exile would appear preferable to forced banishment from his father's presence while living in close proximity to him. His challenge that the king just has to kill him, "if" he bears guilt, rings less true. He was guilty after all of killing his brother in a deceptive and cowardly fashion; he has never expressed his regret over this crime and apparently is not ready to do so now. Rather, he covers his guilt behind a facade of innocence: "if I bear guilt, let him put me to death." That kind of claim would issue more appropriately from the mouth of someone who is innocent (Fokkelman 1981, 153). At the end of the day, Joab convinces the king, and father and son meet. Absalom makes prostration, and the king responds with a kiss. Yet, somewhat strangely, no conversation between the two ensues, nor do they shed a tear. In this unit, King David is always simply "the king," with no mention of his name or of the relationship between him and Absalom. Three persons make prostration before this king—the Tekoite, Joab, and Absalom. Yet all the bowing and scraping, connoting the power and majesty of David, cannot prevent the tottering throne of "the king" from almost coming to a premature end.

Cross and Double-Cross (2 Sam 15:1–18:32)

The next four chapters tell of Absalom's rebellion, King David's flight, and the battle between the two protagonists' armies that results in Absalom's death. While four years go by in the initial six verses of chapter 15, the next episodes decelerate to a span of days, with the tempo of the story at times exceedingly slow, forming a stark contrast to the emergency and the need of haste in which King David finds himself. Conversations and speeches get close attention and take up a large part of the narrative. In addition, a great number of personages appear on the stage, each in relation to the main characters, Absalom and David. All of them are important for our understanding of events and of how they affect the central figures. We meet Ahitophel and Hushai, counselors to Absalom, one a true supporter of the revolt and one a pseudo-friend. Men come to support or curse David: Ittai, Ziba, Barzillai, and Shimei. Alongside Joab, a familiar character in the David stories, we meet Amasa, his younger relative, a commander appointed by Absalom. The priests Zadok and Abiathar with their sons Jonathan and Ahimaaz play an important role as spies for David. In addition to these named characters, masses of servants, soldiers, and people side with either Absalom or David. In addition, there are a number of unnamed women: ten concubines left behind to "guard" the palace, a female servant who is intermediary, and a woman who hides David's spies from their pursuers. Women without names function as characters to set the force of Absalom's takeover in stark relief or as those who move the plot along at a moment when men's fates hang in the balance. As is mostly the case in these narratives, these women are only important as they enhance male power and activity.

The verb "to cross" (Hebrew *avar*) is central to all the episodes. In a literal sense, the king and his retinue cross the Kidron valley, east of Jerusalem, with the purpose of eventually crossing the Jordan. In 15:17-24 the verb occurs eight times and appears with great regularity from that unit on. Chapter 17 makes the urgency of the Jordan crossing clear through the repeated use of *avar,* as David's spies counsel him to

> Rise and cross over the water in haste. . . .
> So David arose and all the troops that were with him,
> and they crossed over the Jordan until morning light,
> until no one was left who had not crossed the Jordan. (2 Sam 17:21-22)

Crossing over is also key to the actions of many in a figurative sense. A great number of people cross over to Absalom, among them Ahitophel, a royal counselor, whose taking Absalom's side deals a severe blow to David's chances of regaining his kingship. Hushai pretends to have crossed over to Absalom but in reality acts as Absalom's servant on David's request and thus double-crosses Absalom. His advice runs counter to ("crosses") Ahitophel's to the disadvantage of the latter and ultimately of the cause of Absalom. There is a constant crossing of boundaries, both geographical and personal. The king and his followers cross the city of Jerusalem and the valley beyond. The Jordan is the major boundary, one side of which spells danger and the other a measure of safety for David. Absalom beds his father's concubines, crossing a boundary that seals the break between him and his father definitively, while Joab crosses the command of the king to treat Absalom gently. Ironically, Absalom's mule, once his rider is caught in a tree, leaves him and "crosses over," indicated with the same Hebrew verb that can also mean "to pass on." Even his mule betrays him at the crucial moment. Finally, two major characters, Ahitophel and Absalom, cross from life to death, both in a way hanging themselves. It is a sad story. On the surface, it has a good outcome for David, as his army is victorious. For the king, this triumphant outcome is, however, a source of a bitter and debilitating grief that will open the final scenes of the decline of David's grasp on his kingdom and throne in chapters 19 and 20.

Another organizing image, not always apparent in the translations, involves the "head" of someone or something. The Hebrew word *rosh* signifies both a person's head and the top of a structure or mountain. Polzin has noted how often "heady violence" occurs in the Deuteronomistic History. David goes up to the "head" of the Mount of Olives with his head covered, followed by the people showing the same sign of mourning (15:30); Hushai has put dirt on his head (15:32), and Abishai is ready to cut off Shimei's head (16:9). In these chapters both head and heart play significant roles. Absalom steals "the hearts of the men of Israel" (15:6, 13); David has significant encounters at the "head" of the Mount of Olives; Absalom is struck to the "heart" while he hangs by the "head" in the "heart" of the tree (Polzin 1993, 165–67; Alter 1999, 290).

Throughout this part of the narrative, the writers reveal little of Absalom's inner life. While his actions speak clearly of his ambitions and ruthlessness in preparation for and during his coup d'état, he gets relatively little speaking time, and most of it occurs in the lead-up to the coup. Afterward, his brief exchanges with Hushai and Ahitophel disclose only the business at hand. His vanity, already apparent in the previous chapter, is once again an issue and almost certainly plays a role in the exchange with Hushai. On the other hand, he is able to charm people and draw them into his orbit. He is able to gather a large following, and no less a person than Ahitophel joins his side. Yet, in spite of his central part, he remains somewhat of a flat character. The real story is, after all, about David and the aftermath of his ruinous dealings with Bathsheba and Uriah that bring to pass Nathan's foretelling. David's thoughts and feelings receive more attention in these texts than perhaps at any other point in the story. He weeps, speaks supportively, prays, expresses his confidence in God, keeps his temper in the face of great provocation, and refrains from gratuitous violence. In the midst of all the turmoil, he is able to devise a scheme to plant spies in Absalom's house and to send a counterforce to the enemy that may overturn the advice of a counselor, whose word was "like God's word" (16:23). He mentions his son's name only a few times, once just before and once during his flight from Jerusalem (15:14, 34), and then again before the battle when he bids his commanders to protect his son from harm, referring to him again as "the lad" (18:5). In that instance, his royal self certainly takes a backseat to his fatherly self. At moments he gives evidence of his typical canniness and ability to strategize, especially when he sends Hushai back to Jerusalem (15:34), while at other times he is simplistically ready to believe bad news about his protégé, Mephiboshet (16:4). Overall, these texts paint a complex and human portrait of a man who must have hovered between hope and despair, between trust and suspicion.

A Son's Rebellion (2 Sam 15:1-12)

"Absalom is indeed the son of his father." (Goldingay 2000, 278)

The scene opens with Absalom in the center. He achieves his goal of usurping his father's throne in two stages of unequal length in terms of time. The time span that leads up to the proclamation, "Absalom is king in Hebron!" (v. 10), takes up four years and is told in six verses. During this period, Absalom displays great pomp and circumstance, illustrating his vanity and pride once again, although perhaps also signaling that he has his eye on more important things than weighing his hair. In a more significant detail, the text elaborately relates his manner of drawing people to his side. He does this by getting up early and approaching individuals who came to the city to have a legal case heard, asking personal information (where are you from?), declaring their case "good and just," and sighing that if only he were judge, he would see that everyone would receive justice, something they currently would not get from the king! If they made prostration before him, he would lift them and kiss them, pretending to be just one of the folks perhaps. The kiss also raises some questions. His father had reconciled with him by a kiss. But were they truly reconciled? He kisses, but is prince Absalom just one of the folks? He did this for four years, the unit describing what he did habitually. It ends with the words, "So Absalom stole the heart of the men of Israel." He does so by manipulation, of course, for not everyone's cause can have been "good and just," and by maligning his father. On the other hand, Absalom may have had a genuine mistrust of his father's capacity to deal with his people with justice and equity. We remember that the anger of Absalom began when his father failed to deal justly with his rapist son Amnon. We have not seen David act in any particularly just or wise ways after that event either.

As he did before (14:24), Absalom asks his father for permission to go make a visit, to Hebron this time, because he had made a vow to God during his exile. The apparently unsuspecting king gives him permission and sends him off with words of peace. Once in Hebron, Absalom engages in intense activity. He sends runners throughout Israel (the Israel whose hearts have already been stolen!) to tell the tribes to proclaim Absalom king at the sound of the ram's horn. He sends for Ahitophel, David's counselor, and gains a good following, no doubt helped by the foundation he had so carefully laid during the previous years. The support of Ahitophel alone was probably worth a thousand followers. One may wonder how David could have been so unsuspecting all this time as not to intervene in Absalom's plots. Were his eyes closed the entire four years? Did he suspect nothing when this son, who once before off on a "visit" had murdered his brother, asks again for permission to go visiting? Is his sense of justice indeed asleep?

In an ironic note, Absalom's name occurs with great frequency within a few sentences (six times in vv. 7-12). The ending of that name signals "peace" in Hebrew. In addition, the root peace is embedded in the name Jerusalem, and the king sends his son on his way "in peace" (v. 9). It was certainly not for peace that Absalom went to Hebron; peace is in fact the farthest thing from his mind as he has himself declared king while in Hebron, the place where the people of Judah first proclaimed his father king (2 Sam 2:4).

Crossing Over (2 Sam 15:13-16:15)

"David has not wholly lost his touch." (Goldingay 2000, 291)

At the first word of his son's rebellion, David decides to flee, and the rest of chapter 15 and much of 16 is taken up with the account of his flight eastward. While the haste is palpable, numerous details and conversations lend the account an air of slow motion. It takes twenty-nine verses to get David and his entourage as far as the eastern slope of the Mount of Olives, a stone's throw from Jerusalem. The slow tempo of the narrative thus provides its own strain, offering a counterpoint to the many verbs of motion that testify to the desperation of David's flight. It is not clear why David is in such haste to get out of Jerusalem or whether this is indeed the right move to make. According to his words, his ostensible reason for the hasty flight is to avoid slaughter in the city, for he fears Absalom will "strike the city with the sword" (15:14). In addition, the city is a place where he would be less able to deploy an army. Perhaps, rather than being motivated by panic, he departed from the city together with his entourage, which includes his guard of 600 (v. 18), because he swiftly calculates that his best chances lie not inside the city but outside. His flight will buy him some time and an opportunity to assess his chances and move a few pieces on the chessboard that may tilt the outcome of the struggle at least somewhat in his favor. Leaving ten concubines behind to "guard" the palace (v. 16) does not sound like one of his smarter ideas, but he may not have wanted to encumber himself too much with family members. We note also that the story does not mention wives and offspring, although we may perhaps assume from later developments that they did accompany him. As often, the women of his household do not merit mention; the concubines receive attention only because they will have a further role to play. Children appear in the company of the Philistines (v. 22).

As the faithful guard from Gath, presumably dating back to David's days in the service of the Philistines, files by, David has his first conversation. He addresses one of them, Ittai, to convince him to return with his men, not wanting to drag them with him while he wanders to an unknown destination (v. 20). Ittai, however, swears loyalty to the king and promises to stand by him at all costs (v. 21). Thus, the first individual to be faithful to David is a foreigner and a Philistine at that, underlining the perfidiousness of his own son and his former counselor. At this time, they are in the outskirts of Jerusalem where all the people are "crossing over," Ittai with his men and children with them, and all the land is weeping (v. 23). The next cluster of people consists of Zadok and Abiathar, the priests, who are carrying the Ark, which they put down until all the people have crossed over the Kidron. This placement of the Ark, with the priests waiting until the crossing is complete, signals that the presence of God represented by the Ark watches over the king and his entourage until they have safely crossed. There is an echo here of the people under Joshua finishing their crossing of the Jordan while the priests with the Ark of the Covenant stand in the middle of the river (Josh 3:17). The king then urges Zadok to bring the Ark back to the city, where Zadok's and Abiathar's sons may be able to play an important role, spying on David's behalf and bringing him reports (vv. 25-29), again reminiscent of an episode in the Joshua stories when Joshua sends spies to Jericho (Josh 2:1). The frame around this unit consists of the verb "to bring back."

> The king said to Zadok,
> "Bring the Ark of God back to the city.
> If I will find favor in the eyes of the Holy One,
> He will bring me back and let me see it and its abode." . . .
>
> Then Zadok and Abiathar brought back
> the Ark of God to Jerusalem and stayed there. (2 Sam 15:25, 29)

With these words David acknowledges that the reclaiming of his kingship and eventual return to Jerusalem are in the hand of God. At the same time, he sets up a line of communication with the headquarters of the enemy, his first move in a direction of hope for a positive outcome (Fokkelman 1983, 187).

In counterpoint to his hopeful words, David and his people climb up the Mount of Olives while weeping, a dark moment made bleaker by the report that Ahitophel has joined the Absalom party. This news affects David deeply, causing him to utter the prayer that God may confound the counsel of Ahitophel (v. 31). It is then perhaps not accidental that Hushai crosses his path immediately after his prayer at a place of worship "where one bowed down to God" (v. 32). Visibly carrying signs of mourning, Hushai is clearly on David's side, and David asks him to go back to the city; the immediate need is to provide a counterweight to Ahitophel's advice. David reminds Hushai that he will not be alone but will have the support of the priests, Zadok and Abiathar, along with Jonathan and Ahimaaz, their sons. The chapter ends on both a positive and a negative note:

> Hushai, David's friend, came to the city
> when Absalom came to Jerusalem. (2 Sam 15:37)

In contrast to the positive remark about Hushai's return to Jerusalem stands the report on the entry of Absalom when David is still only a short distance outside the city!

The next encounter is with Ziba, the servant of Mephiboshet, Jonathan's son and David's protégé. Ziba himself comes with gifts, no doubt to provide assurance of his trustworthiness while he reports treachery on the part of his master. David may be all too ready to believe in the nefarious role played by those close to him; he believes Ziba and gives him all the property that was Mephiboshet's (vv. 1-4). His overeager acceptance of this betrayal, with no word but Ziba's to support it, is a sign of how David hovers between despair and hope, trust and mistrust. On the heels of this encounter, a descendant from the clan of Saul comes out to curse David and throw stones at him, shouting invective and insult. In Hebrew the words "Get out! Get out!" convey clearly the hiss of Shimei's rage and hatred: *tse! tse!* he cries (v. 7). Abishai, always ready to take out those that are threats to his master, enters offering to behead "this dead dog" (v. 9). David, however, restrains him, distancing himself from his bloodthirsty nephew at the same time, as he did once before (2 Sam 3:39). He utters again the hope that God may bring "good" back to him in place of these curses. As for the curses themselves, coming as they do from one of the house of Saul, how hurtful can they be for one whose own son is aiming to kill him (v. 11)?

The movement to and from Jerusalem ends with David and his people arriving at their destination, most likely the Jordan, and taking time to rest, while Absalom reaches Jerusalem (vv. 14-15). The phrasing of these two arrivals is significant, contrasting the supporters of David, "the people who were with him," with "all the people, the men of Israel" at Absalom's side, adding for good measure Ahitophel, whose presence weighs heavily in the balance in Absalom's favor. It remains to be seen whether Hushai, the Arkite, may be able to outmaneuver him.

Counselors (2 Sam 16:16–17:14)

"This is the logic of patriarchal power. That the son has entered his father's city is not enough; he must enter his father's women." (Fewell and Gunn 1993, 139)

Like his father on the way out, Absalom encounters people on the way in, not all of them people he expected to meet. He does not even have time to open his mouth when he confronts Hushai, who, before anyone can ask questions, utters his "Long live the king! Long live the king!" (v. 16). Hushai does not say which king he has in mind, thus preserving for himself a shred of truthfulness because Absalom with his inordinate pride will naturally apply it to himself. Absalom's words clearly indicate a belief that Hushai has betrayed David, calling into question Hushai's loyalty toward "his friend" (v. 17). Hushai gives a clever reply to this accusation, avowing that it is not for him to choose the rightful king but that this is up to God's choice and the people's confirmation. As for him, he will stay with God's preference. Again, it is up to the listener to decide whom he has in mind as God's choice. Absalom is all too ready to insert himself into that position. For good measure, Hushai adds that he will serve the son as he has served the father. Never mind that, to all appearances, he has just betrayed the father! He shows himself in this exchange to be not only a clever manipulator of words but also an able reader of Absalom's outsized ego.

It is, however, not Hushai but Ahitophel who gets to strike the first blow in terms of advice (vv. 20-23). When Absalom asks him what he should do, the first important matter to Ahitophel's mind is to take possession of all that belonged to David, including his women. Ahitophel counsels his master to engage in sexual intercourse with the concubines David left behind. Then the sorry spectacle takes place of Absalom raping his father's concubines in full view of the populace. Both Absalom and David have reached a kind of nadir with this action. Absalom, although believing himself at the height of his power through taking possession of his father's women, has now sunk a great deal lower than his brother Amnon, while for David the full unfolding of his fate announced by the prophet Nathan becomes reality (2 Sam 12:11). There is little doubt that he heard of this event, having planted his own spies in Absalom's court. The direct purpose of the act for Absalom is to enrage his father, to make himself "odious in his father's nostrils," and to strengthen the confidence of those who have joined his side (v. 21). Ahitophel hereby proves himself an able advisor. That he considered this debauchery essential to cement Absalom's power is clear from his willingness to waste valuable time that could have gone into the pursuit of David. To confirm the value of Ahitophel and his advice, the narrator inserts a comment on the quality of Ahitophel's counsel, noting that both David and Absalom valued it as if it were a word from God. This comment sounds a note of warning for what may be around the corner and once again introduces the tension that surrounds the two counselors on opposite sides of the struggle between David and Absalom.

Without further circumlocution, Ahitophel urges Absalom for permission to take troops and that same night pursue David, to capture him in a worn-out and debilitated state:

> Let me, please, choose twelve thousand men,
> so I can get up and pursue David tonight

> I will come upon him and he will be tired and slack-handed
> and I will panic him, and all the people with him will flee.
> Then I will strike down the king by himself. (2 Sam 17:1-2)

His speech is short and to the point, wasting not a word, and it is clear what he has in mind. David matters most. In order to catch him and kill him, it is crucial that pursuit start right away. In this manner not only will Absalom prevail, because David will be dead, but there will also be no further bloodshed. Perhaps Ahitophel too was tired, or too excited about the prospect of the hunt, or disgusted by what he had just witnessed, for he forgets to wrap his counsel in a flood of pretty words. He barely manages to add a "please" to his request.

The narrative makes clear that Ahitophel's advice went over well with Absalom and the people (v. 4), so it would seem superfluous to go elsewhere for guidance. In view of this general acceptance, Ahitophel will not have counted on Absalom going to Hushai for a second opinion, but it seems that the prince does not intend to ignore the fact that he now has two of his father's counselors at his side. He calls in any case for Hushai and then makes what is probably the first misstep in his carefully calculated machinations. When he tells Hushai what Ahitophel has said, he thereby hands Hushai the weapon he needs, for he must know what the opposing counsel said in order to offer counter-advice (Fokkelman 1981, 214). His first words are blunt and go straight to the point: "Not good . . . ." These words come in the first place in the Hebrew sentence, startling Absalom to attention. "Not good is the counsel that Ahitophel counseled," and to soften the blow of his negative judgment somewhat Hushai adds "this time" (v. 7). Then he gives his own advice, wrapping it in all sorts of circumlocutions, playing with the prince's vanity and his knowledge of David's history, drawing on old fears that a son may have had of so valiant a father who had cut such a swath in the course of his life (vv. 8-13). He flatters Absalom, making grandiose promises and using exaggerated metaphors, countering the feeble "slack-handed" David of Ahitophel's speech with the image of a ferocious bear (v. 8). Cleverly, Hushai makes clear that Absalom will be part of the pursuing party, something Ahitophel overlooked, together with the multitudes that follow him (v. 11). Never mind how strong the father was and is; the multitudes following Absalom will be too much for David, and there will be no place left for him to hide. The intent of his speech is to cause delay, of course, in opposition to the urgency called for by Ahitophel. It is all too obvious, but not for one with an ego the size of Absalom's, one who just had his first taste of what it means to take his father's place by bedding his father's women. Absalom falls for it.

Once again, the narrator inserts a note, this time providing the information that in reality it was not Hushai's but God's doing that Ahitophel's counsel be overturned (v. 14) in answer to David's prayer. After all, God is still guiding the path of his anointed in spite of his many missteps and the flaws that have become visible in his character. Whether this path will ultimately spell peace for the nation is much in doubt, certainly from the vantage point of the ones who wove the stories together at a time when it would seem that kingship had been of little benefit. David will not arise from the debacle of this uprising with his head held high, and the sword will not have departed from his house.

Getting It Across (2 Sam 17:15-29)

"Ahitophel is a man with true inner freedom." (Fokkelman 1981, 230)

It has become important to get word of the advice to David so that he may take steps to avoid capture. Hushai resorts to informing Zadok and Abiathar so they may bring a report to their sons, Jonathan and Ahimaaz, who, as it turns out, have been hiding outside the city while a mediator brings messages from fathers to sons. These two, the faithful priests and their faithful sons, provide counter-images to the faithless son of David. Where David's son does everything he can to seek his father's life, the priestly offspring risk their own lives in order to preserve the life of their king. It is not clear that Hushai reports to the priests which advice has met with the more favorable reception, his or Ahitophel's; he may not have known, or he may not want to count on anything. In any case, he reports what both men have said and includes a plea for David to cross the Jordan as soon as possible.

The focus now turns briefly to Jonathan and Ahimaaz, who were stationed close to the city at a place called Ein Rogel, "Well of the Scouts" or "Well of the Runner." In either case, it is an apt name for a place where messengers bring reports in haste to spies who forward the news to their master. The narrative provides the information that they have already gone back and forth to King David, no doubt bringing news of Absalom's possession of the king's concubines. At this point, however, a member of Absalom's household sees them and runs back to Absalom with the tale. The two messengers are aware that they have been discovered and manage to find a hiding place in the well of a nearby house with the help of a woman who spreads a cover over the well on which in turn she spreads out grain. Again, the story of the spies in Jericho, hidden by the prostitute Rahab, comes to mind (Josh 2:6). Earlier, the story identified the person who functioned as go-between from the city to the men stationed outside as a woman (v. 17), perhaps the same person who hides them or the wife of the homeowner with the well. In any case, now women step in to function as important agents on behalf of David. The king's fate surely hangs in the balance with the detection of the spies, whose discovery might well have betrayed the presence of more than one untrustworthy supporter at Absalom's court! As it is, the woman misleads the servants of Absalom who have come to find the spies, and they go back to the city after a fruitless search (Josh 2:5-7).

The two come out of their hiding place and make their way to David to report. Curiously, they are said to convey only the counsel of Ahitophel. Perhaps they did not think Hushai's advice worth mentioning, or the information that came to them from the priests may have only included Ahitophel's words, or caution and Ahitophel's previous record may have caused them to believe that Absalom would certainly follow his counsel. In any case, they bid David arise and cross the water quickly, based on what Ahitophel has urged. David follows their bidding and shortly all find themselves on the other side of the Jordan. Jonathan and Ahimaaz most likely remain with their king because for them there is now no going back.

While many are thus heeding the counsel of Ahitophel, he himself wakes up to the fact that his words have fallen on fallow ground (v. 23). Convinced that the only chance of a favorable outcome for Absalom had rested in quick action to capture David, he goes home and commits suicide. At every turn, the narrator has shown respect for Ahitophel, one who may also have been disappointed in his king and viewed Absalom's rise as a fresh start, and spends some time describing his final moments. He rides home on his donkey, puts his affairs in order, and hangs himself, choosing what he may have felt was the only honorable way out. Although such a fate usually draws strong criticism in the Bible, the narrative lets him go to his grave in good order, and he is buried with his ancestors. In exercising this choice, his death forms a contrast to that of helpless Absalom hanging from the tree, waiting for the fatal blows.

The end of the chapter recounts the movements of both David and Absalom in the region of the Transjordan where the eventual battle will take place. The crossing of the Jordan, which for David meant a measure of safety and the regaining of his equilibrium, spells danger for Absalom. He has waited too long, and David has had time to organize and to receive support. While David encamps at Mahanaim, three individuals—the son of a former enemy, Shovi the son of Nachas; the previous protector of Mephiboshet, Machir the son of Amiel; and Barzilai from Gilead—bring provisions for

David's army. A sign of outside support arrives at a desperate time and simultaneously highlights the dissimilarity of this benevolence from outsiders with the treachery of the insider, the son. Events appear to be moving in a direction favorable to David's regaining his throne. A note reports the appointment of Amasa, another of David's relatives, as commander of Absalom's army. This Amasa will have a further role to play in subsequent events.

Death of a Son (2 Sam 18:1-18)

"Once Absalom is dead there is no more need for fighting." (Fokkelman 1981, 247)

With his army arrayed for battle, David appoints his commanders and prepares to go out with them himself (vv. 1-2), but his troops wisely counsel him that this is not a good idea, for they understand that the struggle is in reality about David, and he consents to their wishes. He then orders his generals, Joab, Abishai, and Ittai, to "(go) easy for me on the lad, on Absalom" (v. 5). The Hebrew expression used here is rare and somewhat unclear. Those following the King James translation render the phrase "deal gently" or something like it, and some derive the command from the root "to cover," with the attendant meaning of protect. All heard him say this, as the text makes clear through the mention of "all the commanders" and "all the troops." All heard it, but what did they understand? That they should spare his life or give him an easy death? It is hard to say. Even David must have realized how unwise it would be to keep Absalom alive under the circumstances. He speaks here entirely as a father rather than as a king. In the event, Absalom's life is neither spared nor does he get an easy death. Three verses follow to recount quickly the battle itself, with the text, as so often, affording only a general picture of the fight beyond noting numbers and the fact that the forest swallowed up many victims on Absalom's side (v. 8). All the attention goes to the person of Absalom and the manner of his death. First, a tree "captures" him:

> Absalom happened to be in front of David's servants.
> Now Absalom was riding on the mule
> and when the mule entered under the branches of the great oak,
> his head was grabbed by the oak,
> so he dangled between heaven and earth.
> And the mule that was under him passed on. (2 Sam 18:9)

Although presumably his hair is caught, the same hair that he had so proudly shaved and weighed, the text mentions only his "head," emphasizing the key word for this part of the narrative cycle. It could also be that it was actually his head that got stuck in the fork of the tree branches and that the common understanding of the hair caught in the tree comes from the listener's awareness of Absalom's vanity and his involvement with his hair. Would, however, even a vain warrior go to the battlefield with unbound hair? Perhaps an untrained one, as Absalom must have been, would do so. Whichever the case may be, there he hangs, while his mule passes blithely on, "crosses over." He is caught by the forces of nature, the forest has turned against him, and his mule, perhaps the means of escape, is his no longer; soon human enemies will join to send him to his death.

Absalom is not yet dead, and first a soldier finds him there and reports it to Joab. The anonymous soldier is eloquent in his own defense to Joab, who questions him angrily about his lack of action. He reminds Joab that everyone heard the king order the generals to guard Absalom, to keep him safe, evidence of how at least this soldier interpreted David's command. He was not about to go against the king's orders. Indeed, if he had done so he knows that Joab would have washed his hands of him. Joab has heard enough, listens no further, and knocks Absalom out of the tree. Although he strikes him to the "heart," it is clear that he is not yet dead, for Joab's ten weapon-bearers administer the fatal blows (v. 15). Perhaps ten blows symbolize the violence of a man who raped his father's ten concubines (Goldingay 2000, 284). The death of Absalom spells the end of the battle, and the troops throw Absalom into a pit. All that remains of him is a heap of stones and the memorial he had erected for himself in view of his lack of offspring—an ignominious end for the beautiful prince.

Joab, it seems, could have done little else. Throughout the story, sometimes in distasteful ways, he is faithful to David. He had at least one unpleasant experience with Absalom and may feel even more betrayed by the prince's coup d'état than David does. Was he not the one who had helped Absalom to return to his home to be reconciled to David? He is well aware that leaving the prince alive, even under house arrest, would be extremely unwise. As a man of action who has always acted on behalf of his king, he takes action. He is also aware that David will not receive the report of Absalom's death as good news, as the sequel shows.

News Comes to the King (2 Sam 18:19-32)

"Ethiopians are of course world-class marathon runners." (Goldingay 2000, 293)

At crucial times in the stories, messengers have reported the outcome of a fight to a character who was absent from the battlefield. We first encountered Eli waiting anxiously at home to hear about the fate of the Ark and his family (1 Sam 4:12-18). A messenger brought news to David about the deaths of Saul and Jonathan (2 Sam 1:1-16), and another came with a report of the fight with Ammon and the death of Uriah (2 Sam 12:22-25). Once again, the king waits away from the scene of the struggle, and there are those around who are eager to bring him the good tidings that his army has been victorious. The first is Ahimaaz, the same who risked his life earlier as a spy for David. He requests Joab to send him with "the good news," a word that will play a key role in what follows. Joab's reply, his first attempt to dissuade Ahimaaz, employs the term "good news" three times, twice to indicate that the news will be far from good for the king, for "the son of the king is dead" (v. 20). He sees someone else standing around, a foreigner on whom the wrath of the king will fall more acceptably than on courageous Ahimaaz. He commands the Ethiopan to do the job. When Ahimaaz begs to be a member of the running party, Joab tries for the second time to keep him from the task, again assuring him that there is no "good news." Then, when it seems there is no holding Ahimaaz back, he tells him to run. Ahimaaz, being the better runner, soon overtakes the first man.

A shift of scene moves the action from the running messengers to the sitting David, who is between the inner and the outer gate with a lookout posted on the wall. We recall Eli sitting outside the gate of Shiloh, awaiting the news of the death of his sons. An exchange between the lookout and the king takes place, making clear that what appears first to be one runner turns soon into two. The king, who first declared that one man alone would be sure to bring good news, assures himself that the second one also will have good news, illogically connecting a "good" man with "good" news (vv. 25-26). And that is how it appears, as Ahimaaz, having gotten there first, cries out, "All is well!" (v. 28). He reports the victory of David's army over "the men who lifted their hand against my lord, the king," but David only has ears for news about Absalom and immediately wants to know whether the announcement includes the well-being of his son: "Is it well with the lad, with Absalom?" (v. 29). At this question, twice warned by Joab, Ahimaaz begins to stutter without being able to finish his sentence. In the meantime the Ethiopian runner has drawn up and the king waits for his tidings. Like Ahimaaz, the second runner announces the positive results of the battle, and again the king wants to know only one thing, repeating the question about Absalom (v. 32). The Ethiopian has not heard Joab's warnings to Ahimaaz and, without hesitation, declares,

May they become like the lad,
the enemies of my lord the king,
and all who rose up against you for evil. (2 Sam 18:32)

An account that should have ended in good tidings instead rings out the return of David to his throne with the word "evil" (Hebrew *ra'ah*). Its harsh sound reverberates in the story, confirming expectations that all has not ended well.

A House Divided (2 Sam 19:1–20:24)

"The old David has died and no new David has been born." (Goldingay 2000, 294)

In the two chapters that deal with the aftermath of Absalom's revolt, it becomes increasingly clear that the reestablished national unity is fragile and easily broken. First, David's extravagant grief over the death of his son jeopardizes the accomplishments of the recent victory and his standing with the people. General Joab rudely shocks David out of his isolation and mourning, but David's actions afterward give some evidence that he has a difficult time making sound judgments in service of his kingship as well as his realm. Having regained his throne, he must set his mind to healing the deep divisions that simmer just below the surface. Instead, he does nothing to quell and reconcile a quarrel between the people of his tribe, Judah, and the rest of the nation, here consistently called "Israel." The fissures that will eventually split the small kingdom already surface in the form of quarrels about who has more at stake in "bringing back" the king to Jerusalem. David fans the flames of the incipient quarrel rather than quenching them by encouraging members of his own clan, Judah, not to be "the last to bring the king back to his house" (19:12, 13). He may be concerned with regaining the support of many Judahites who had been followers of his traitorous son. It was certainly a difficult task to build a harmonious realm out of the recent sharp divisions.

As during the flight from Jerusalem in the previous chapters, David has encounters on the way back with both enemy and friend. Shimei appears again, this time in deep distress over his earlier behavior (19:17-24). Instead of Ziba, Mephiboshet himself comes to meet David and presents a moving and convincing defense of his earlier absence from the flight, while accusing his servant Ziba of slander against him (19:25-31). Finally, Barzillai, the friend who had provided for the army on the eve of the battle, has a conversation with the king just before he makes the journey back across the Jordan

(19:32-40). The chapter ends with renewed quarrels breaking out between Judahites and Israelites. It is not surprising, then, that soon a clash of swords follows this clash of words (Alter 1999, 320), when another rebellion breaks out under the leadership of a Benjaminite, Sheba by name, with the Israelites throwing their support to this "worthless fellow" (20:1-2).

David, in the meantime, reaches Jerusalem and undertakes two measures: one regarding his violated concubines and one regarding his army. He confines the concubines for the rest of their lives (20:3) and sends his kinsman Amasa, whom he had appointed over the army instead of Joab (19:14), to deal with Sheba. In the place of an account of a battle to rid the kingdom of this renewed threat, there follows a report of an encounter between Amasa and Joab, one that turns deadly for Amasa. The army then proceeds to the city where the rebel Sheba is holed up, with Joab once again in charge of the army. A "wise" woman convinces Joab, initially ready to lay siege to the city of Abel, that getting rid of Sheba alone would be more expedient. The exchange between the wise woman of Abel and Joab takes up the larger part of this section and brings to mind other women, mostly unnamed, who have intervened in the affairs of men to bring about a conclusion that avoided unnecessary bloodshed. Like others before him, Sheba loses his head. The entire episode ends with a note on David's cabinet that lists Joab "over the entire army of Israel."

The desired unity and harmony that should have followed David's reinstatement thus appear to be far to seek. Renewed fights, personal and communal, mar the triumphant return of the king to his city. Although there are friendly encounters on the way back, there is ongoing contention among different sections of the population with respect to their king. Although the king listens to general Joab concerning his excessive outpouring of grief, he clearly tries to distance himself from his all-too-powerful cousin. Joab obviously will not accept his removal as commander of the troops and gets rid of his replacement in the same violent way he eliminated his erstwhile rival Abner (2 Sam 3:27). His killing of Amasa is, however, also the murder of a relative and therefore puts Joab in an even less favorable light. In some ways the end of this part of the story harkens back to its beginning, when there were two kings in the land and violence and bloodshed were the order of the day (2 Sam 2–4).

The Pit of Despair (2 Sam 19:1-9)

"The human spirit will endure sickness,
But a broken spirit—who can bear?" (Prov 18:14)

The scene opens on David removing himself to an "upper room" after receiving the news of Absalom's death, weeping and crying Absalom's name. Opening and closing lines of the unit (vv. 1-5) repeat the cry, "My son, Absalom, Absalom, my son, my son!" The expression "my son" (Hebrew *beni*) occurs six times surrounding the triple mention of the son's name, creating an echoing wail. What the king never did in response to the death of the child born to him and Bathsheba, what he did not utter when his eldest was murdered, he now voices in full force. Who knows whether David's exorbitant grief is not the result of accumulative grieving that never found its way out of his soul? From a bystander's point of view, this son certainly did not deserve his father to mourn over him. Nevertheless, who is to judge a parent's lament over even the most wayward of her children? Similarly, the prophet Hosea has God lament over God's people as rebellious children on whose behalf God's heart is moved and God's compassion "grows warm and tender" (Hos 11:8). Perhaps David had hoped that somehow both his son and he could come out of the debacle alive. Perhaps he thought that once Absalom realized who was boss, he would come to his senses and toe the line.

We, who know Absalom, are aware how unlikely a scenario this seems. In all of the accounts of the rebellion, he offers not a word of concern for his father but is rather all too eager to entrap him and, in the first instance, to follow the advice of Ahitophel who wanted to strike David down (17:2). From all that went before, it appears that David was an indulgent father, like Eli and Samuel before him, not capable of disciplining his sons. He was unwilling to punish one son for violating his sister, David's own daughter, an injustice that he should have addressed, and in doing so he might have forestalled much disaster that followed. In the same vein, he did not directly deal with the wrong done by Absalom in murdering his brother, and things went on from there. It became clear that as a parent David lacked the competence and adroitness he possessed as a leader. He has now reverted to his parental self rather than taking into account the political consequences of this withdrawal into his emotions and the effect it will have on his people. In ironic contrast to this reality, the references to David as "the king" throughout this first unit omit his proper name. This title occurs in almost every sentence of the first five verses coupled with verbs connoting grief, thereby creating accumulated images of despair: "the king wept and spoke" (v. 1), "the king is weeping and mourning" (v. 2), "the king is sorely pained" (v. 3), "the king had covered his face," and "the king cried in a loud voice" (v. 5).

Surrounded by this outpouring of misery, the people "stole away," as soldiers do when they have lost courage or faced defeat (v. 4). As the living

Absalom had once "stolen" the hearts of the people (15:6), so now dead Absalom steals the joy of the victory from the people, and he may turn out to be more dangerous dead than alive (Fokkelman 1981, 270). What should have been a moment of triumph, a turn of the tide in David's favor, evolves instead into the most dangerous juncture of David's long reign. The people's "stealing away" means also that they are leaving his side, a fact that Joab does not fail to notice. He launches into a sharply invective speech (vv. 6-9).

Joab, the realist who had been the cause of Absalom's death, may have felt a degree of guilt because he of all people had taken measure of the king's attachment to his son. Possibly, his own conflicted feelings feed the mood that produces the tongue-lashing he unleashes on the king. No doubt, only such a harsh attack as the one Joab mounts could have brought David to his senses. Without any address, Joab begins with an accusation, hammering down how David's behavior affects everyone—his servants, his family, and his army and generals. David acts as if he hates those who love him and loves those who hate him. Fokkelman observes that Joab walks "right over the completely defenseless David with the sheer force of his jackboots" (Fokkelman 1981, 277). Joab's complicity in a number of deaths, some in the past, some still to come, will eventually cost him his life (1 Kgs 1:31-34), but that day is not yet. For now, he is the powerful general and loyal ally of David, who threatens him with the desertion of the troops unless David shows himself and addresses them. David, shocked into awareness as a slap in the face may bring someone to consciousness, complies:

> Then the king arose and sat in the gate
> and all the people were told,
> "Look, the king is sitting in the gate." (2 Sam 19:9)

Although conceding the point, David is still only "sitting" and thus only partially acceding to Joab's command to "go out and speak to the heart of your servants" (v. 8). In addition, David speaks only through representatives and addresses only one part of the people.

The Return of the King (2 Sam 19:10-41)

". . . do they really want the old king back?" (Goldingay 2000, 296)

Before the king can even cross the Jordan, squabbles break out. First, the part of the nation now called "Israel" deliberates too long about escorting their king back over the river. In the meantime, David exhorts his clan, his "family" members, not to be "the last to bring back the king" (v. 13). This same clan, of course, had also been disloyal in following his son in the rebellion, so he may have been eager to assure them of his goodwill. This call on the support of Judah helps widen the wedge between his tribe and the rest of the nation rather than healing the potential rift. At the same time, he appoints Amasa, his relative chosen by Absalom to lead his army (17:25), as commander in place of Joab. This choice may show David's resentment of Joab, whether in the face of his rude speech or because David had knowledge of Joab's role in the death of Absalom. Alternatively, David has a more nefarious purpose with this appointment. As is often the case, the narrative provides no information about motivations for an action. Further, we do not hear how Joab received his dismissal, although his reaction will eventually become clear.

Now the king arrives at the Jordan, and a number of individuals encounter him on his way back as they did on the way out. The effect of the meetings and exchanges is to delay the arrival of David on the west side of the river. Just as the flight out of Jerusalem up the Mount of Olives and over the Kidron seemed to take place in slow motion, now the victorious return begins at a slow pace. The account does not report that David finally reaches the Jerusalem side of the Jordan until v. 41. David treads the verge of Jordan, and Judah is ready to "bring the king across" (vv. 16, 19), but delays occur. First, he must deal with Shimei, the Benjaminite who had cursed David as he fled before Absalom (16:5-12). Shimei has seen the error of his ways, but he takes no chances on the king's pardon and surrounds himself with a considerable force of men (vv. 17-18). He begs forgiveness and points out that, of all the "house of Joseph," he is the first to come and meet the king (v. 21). In an almost comic turn, Abishai is once again ready to take care of Shimei, although he does not offer to do it himself this time, but David will hear none of it and swears to Shimei that he will not "die" (vv. 23-24). In answering Abishai, David tellingly refers to the "sons of Zeruiah," including Joab, thereby establishing distance and revealing something more of his discontent with his cousin. David will stay true to his oath to Shimei only in the narrowest sense, as Shimei will eventually die under King Solomon, whom David instructed toward this end before his death (1 Kgs 2:36-46).

The next to appear is Mephiboshet (vv. 25-31), about whom his servant Ziba had given a report to David on his exit from Jerusalem that branded him a traitor. Ziba himself had joined the company of Shimei (v. 18) on his way to seek the returning king's pardon. Mephiboshet comes alone, displaying visible signs of distress over King David's potential failure to regain the throne (v. 25), signs that according to the narrator had begun on the day of David's flight, thus clearing Mephiboshet of all suspicion of treachery. When King David, who does not share the omniscient perspective of the narrator, asks the reason he stayed behind at the time of the king's flight, Mephiboshet's reply sounds honest and devoid of all duplicity. When the king decides to divide the property he had already handed to Ziba between the master and his servant (v. 30), Mephiboshet's response exhibits concern only for David's welfare (v. 31). The encounter puts David in a somewhat unflattering light, since dividing the property equally fails to acknowledge wrongdoing on the side of one of the parties.

The last individual to encounter David before he crosses westward over the Jordan is eighty-year-old Barzillai (vv. 32-40), who had earlier provided the fugitive king and his army with ample provisions (18:27-29). The king urges Barzillai to go back to Jerusalem with him, but Barzillai expresses a preference to "die" in his city (v. 38). Advanced in years, Barzillai may have had little taste for future adventures at the side of his king, loyal servant though he may have been. He will accompany his lord a short distance but then return to his home (v. 37). Finally, the king is ready to cross the Jordan. Barzillai is the only person to receive a kiss and blessing from David as he returns to his city (v. 38), an action that takes place in the midst of a surfeit of crossing:

> Then all the people crossed the Jordan,
> and the king crossed.
> The king kissed Barzillai,
> and blessed him and he went back to his city.
> The king crossed to Gilgal,
> and Kimham crossed with him
> and all the people of Judah brought the king across,
> and also half of the people of Israel. (2 Sam 19:40-41)

A People's Rebellion (2 Sam 19:42–20:13)

"What will Israel in exile do, the Israel of the Deuteronomist's time as well as of David's?" (Polzin 1993, 196)

Barzillai may have done well to return to his home, for renewed squabbling breaks out between the tribes, a quarrel that bodes ill for the immediate as well as the distant future (vv. 42-44). It is of some interest that the contention between Israel and Judah involves the person of the king without his active participation, hinting perhaps at David's failure of leadership (Fokkelman 1981, 316). Already the fragile union of the nation is evident, a union that will break apart for good after the death of King Solomon. As for now, a people's rebellion follows the one that began in the royal house. Another "worthless fellow" (*ben belia'al*) arises, not surprisingly a

Benjaminite, to urge secession from the Davidic house (v. 1). Sheba announces his intentions and calls on "Israel" to follow him. Sheba's rallying cry disturbingly anticipates the one issued in 1 Kings 12:6 at a moment when the nation will break apart for good.

Accompanied by the men of Judah, David reaches Jerusalem and takes action concerning the concubines he had left behind to guard the palace, the ones Absalom had violated in full view of the populace. These women have now become taboo for David and, while he does not expel them, he places them under perpetual confinement until the day of their death while denying them sexual intimacy. Echoes resound here of the interruption of marital relations between David and Michal (2 Sam 6:23), and the ruin of Tamar, David's daughter, who lived a "desolate woman" in the house of her brother Absalom following Amnon's violation of her (2 Sam 13:20). Thus the devastation of women's lives follows in the wake of the machinations of men in power. At the same time, the number of the concubines, ten, symbolizes the number of tribes that are breaking away from David. "The violation of the harem and the imprisonment of the concubines now symbolically become the seal on the secession of the ten tribes" (Fokkelman 1983, 321). In some way the Davidic house in its reduced state will mirror the reduced state of the violated concubines (Polzin 1993, 198).

The next task of some urgency for David is to quash Sheba's growing rebellion. He entrusts his newly appointed commander Amasa with mustering troops. Amasa, perhaps for lack of experience, falls somewhat short of his task, a failure the text does not make clear in detail (v. 5). Possibly to guarantee a successful result, David sends Abishai, Joab's brother and another of the sons of Zeruiah, with the order to pursue Sheba before he can ensconce himself too deeply in fortified cities (v. 6). Subsequently, and inexplicably, the narrative states that Joab's men followed Abishai (v. 7), thus introducing Joab's name via his troops. Nothing of what follows concerns a battle with Sheba and his followers. Instead, the story reports the location of a meeting between Amasa and Joab, who makes an abrupt personal appearance. While Joab embraces the unsuspecting Amasa, he drops his weapon and, picking it up with his free hand, disembowels him. It is a bloody revenge, similar to the one he took on Abner (2 Sam 3:27). Likewise, he faced in Abner a formidable rival. Amasa was clearly in his way and had also recently switched loyalties. Once again Joab manages to dispatch both a rival and someone whose loyalty to his lord, David, was questionable. This bloody spectacle occurred in the same location where some time ago twelve young men had died in a similar bloody struggle (2 Sam 2:16). Now, as then, the nation is divided in its loyalties, kingship having proven to be less than a stabilizing factor. Now, as then, a bloody corpse proves a distraction for the troops moving ahead (2 Sam 2:23; cf. 2 Sam 20:12).

In reflecting on what has taken place, some questions arise as to David's role in the events. It is true that his replacement of Joab with Amasa could simply be motivated by resentment toward Joab, who had both caused the death of his son and reprimanded him for his grief afterward. In addition, this appointment of a relative who had supported Absalom's coup d'état could be interpreted as a smart move on David's part, guaranteeing the loyalty of one who might otherwise prove dangerous, while at the same time putting Joab in his place. Yet David had known his cousin and loyal general for a long time. He knew both his loyalty and his ruthless inclinations toward potential rivals. Is it likely that he was entirely ignorant of the murderous designs entertained by one who had not hesitated to dispatch Abner in the most brutal way imaginable? Is it just possible that David saw this as the perfect solution for a situation that could cause distrust and instability among the commanders, the troops loyal to them, and by extension to the kingdom? In that way, too, his hands would remain clean, as they did at an earlier time of much mayhem and vengeful action at the beginning of his kingship. In the context of this line of thinking, it is telling that Joab moves into his old position at the end of the chapter without any mention of David's involvement in his reinstatement.

Joab and the Siege of Abel Beth Maacah (2 Sam 20:14-26)

". . . you are seeking to kill a city, a mother in Israel; . . ." (v. 19)

Meanwhile rebellious Sheba has found refuge in the town of Abel Beth Maacah, and the troops, now under Joab's command, hasten on their way to lay siege to the town. There they construct a battering ram to destroy the city wall. Before any hostile engagement can take place, a "wise woman" from the city calls on Joab to come within listening distance and hear her out. First, she points out that from of old Abel has been a center where people have come with their questions, in this way perhaps underlining her credentials. Then she asks him why he would destroy a city, a "mother in Israel," and thus destroy the "heritage of the Holy One" (v. 19). Joab, who is no stranger to the company of "wise women," answers that this is far from his mind, and that they have come for only one person who has "lifted his hand against the king," Sheba, the son of Bichri (v. 21). With the utmost confidence, the woman from Abel Beth Maacah promises Joab Sheba's head. This woman obviously has great influence in the city, for, when she speaks to all the people "in her wisdom," they cut off Sheba's head and throw it over the wall.

The question the woman poses to Joab is reminiscent of the one Abner asked when he inquired of Joab whether the sword would "devour forever" (2 Sam 2:27). Its intention is clearly to stop ongoing hostilities. Then as now, the question has the effect of stopping Joab in his tracks. The precise term the woman uses for the town is "mother-city," the only time this term occurs in the Bible, and its implication is that Joab would engage in matricide. As others have pointed out, at key points in the Samuel narratives, women intercede to avert unnecessary bloodshed: Abigail, who goes out to meet David before he can rain death and destruction on her household; the wise woman of Tekoa, who intervenes between David and Absalom; and once again here at Abel Beth Maacah (Alter 1991, 326). On these occasions, women take initiative on behalf of the well-being of their communities, using persuasive power to turn the protagonist from a destructive path. It is also worth noting that Joab engaged the Tekoite and that at this point he is open to taking counsel from a woman. She makes him aware that in all likelihood the rebellion has not yet taken root among Sheba's followers and that his removal will take the wind out of the sails of the uprising. She is correct and so the hostilities end with the decapitation of Sheba, whose head is tossed over the wall as proof. Joab turns around and goes to Jerusalem "to the king" (v. 22). There is no word on David's reaction, negative or positive, a possible indication that he and Joab had been in agreement the entire time.

The list of David's cabinet at the conclusion of this part of the narrative parallels that of chapter 8 (vv. 15-18), these two accounts forming bookends around the close-up view of David's court. There are some differences between the lists. First, the heading of the list in chapter 8 declares the king as a provider of "justice and righteousness for all his people" (v. 15). The omission of this description of Israel's king after all that has taken place is certainly telling. Lacking also is the mention of David's sons as priests, two of his sons at least by this time having thoroughly discredited themselves. According to the final list, Joab is over "the entire army," indicating an increase in status. Additions are Adoram, the secretary of labor, likely appearing here in anticipation of the role he will play in King Solomon's building projects, and a priest in special service to David's house at the end (Alter 1991, 328).

Calamities, Heroes, and Poetry (2 Sam 21–24)

"The issues here are national rather than personal." (Fokkelman 1990, 284)

The story of relationships and intrigue at David's court is not at an end, but it stops here in the narratives of Samuel, to be continued in the first chapters of 1 Kings. Instead of going on with the ups and downs of David's personal life, the final chapters of 2 Samuel provide an overview of important aspects and events of David's reign in which David plays a role, but without the close-up perspective of the stories in chapters 9–20. The calamities of famine and plague reported here (2 Sam 21 and 24) present threats to the nation more than to David personally. The two disaster stories in chapters 21 and 24 surround lists of heroes and deeds of conquest and the vanquishing of gigantic threats to the Israelite armies, all in the context of battles with the Philistines. Both stories depict a God who, for unaccountable reasons, acts in vengeful ways against the people. In the first, chapter 21, God reveals the reason for the divine anger, an anger subsequently appeased by human sacrifices that decimate the house of Saul, thus creating a link between God's rejection of Saul and God's wrath against the people. In the second story, the last chapter of 2 Samuel, God's anger is even more inscrutable, as it arises from David's taking a census, an action encouraged by the very God who later denounces it and doles out punishment.

Between these two stories we find the lists of heroes, 2 Samuel 21:15-21 and 23:8-35, testimony to the warrior culture of the time and to the strong individuals who surrounded David at the height of his power and martial prowess. These lists in turn surround two poems, one long paean of praise to the God who provides deliverance and acts with loyalty, *hesed,* toward God's anointed (22:1-51), and a short poem titled "The last words of David" (23:1-7). With others, I consider these chapters to be appendices, exhibiting distinct stylistic and thematic features—material that, according to the text's earliest collectors and editors, fit best here. Thus, together with chapters 6–8, they form a framework around the narratives with their focus on David and his court in chapters 9–20. Denoting this material as an appendix by no means identifies it as a random miscellany of haphazardly collected information. To the contrary, these chapters are precisely structured in a concentric fashion: two stories of disaster that end in atonement surround two lists of heroes and accounts of heroic deeds, which in turn surround two songs of praise to God. These texts in themselves speak to the glory as well as the risks of royal power.

The temporal placement of the events recorded in the texts is vague, pointing in general to "the days of David" (21:1), a time indicator that leads one to conclude the events narrated could have taken place at any time during David's reign. The major battles of chapters 21 and 23 appear to be with the Philistines, locating them at an earlier period of David's rise or his reign. Robert Alter claims that in some narrative portions of this material, the theological assumptions and imagination of situation and character are "strikingly different from the David story proper." Especially in chapter 24, God has "the look of acting arbitrarily, exacting terrible human costs in order to be placated. Unlike the deity of 1 Samuel 1–2 Samuel 20 the depiction of God in this section is decidedly interventionist, a God who "Incites David to carry out a census that will only bring grief to the people" (Alter 1999, 353). The overall effect of the depictions in the list of heroes, where the role of David takes a backseat to that of his heroic companions, as well as in the narratives, where God is the major character moving the action along, is to put the power of the royal office, and specifically David's power, in perspective. After all, God, rather than David, is in control of what happens in Israel. The poems in chapters 22 and 23 also testify to a glorification of God's grandeur and majestic command. We may not approve much of this particular perspective on divine intervention, but for the writers and eventual editors there may have been some consolation in the fact that the survival of Israel did not ultimately depend on the royal house.

The Decimation of the House of Saul (2 Sam 21:1-9)

". . . as unsavoury an episode as any we have read . . . ." (Goldingay 2000, 300)

A famine of three-year duration occasions David to question the deity. The text does not even spell out the content of David's prayer but simply states that he "sought the presence of the Holy One." In ancient times people would likely ascribe the cause of a natural disaster, such as a famine most often brought on by drought, to divine wrath. As it turns out, God is indeed angry, once again with Saul and his house because of an alleged crime committed against the Gibeonites. By now, the mention of Gibeon should alert the reader that bloodshed is just around the corner, as we encountered the place in the context of gruesome violence in 2:12 and 20:8. The story of the Gibeonites and how they gained protected status in Israel through deception occurs in Joshua 9, and, although it does not speak particularly well for this group, their ruse resulted in a commitment on the part of the tribes not to destroy them (Josh 9:26). While no other Samuel texts mention Saul committing acts of violence against them, this narrative may draw on different material that preserved such a tradition. In any case, David takes the Gibeonites seriously and asks them what he can do for them and how he can atone (v. 3).

A deliberation ensues, noteworthy for the clever way in which the Gibeonites draw David into a commitment that he may not have foreseen at the beginning of the exchange. Times have changed, but the Gibeonites have not changed their wily ways. First, they make clear that it is not about money. Some translate v. 4, "To us this business regarding Saul and his house is not a question of silver and gold . . ." (Fokkelman 1990, 278). In addition, the Gibeonites point out that on their own they do not have the right to shed blood. To these observations the king replies with a variation on his earlier question. "What shall I do for you" becomes "whatever you say I shall do for you" (v. 4), indicating a much stronger commitment on the part of David to accede to the Gibeonites' request. Perhaps he foresees what is coming, and an act of vengeance against the house of Saul can only be of advantage to the establishment of his own "house." Indeed, the Gibeonites require retribution of the most savage sort: execution of seven of Saul's descendants, a demand to which David agrees (v. 6). The divine word to David has been that the national calamity of famine, a disaster that must have exacted many victims during the three years it lasted, is because of Saul and his "house of blood-guilt." The execution of innocents belonging to Saul's house will thus be the means to atone for the guilt incurred by this house. This implacable logic offends any sense of justice and fairness.

David hands over two sons and five grandsons of Saul—two sons of Rizpah, whom we met earlier in the story (2 Sam 3:7-8), and five sons of Merab, Saul's daughter whom long ago he had promised to David as a wife only to renege on the promise (1 Sam 18:17-19). These seven are executed in a ritual manner, although whether by impaling or hanging is not exactly clear from the rare verbal root that occurs here (v. 9). The writer places the note on the sparing of Mephiboshet, Jonathan's son, within the narration of the handing over of Saul's offspring to the Gibeonites, thus putting Mephiboshet's survival in the context of the slaying of his kin. Elsewhere, this act of generosity takes place on the initiative of David who is actively seeking out survivors of Saul's house (2 Sam 9:1-13). Here the act is called a "sparing," using a verb that functions in a key position in the David-Bathsheba episode (2 Sam 12:7-8). The narrative that unfolds here likely draws on different source material. In any case, the seven are executed, as the text has it, "in the first days of the harvest, the beginning of the barley harvest" (v. 9). "The seven fell together" as once twenty-four contestants fell together at Gibeon during the period of the civil war leading up to David's reign (2 Sam 2:15). The mention of harvest in a period of famine is incongruous and inserts perhaps the first note of hope into this dark and gruesome tale.

Rizpah's Long Watch (2 Sam 21:10-14)

"Rizpah places herself, for a long period, in a pure hell." (Fokkelman 1990, 285)

First the story descends deeper into tragedy as the mother of two of the men takes her place on executioner's hill and keeps watch over the bodies. The time of the barley harvest indicates the month of April. She stayed there until "water poured from the sky" (v. 10). Unless the phrasing indicates occasional showers, this means that she stayed there with the decaying corpses of Saul's descendants, two of them her own sons, from spring until fall. An unburied dead body was a desecration, "a primal sacrilege, a final desecration of the sacredness of the human person" (Alter 1990, 332). Rizpah's purpose is to keep away the vultures and animals from the bodies.

David hears of Rizpah's watch, and her action moves him to gather the bones of Saul and Jonathan from Jabesh Gilead, then collect the bones of Saul's executed descendants and bury them together in the family grave. Only then God relents and restores the land to well-being. We may want to turn our eyes from this distressing story of an angry and vengeful God who can only be mollified by human sacrifice. Yet Rizpah and her actions merit our attention. She appeared earlier as the woman who caused contention between Saul's son Ishboshet and Abner (2 Sam 3:7-9). Both accounts identify her as a "concubine," someone lower than a wife in the hierarchical order of the patriarchal household. Abner may well have been guilty of the act specified in Ishboshet's accusation, but it is of no significance to Abner, who is infuriated that such an unimportant matter would cause reproach from Saul's son. We do not know what happened to Rizpah after the murder of Ishboshet. She has outlived the death of her erstwhile master and that of his son, and we encounter her now preventing the corpses of two of her own offspring and five of Saul's grandsons from further debasement. In the prelude to David's kingship, women had no agency and appeared only to enhance or diminish male power. Rizpah certainly had no agency that was worth mention. So it is startling that here, in the aftermath of one of the most distasteful episodes during David's kingship, Rizpah acts on her own initiative and in her own way furthers at least a type of resolution in the form of the burial that David makes possible for the deceased members of the house of Saul.

She does not seem to do much, just sitting or lying there, shooing away the animals that would come to maul the dead bodies. Although we might assume that she is there only for her sons, the text refers consistently to "them," that is "the seven who fell together." Rizpah, low in the pecking order of the royal court, takes part in a protest action. This very action moves David to give the remains of Saul and his descendants a decent burial. Instead of being a tool in the hands of powerful men, her defiant act of remaining with the dead until a resolution comes about stands out in these narratives as one of singular bravery and authenticity. She joins Hannah and Abigail and the wise woman of Abel Beth Maacah in taking a stance that is entirely her own. Unlike the three of them, she was not able to prevent the violence that occurred, but she halts further violation by the hand of the powerful. Rizpah's watch was long, and it behooves us to pause for a moment in homage to her courage and patience. Her act is inspirational; it at least inspires David to do the correct thing so that at long last the bones of Saul come to rest (v. 14; see Fokkelman 1990, 289).

Heroes of Old (2 Sam 21:15-21; 23:8-35)

". . . when Truth itself is reconceived, understood as proliferating, it becomes truths, or better, stories, that illuminate and enrich each other with their variety and multiplicity rather than being partial installments of the one true story." (Schwartz 1997, 173)

Two lists in chapters 21 and 23 frame the poems considered below. Quickly the text veers away from the heroic act of one woman to focus on the valor of the heroes that surrounded David in his exploits. All the rest of chapter 21 and the larger part of chapter 23 consist of lists naming those who fought with him in battles, who accomplished heroic deeds, and who saved David's skin at times, thus creating an impression that the valiant leader of armies would not have got far without the help of these comrades-in-arms. In fact, already in the first list, David grows faint, and Abishai does the job of killing the Philistine champion (vv. 15-17). Then the troops tell David not to go out with them any longer to fight "lest you extinguish the lamp of Israel" (v. 17). This phrase, in content similar to the plea from the soldiers on the eve of the battle at Mahanaim (2 Sam 18:3), and certainly highlighting the significance of David's stature for the nation, in fact moves David to the background of the action.

The context for the exploits in 21:15-21 is the war with the Philistines; the phrase "there was a new fight between the Philistines and Israel" occurs four times (vv. 15, 18, 19, 20). Within this framework, four Philistine champions come forward, all descendants of the "Raphah," a legendary gigantic race that preceded Israel in Canaan. These giants had enormous physical size, and it is no surprise that Goliath is among them (v. 19). One of David's servants defeats each of the four Philistines: Abishai, Sibbechai, Elhanan, and Jonathan, a nephew of David, are the four who step forward. Elhanan's defeat of Goliath contradicts the story of David's killing of the same (1 Sam 17:50), and again testifies to the way this part of the story draws those around David into the limelight rather than David himself. This version is probably the more original of the tales of Goliath's defeat, since great deeds of valor would more naturally accrue to a known hero in the stories rather than to an otherwise unknown character (Alter 1999, 334). That we find both traditions preserved in the text of Samuel is quite remarkable and underlines the importance the narrators placed on telling the story in multiple versions (see Schwartz above). The concluding lines of this list include David as subject, but the preceding account denies him a leading role in the defeat of the gigantic opponents:

> These four were born to the Raphah in Gath,
> and they fell by the hand of David
> and the hand of his servants. (2 Sam 21:21)

The list in 23:8-35 differs from the first one in presenting the "three" and the "thirty," the "three" receiving the greatest accolades with the "thirty" just below them in significance. According to Alter, this list may date back to David's own time. It is an epic list with some narrative elaboration, dating back perhaps to the early phases of David's career when the Philistine threat had not yet been laid to rest. Asahel is still an active member of the elite corps (Alter 1990, 348). We find here also Abishai and Joab, although Joab's name is among neither the three nor the thirty. Uriah the Hittite is at the end of the list.

A short narrative embedded within the recital (vv. 13-17) tells the tale of three heroes breaking through the enemy lines (at Bethlehem!) to draw water for a thirsty David. Instead of drinking it, David offers it as a sacrifice to the Holy One (v. 16), for he considers it bought at the risk of his men's lives (v. 17). A small portrait emerges of a modest and pious leader whose men will go through enemy fire for him, but not of the valiant commander we find elsewhere in the texts.

Sweet Singer of Israel (2 Sam 22:1-51; 23:1-7)

"There is, of course, a persistent biblical notion of David the poet as well as David the warrior-king." (Alter 1999, 336)

Two poems attributed to David, one long and one short, consist mainly of praise for God's help for David in situations of distress. Long poems at times close biblical books, and in our case poems of praise virtually frame the entire text of 1 and 2 Samuel. In addition, the poems of praise in these last chapters also balance the lament with which the material in 2 Samuel opened. The Hebrew text of chapter 22, with its near duplicate in Psalm 18, is notoriously difficult, although the overall theme is not hard to make out. The content evinces the warrior culture that was such an overwhelming reality in the days of early Israel and in the texts that record the beginnings of kingship. The poem uses the first person for the poet throughout, while God appears in third person description or in second person address. The shift to second person is apparent in the second half of the poem, vv. 26-51, which lends the song its strong aura of intimate relationship between God and the speaker.

Three opening stanzas describe God as the essence of rescue and deliverance. God is a "crag," "fortress," "rock," "shield," "bulwark," and "refuge." Each image receives the personal possessive pronoun, which lends the lines the quality of personal experience. God is not only a rock and a deliverer but also *my* rock, *my* fortress, *my* savior. Words for deliverance occur multiple times in the opening verses. As in Hannah's praise song, the "horn" is the image of strength (cf. 1 Sam 2:1, 10). As it does in Hannah's poem, reference to God's favor for God's "anointed" closes the prayer. References to God as "rock" punctuate the poem, occurring in the opening lines (v. 3), in the middle (v. 32), and at the end (v. 47). The situation of the poet, addressed in general beginning in v. 4, is one of deepest distress, expressed in standard imagery of "enemies," "breakers of death," "torrents of Belial," "cords of Sheol," and "snares of death" (vv. 4-6). Out of this pit of despair, the poet cried to God, who heard his voice (v. 7).

Before elaborating further on this theme, the poem turns to a vivid description of a divine appearance (vv. 8-16). Borrowing from archaic imagery of other literary traditions of the region, the theophany depicts cosmic tumult, earthquake, and eruptions accompanying the descent of the divine rescuer, thunder and lightning, and what sounds like a tsunami (v. 16). This then is the God who rescues the one beset by enemies "stronger than I" (v. 18). The moment of deliverance is all the more impressive as it follows on the turbulent descriptions of the appearing of the mighty God. Then the poet turns inward and begins to attest personal innocence (vv. 21-25): righteousness and purity frame the lines that describe the state of this human being before God (vv. 21, 25):

> For I kept the ways of the Holy One,
> and did no evil before my God.
>
> For all His statutes are before me,
> from His laws I have not turned aside.
> I was wholehearted toward Him,
> and kept myself from sin. (2 Sam 22:22-25)

This assertion clearly does not refer to the David who violated another man's wife and had her husband murdered. God's protection of David here takes place as a reward for David's "righteousness."

Verses 26-37 begin by addressing God in the second person, moving from attestations of God's faithfulness in general ("With the loyal you keep loyalty" [v. 26]; "With the pure you are pure" [v. 27]) to more personal testimony ("You are my lamp," "my darkness," "I rush," "I leap"). Once again turning to a description of God's protection for all who flee to God for refuge, this set of stanzas concludes with a strong statement of personal reliance on God to lend strength in battle. These last lines inaugurate the theme that comes to the fore in the following verses, the defeat of the enemies in telling detail.

Verses 38-43 describe the completeness of the destruction heaped on the opponents of the poet made possible by God's helping hand. What begins in pursuit ends in destruction (v. 38), battering, smashing, and annihilation. Unlike the cries of the poet, the cries of the enemy go unanswered by the Holy One (v. 42). The entire scene ends with violent images of total annihilation:

> I crush them like dust of the earth,
> like street dirt I pulverize them, I stomp them. (2 Sam 22:43)

This theme of crushing the enemy continues with images of foreign nations adopting the posture of servitude as they have heard of the renown of this conqueror king (vv. 44-46). Finally, the song of praise concludes with expressions of praise and gratitude for the God who so defends God's anointed. In three verses God is the subject in every line (vv. 47-49), recapitulating the theme of the God who delivers. The poem ends with praise for a God,

> Who multiplies deliverance to His king,
> and acts loyally to his anointed,
> to David and his seed everlasting. (2 Sam 22:51)

Although there are similarities with the praise song of Hannah at the beginning of the books of Samuel, especially in terms of key words, there are also striking differences. Hannah's prayer fit the position of a woman who was once bereft of social standing, wounded by the misery of childlessness, one who could sing of a God who lifts up the lowly and raises the poor from the dust (1 Sam 2:8). In her prayer God breaks the bow of the mighty in pieces, and a man is not a hero by strength. In David's poem God is no less powerful, but God's power mainly serves the battle strength of the warrior king. War and its violence permeate the imagery and themes of this chapter. The two poems align in the idea that all power, whether of a fertile womb or a victorious battlefield, belongs to God and is God's to bestow. David has no strength or power of his own but that lent to him by the Most High.

A short poem ends the poetic section of this material. Second Samuel 23:1-7 is presented as "an oracle of David," thus cast within the framework of prophetic speech. For such a short passage, there is a long introduction. David is "the son of Jesse," "the man raised up high," "the anointed," and "the sweet singer of Israel" (v. 1). The first labels are contrastive: a son of a farmer, even if a well-to-do one, is the one who is raised up. Terminology takes us back once more to Hannah's prayer in which God raises the poor. The next identifications pair "anointed" with "sweet singer" (retaining the King James translation). Here then we find a description of the side of David first highlighted when he appeared at Saul's court (1 Sam 16:18). There, too, the reference to him was to a man "prudent in speech." While the preceding poem celebrates David's prowess as a warrior, even if guided and protected by God, the present text emphasizes the poetic, artistic, perhaps even prophetic side of David. That side, too, is subject to divine inspiration, as the next four lines make clear. What David speaks is through "the spirit of the Holy one"; God's utterance is on his tongue and it is God who speaks through him (vv. 2-3).

Only after this long introduction validating the words of David does the subject of the speech arise with its focus on righteousness rather than battle strength:

> A ruler of humanity, a righteous one,
> Is a ruler in awe of God. (v. 3)

Here the root "to rule" (Hebrew *mashal*) connects to "righteousness" (Hebrew *tsedakah*), the quality that marks rulers who extend special protection to the downtrodden and forsaken, as described in Psalm 72 with the picture of the ideal king who partakes of God's "justice" and "righteousness" (Ps 72:1-4). In that psalm, such righteousness explicitly consists of defending the "cause of the poor" and giving "deliverance to the needy." Second Samuel 23:4 goes on from this notion to draw an analogy from nature with its references to the morning light, the rising sun, and the showers that produce grass. Psalm 72 moves also in the same direction with its mention of sun and moon and comparison of the ruler to "the rain that falls on the mown grass, like showers that water the earth." Verse 5 returns to the thought that God has established David in his position with "an enduring covenant," with the final phrase bringing the metaphors around once more to nature.

As in some psalms that compare the way of the righteous with the way of the wicked, the poem ends on a negative note (cf. Ps 1:4-6). The final lines focus on the "worthless man," the *beliya'al*, a category of people we met first in 1 Samuel 2 designating the sons of Eli (1 Sam 2:12) and later Nabal, as his wife, Abigail, referred to him (1 Sam 25:17). More recently, the text indicated rebellious Sheba with this epithet (2 Sam 20:1). Psalm 1 compares the wicked to "chaff whirled about by the wind" (v. 4). Here the worthless one, in contrast to the righteous person, does not partake of anything enduring but is like blown-around thorns, hard to pick up and easy to destroy. Although 2 Samuel 23:1-7 differs in theme from the preceding poem, here as there the ultimate source of human rule, whether in war or in peace, belongs to God, and the human ruler, whether as warrior or just ruler, is dependent on this God.

Illusions of Power (2 Sam 24:1-25)

"Who is the hero of this story?" (Fokkelman 1990, 308)

Another story of God's anger, trespass, punishment, and atonement closes the books of Samuel. It feels disturbing that God incites David to engage in an act that may have been considered taboo, namely a census. In the prelude (vv. 1-3), David orders Joab to complete the task and this time Joab demurs. Naturally, the king's word prevails and Joab makes a circuit of the country, arriving at the number cited in v. 9 of one million three hundred thousand military-able men. Numbers are almost always inflated in biblical history, and it is highly unlikely that the country could have sustained a population anywhere near the size obtained if one adds women, servants, and children to able-bodied males. Be that as it may, before any consequences of this supposedly wicked act on David's part can take place, David engages in a confession because his heart "smote him," an expression we encountered in the cave at Engedi when David spared the life of Saul (1 Sam 24:6). The prophet Gad faces David with three choices of punishment, all of them affecting the nation. David chooses without explicitly stating a preference. Rather, he opts for falling "into the hand of the Holy One" (v. 14).

In the next unit, a messenger of God brings a plague upon the people, and God stays the messenger's hand so that most likely only one day of plague ensues. David intervenes on behalf of his people in ignorance of the fact that the punishment is already halted (v. 17). As Fokkelman points out, "David has no insight whatsoever into the fact that his position as a sinner is at the same time that of a puppet" (Fokkelman 1990, 318). While David's confession thus has no effect on the discontinuation of the punishment, it is remarkable that this confession, his second one, takes place at the same time that the plague halts. The effect of David's witnessing the destruction of his people is that he grows in his role of compassionate leadership, his role of shepherd:

> He said, "Look it is I who have sinned,
> I who did wrong.
> And these sheep what have they done?" (v. 17)

Even after the plague has stopped, David is ignorant of the fact, for in his negotiations with Arauna for the threshing floor he mentions the building of an altar to God as a means to avert the "scourge of the people" (v. 21). Then David buys the threshing floor and builds the altar, heralding the moment that Solomon will construct the temple on that very spot. The foundation of the future temple thus connects to a troublesome story, a "crisis between God and his people, in which the Lord has wielded the classic catastrophes of famine, the sword and pestilence" (Fokkelman 1990, 331).

Of course, this particular episode is also disturbing because the opening lines show God as the instigator of an action that subsequently deserves punishment. Even among biblical storytellers, this aspect raised uneasiness so that the version of the tale in Chronicles transfers the antagonism toward Israel and the provocation to take a census to Satan (1 Chr 21:1). In our version, the story is decidedly offensive and raises questions about the arbitrary nature of God's actions, as happened with the rejection of Saul. There are no satisfactory answers to the conundrum this perspective on God poses. At least in this story, unlike that of chapter 21, there are no human scapegoats around, and the atoning action takes the form of building an altar and regular animal sacrifice. Both the narratives, in chapter 21 and in this concluding chapter, together with the lists and the poems, create a picture of David who depends on God's favor and God's continued support. The stories are stories of national disaster and the lists elevate those around David to heroic status, while the poems depict the utter dependence of the ruler on God's mercy and protection. In their own way, these last chapters of 2 Samuel explore the boundaries set to the power of the ruler.

We have come to the end of the books of Samuel. The story of David will continue, and more dysfunction and turbulence at the court are around the corner. We say farewell, however, to these sometimes inspiring, sometimes alienating, but at all times utterly absorbing narratives and poems that recreate aspects of life in ancient Israel with all that goes into the relationships of human beings with each other and with their God.

Works Cited

Alter, Robert. *The David Story: A Translation with Commentary of 1 and 2 Samuel.* New York: W.W. Norton, 1999.

Amit, Yairah. "Am I Not More Devoted to You than Ten Sons (1 Samuel 1:8): Male and Female Interpretations." In *A Feminist Companion to Samuel and Kings*, edited by Athalya Brenner, 68–76. Sheffield: Sheffield Academic, 1994.

Bar-Efrat, Shimon. *Narrative Art in the Bible.* Sheffield: Almond, 1989.

Biddle, Mark E. "Ancestral Motifs in 1 Samuel 25: Intertextuality and Characterization." *Journal of Biblical Literature* 121 (2002): 617–38.

Botterweck, G. Johannes, and Helmer Ringgren, editors. *Theological Dictionary of the Old Testament.* Grand Rapids: Eerdmans, 1974.

Bronner, Leila Leah. *From Eve to Esther: Rabbinic Reconstructions of Biblical Women.* Louisville: Westminster John Knox, 1994.

Brueggemann, Walter. *First and Second Samuel.* Interpretation: A Bible Commentary for Teaching and Preaching. Louisville: Westminster John Knox, 1990.

———. *Ichabod Toward Home: The Journey of God's Glory.* Grand Rapids: Eerdmans, 2002.

Buber, Martin. "*Die Erzählung von Sauls Königswahl.*" *Vestus Testamentum* 6 (1956): 113–73.

———. "The Man of Today and the Jewish Bible." In *On the Bible: Eighteen Studies by Martin Buber*, edited by Nahum Glatzer, 1–21. Martin Buber Library. New York: Schocken Books, 1982.

Caquot, André, and Philippe de Robert. *Les Livres de Samuel.* Geneva: Labor et Fides, 1994.

Clines, David J. A. *Interested Parties: The Ideology of Writers and Readers of the Hebrew Bible.* Sheffield: Sheffield Phoenix, 2009.

Clines, David J. A., and Tamara Cohn Eshkenazi, editors. *Telling Queen Michal's Story.* Sheffield: *Journal for the Study of the Old Testament* (JSOT), 1991.

Cook, Joan E. *Hannah's Desire, God's Design: Early Interpretations of the Story of Hannah.* Journal for the Study of the Old Testament: Supplement Series 282. Sheffield: Sheffield Academic, 1999.

Davis, Ellen F. "Losing a Friend: The Loss of the Old Testament to the Church." In *Jews, Christians and the Theology of the Hebrew Scriptures,* edited by Alice Ogden Bellis and Joel Kaminsky, 83–94. Atlanta: Scholars, 2000.

Eslinger, Lyle M. *Kingship of God in Crisis: A Close Reading of 1 Samuel 1–12.* Sheffield: Almond, 1985.

Exum, J. Cheryl. *Tragedy and Biblical Narrative.* Cambridge: Cambridge University Press, 1992.

Fewell, Danna Nolan, and David M. Gunn. *Gender, Power, and Promise: The Subject of the Bible's First Story.* Nashville: Abingdon, 1993.

Fokkelman, J. P. *Narrative Art and Poetry in the Books of Samuel, Volume 1: King David (II Sam. 9-20 & 1 Kings 1-2).* Assen: Van Gorcum, 1981.

———. *Narrative Art and Poetry in the Books of Samuel, Volume II: The Crossing Fates (1 Sam.13-31 & II Sam.1).* Assen: Van Gorcum, 1986.

———. *Narrative Art and Poetry in the Books of Samuel, Volume III: Throne and City.* Assen: Van Gorcum, 1990.

———. *Narrative Art and Poetry in the Books of Samuel, Volume IV: Vow and Desire.* Assen: Van Gorcum, 1993.

———. "Algemene Inleiding – Oog in Oog Met De Tekst Zelf." In *De Bijbel Literair: Opbouw en Gedachtengang van de Bijbelse Geschriften en hun Onderlinge Relaties,* edited by J. Fokkelman and W. Weren, 7–32. Kapellen: Felckmans, 2003.

Fox, Everett. *The Five Books of Moses: A New Translation with Introductions, Commentary, and Notes.* New York: Schocken, 1995.

Gafney, Wilda C. *Daughters of Miriam: Women Prophets in Ancient Israel.* Minneapolis: Fortress, 2008.

Garsiel, Moshe. *The First Book of Samuel: A Literary Study of Comparative Structures, Analogies and Parallels.* Ramat-Gan, Israel: Revivim Publishing, 1985.

Goldingay, John. *Men Behaving Badly.* Carlisle UK: Paternoster Press, 2000.

Good, Edwin M. *Irony in the Old Testament.* Sheffield: Almond, 1981.

Gordon, Robert P. *I & II Samuel: A Commentary.* Grand Rapids: Zondervan, 1986.

Green, Barbara. "Enacting Imaginatively the Unthinkable: 1 Samuel 25 and the Story of Saul." *Biblical Interpretation* 11 (2003): 1–23.

Gunn, David M. *The Fate of King Saul: An Interpretation of a Biblical Story.* Sheffield: JSOT Press, 1980.

Hertzberg, Hans Wilhelm. *I and II Samuel: A Commentary.* Translated by J. S. Bowden. Philadelphia: Westminster, 1964.

Hester, David C. *First and Second Samuel.* Interpretation: A Bible Commentary for Teaching and Preaching. Louisville: Geneva Press, 2000.

Jacobs, Jonathan. "The Role of the Secondary Characters in the Story of the Anointing of Saul." *Vestus Testamentum* 58 (2008): 495–509.

Jobling, David, and Catherine Rose. "Reading as a Philistine: The Ancient and Modern History of a Cultural Slur." In *Ethnicity and the Bible,* edited by Mark Brett, 381–417. Leiden: Brill, 1996.

Jobling, David. *1 Samuel.* Berit Olam: Studies in Hebrew Narrative and Poetry. Collegeville MN: The Liturgical Press, 1998.

Klein, Lillian R. "Hannah: Marginalized Victim and Social Redeemer." In *A Feminist Companion to Samuel and Kings,* edited by Athalya Brenner, 77–92. Sheffield: Sheffield Academic Press, 1994.

Lehnhart, Bernhard. *Prophet Und König im Nordreich Israel: Studien zur sogenannten vorklassischen Prophetie im Nordreich Israel anhand der Samuel-, Elija- und Elischa- Überlieferungen.* Leiden: Brill, 2003.

Levenson, Jon. "1 Samuel 25 as Literature and as History." *Catholic Biblical Quarterly* 40 (1978): 11–28.

Levenson, Jon, and Baruch Halpern. "The Political Import of David's Marriages." *Journal of Biblical Literature* 99 (1980): 507–518.

Madigan, Kevin J. and Jon Levenson. *Resurrection: The Power of God for Christians and Jews.* New Haven: Yale University Press, 2008.

Miscall, Peter D. *1 Samuel: A Literary Reading.* Bloomington: Indiana University Press, 1986.

Nicholson, Sarah. *Three Faces of Saul: An Intertextual Approach to Biblical Tragedy.* Sheffield: Sheffield Academic, 2002.

Niditch, Susan. *War in the Hebrew Bible: A Study in the Ethics of Violence.* Oxford: Oxford University Press, 1993.

Lozovyy, Joseph. *Saul, Doeg, Nabal and the "Son of Jesse": Readings in 1 Samuel 16–25.* The Library of Hebrew Bible/Old Testament Studies 497. London: T&T Clark International, 2009.

McCarter, Kyle, Jr. *1 Samuel: A New Translation with Introduction, Notes & Commentary.* Anchor Bible 8. New York: Doubleday, 1980.

Meyers, Carol. "Hannah and Her Sacrifice: Reclaiming Female Agency." In *A Feminist Companion to Samuel and Kings,* edited by Athalya Brenner, 93–104. Sheffield: Sheffield Academic Press, 1994.

Polzin, Robert. *Samuel and the Deuteronomist: A Literary Study of the Deuteronomic History, Part Two, 1 Samuel.* Indiana Series in Biblical Literature. Bloomington: Indiana University Press, 1989.

———. *David and the Deuteronomist: A Literary Study of the Deuteronomic History, Part Three, 2 Samuel.* Indiana Series in Biblical Literature. Bloomington: Indiana University Press, 1993.

Rudman, D. "The Commissioning Stories of Saul and David as Theological Allegory." *Vestus Testamentum* 59 (2000): 519–30.

Scholz, Susanne. *Sacred Witness: Rape in the Hebrew Bible.* Minneapolis: Fortress, 2010.

Schwartz, Regina M. *The Curse of Cain: The Violent Legacy of Monotheism.* Chicago: University of Chicago Press, 1997.

Smelik, K. A. D. "De Ark in het Filistijnse Land." Amsterdamse Cahiers voor Exegese en Bijbelse Theologie. Vol. 1. Eds. K. A. Deurloo, B. P. M. Hemelsoet, et al. Kampen: J. H. Kok (1980):42–50.

Smith, Henry Preserved. *A Critical and Exegetical Commentary on the Books of Samuel.* International Critical Commentary. Edinburgh: T&T Clark, 1899.

Spijkerboer, Anne Marijke. "Geheimzinnigheid en Geheimenis in 1 Samuel 9–10." *Amsterdamse Cahiers* 11 (1992): 35–42.

Terrien, Samuel. *The Elusive Presence: Toward a New Biblical Theology.* New York: Harper & Row, 1978.

Tsumura, David Toshio. *The First Book of Samuel.* New International Commentary on the Old Testament. Grand Rapids: Eerdmans, 2007.

Vikander Edelman, Diana. *King Saul in the Historiography of Judah.* Sheffield: Sheffield Academic, 1991.

Van Wijk-Bos, Johanna W. H. *Making Wise the Simple: The Torah in Christian Faith and Practice.* Grand Rapids: Eerdmans, 2005.

Van Wolde, Ellen. "A Leader Led by a Lady: David and Abigail in 1 Samuel 25." *ZAW* 114 (2002): 355–75.

29087269R00145

Made in the USA
Lexington, KY
12 January 2014